"If sometimes you don't heed your conscience, you need to read this book."

Jack Anderson, Nationally Syndicated Columnist

"This book is a combination of good common sense, appropriate data, and powerful logic. Its persuasive reasoning appeals to one's inner sense of truth. Most parents—no matter how libertarian—will appreciate it, because it provides some thoughtful ideas to discuss with their growing children."

Victor B. Cline, Ph.D., Clinical Psychologist, specializing in sexual addictions

"A real contribution! Worthy treatment of a challenging topic in today's society."

Neil Flinders Ed.D.

"The Forgotten Virtue logically, with solid roots in the Judeo-Christian code, justifies, illuminates, and defends the sanctity of the fountain of life."

George W. Pace, Ph.D.
college professor/parent

"The power of chastity is simply peace in all interpersonal relationships. This book shows this. A tremendous tool for counseling."

John Olsen, private investigator

"Just finished reading 'Virtue' and I'm in awe. This book illuminates all that makes chastity a cherished virtue. The case studies and dialogues are stimulating. It helps the reader take a powerful look at healthy living and loving."

Jane Ann Olsen, parent/author

"Only a mother could have written this book; it's a labor of love. A superb job!"

Cheri Loveless, Co-founder Mothers at Home, parent/editor

"An excellent perspective on a subject that cries for enlightened voices. Fresh; nothing like it out there. Strong without being offensive."

Darla Isackson, author/editor/mother of five sons

"This book has the power to heal shattered lives. It did mine."

Jason Alkema, college student

"This book is for everyone—young, old, married or single. As a teacher of teenagers, I've found fear tactics don't work. Teens want to know the solid reason and rewards for waiting to have sex until marriage. This book does it."

Lyn Walkenhorst, parent/music teacher

"This book's title, the book's author, the book's contents bespeak excellence—something to be chosen and cherished. Mollie Sorensen no longer stands alone to guard the bridge."

Ralph V. Larson, Ph.D

"As a mother of five young men, I always wanted a book that would make it easier to explain the benefits of chastity—this is the help I've been looking for. It gives parents a blueprint for building trust and understanding that's needed to begin teaching the principles."

Susan Maughan, parent/educator

"This book is not a guilt trip or an argument for one way. It shows the joy, the peace and the freedom of chastity. The ideas stimulate the desire to see each other's divine nature, to love and to respect. It renewed my devotion to my husband."

Francine Cardone-Miller, parent/educator

"The Forgotten Virtue guides the human spirit towards truth, and self-respect. It's a celebration of love and self-discovery."

John Miller, Jr. parent/professional golfer

"The Forgotten Virtue should be in the home of every family who truly loves and cherishes their children, and wants to fortify them against the evils of sexual promiscuity."

Michael Chadwick, author, and foreign
policy advisor for the United States Senate

THE FORGOTTEN VIRTUE

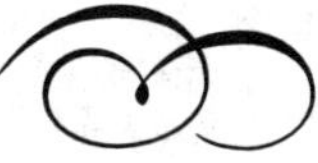

Rethinking the Sexual Revolution

Mollie Hobaugh-Sorensen

Sun West

First Edition

Book design by Don Sorensen

For information write to:

Sun West Publishing

P.O. Box 716

Napa, CA 94559

For information about seminars, and other books by Mollie Hobaugh-Sorensen visit the web site at:

http://www.mollie.com

Send e-mail to:

mollie@mollie.com

ISBN 0-9659261-0-9

Contents

Acknowledgments

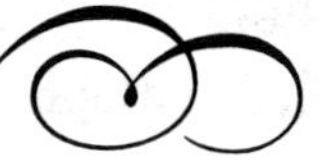

Classical literature has within it time-honored treasures of truth and common sense—a gift to each generation. I am grateful to authors who have taught me so much: Leo Tolstoy, Charlotte Bronte, Charles Dickens, Thomas Hardy, Fyodor Dostoyevsky, Kahlil Gibran, and to thoughtful Christian philosophers: Jacques Maritain, Henry Drummond, and C.S. Lewis. I'm indebted to my contemporaries who added insights: psychologist Dr. Victor Cline who allowed me to use his brilliant work on pornography, and Dr. Neil Flinders who provided the wide-angled perspective on the ideas behind the sexual revolution.

I am indebted to the many editors who so generously gave of their time and talents: Sharon Elwell, Cheri Loveless, Darla Isackson, Michael Chadwick, Ingrid Jacob-Sorensen, our daughter-in-law, and Signe Sorensen-Knapp, our daughter. I am especially appreciative of those who so generously shared their stories and experiences so that others could benefit. These stories illustrate and illuminate the concepts.

I am forever appreciative to my husband, Norman Allen, my soul-mate who is ever-constant, and to each of our eleven children: Donnie, Norman Ray, Signe, Adam, Aaron, Shiloh,

Anna, Jennifer, Micah, Mary and Jessica. They are my jewels, my friends, and my counselors! They called me over and over to ask, "How's it coming, Mom? Are you finished with the book?" I desperately needed their encouragement. Without it, this book may never have been completed.

I am grateful for my parents, Harry and Anita Hobaugh, who have shown me the meaning of "romantic love" all of my life. Most of all, I am eternally indebted to the light within—the Author of all truth who has taught me more than I thought possible—even more than I thought I could handle.

Preface

"The victory of pure reason over superstition will not be achieved without tremendous struggle."

Haeckel

You are holding a miracle. Over and over I threw my hands up in exasperation and cried to my husband, "I can't do it. The subject—chastity—is too delicate, too controversial, too broad, too misunderstood. I'm afraid I could create more misunderstanding. I don't know if they'll be able to overcome the prejudice and hang with me long enough to get a glimpse of the vision I've gained."

"The topic seems pretty clear cut," he said, "No sex outside of a legal marriage."

"That's one of the problems, it's not clear cut," I said, "Chastity is in a whole different realm. If we say to our children 'Don't steal' we would mean also, 'Don't covet other people's belongings'. Sex, though, is altogether different. Sexual desire is a part of being human—it's natural and normal. The desire to steal or lie comes from the dark side of our natures, while wholesome sexual desire is God-given.

"We seem to run from one extreme to another; some

people can't stop talking about sex, and others never begin. There are those who only mention it with a snicker—like it's all a joke we play on each other. Some think it's all just a physical itch that must be scratched. We seem to have lost our balance; we don't know what's normal, wholesome, or right.

"Sex is not just great because it's so pleasurable, it's great because it's so grand, grand in depth and grand in scope. Men and women were created to be attracted to one another, and that attraction creates bonds of love that inspire like nothing else. It can be the height of virtue, the super-glue that creates circles of love and holds marriages and families together. It's a refuge and a strength. It's all so awesome, we're lucky if we can even begin to appreciate it.

"Through this process babies are created—the most innocent, sweet, angelic beings on earth. Chastity is the immortal virtue; it affects not only our own lives but those of our children, and their children.

"Sometimes, I want to run up and down the streets shouting like an over-zealous fanatic that sex is too important, too wonderful to take lightly. I've been given a glimpse and I need to share it. But, how can I share such a vision? It's impossible! Now you see why I want to give up."

"You can't give up," he said. "Capture the perspective that you've gained. Show how chastity sets the stage for love and sexual fulfillment. I know it's frustrating, but just keep going."

This conversation with my husband took place over and over as I faced the Goliath of my life: to shine the soft light of logic and reason in an arena ruled by anger, prejudice and false traditions. I wanted to assist the reader to make responsible and ethical sexual decisions, but the process has been maddening—my most difficult labor ever; which says a lot for a mother of eleven who has experienced gut-wrenching labors.

Research was difficult. Books on moral virtue—or chastity—are no longer politically correct. Like the Communists who burned the books that disagreed with the Almighty State, our society has suppressed ideas that disagree with the Almighty Popular Opinion. Even collections of famous quotations have only a few items under the heading of "chastity," and these comments most often take a negative slant.

The word chastity has become so misunderstood that at one point I attempted to discard it altogether. I spent hours searching for a non-controversial substitute, but eventually decided that there is no substitute. The term "abstinence" is only a small part of a greater picture. Moral virtue comes close, but not close enough. Chastity is the only word that fits, but heaven forbid, not the chastity that causes us to love less and feel self-righteous, but the kind that causes us to love more and feel wonderful about it. I call it *enlightened chastity*.

Another challenge I faced was conveying the message in a non-denominational manner. The insights are based upon fundamental American principles: there is a Supreme Creator, we are His children, and we have the power within to direct our own lives in the "pursuit of happiness." The Founding

Fathers called these: *self-evident truths.* To this foundation, I have added ideas, quotes from inspirational literature, personal conversations and stories that enlighten as well as entertain.

Another struggle with this writing was discovering the right approach. The first draft was authoritative and scriptural, but it didn't feel right. The second was less authoritative, but still not right. I prayed with all my heart and soul for the strength to get it right. I remember a professor saying, "There's a time when virginity is virtue, and a time when it's a vice." In other words, there's a "time to embrace, and a time to refrain from embracing". (Ecc. 3: 5) I certainly didn't want anyone to refrain from embracing when it was the "time to embrace".

Gradually, a new and exciting view came into focus, so new it seemed impossible to share; I barely knew it myself. I was haunted with the fear that my words would be inadequate. Writing is a lonely business; isolated from the world, you labor at creating a mosaic of ideas and hope that the reader will capture the same vision. Through the grace of God, and despite my weaknesses, the miracle has occurred: those who have read this manuscript have arrived at the vision I hoped to create.

After reading the book, men have made such comments as: "I never understood before, if only someone had told me; I never realized what I was doing . . .I would have never treated women in that way. . .I want to be a better husband. . .I love my wife so much more after gaining the understanding." One middle-aged university professor said, "It made me realize how I have taken my wife and the love that we have shared for so many years for granted. It's given me a new depth of gratitude."

Women have said, "Where was this book when I needed it? I would have lived my life completely different if I had only known." One young mother said, "If I had read one page of this book while a teenager, I would have chosen to remain virgin until marriage; no one ever told me these things before."

I was thrilled one Sunday afternoon when a friend of our daughter's came to visit. After we exchanged greetings, she said, "I want you to know that before I had a chance to read your book, my mother read the entire thing—and it has changed her life. She's no longer promiscuous. I don't know whether you know it or not, but I left home during high school because I hated to see my mother living with so many different men. She's given birth to seven children—all by different fathers. During high school, I just couldn't handle it anymore, so I moved in with a friend. About a year ago I decided to move back home to see if my Mom and I could get along. Not too long after that, she saw your book in my room, and asked if she could read it. The change is amazing. She doesn't sleep around anymore; she even looks and dresses different. She says she'll never be the same again."

The miracle has happened. There's great power in ideas, power to chart the human soul in it's "pursuit of happiness." My hope is that your journey to discover the mosaic of understanding will enlighten your life, and fill you with the desire to restore the treasure of the forgotten virtue.

The Forgotten Virtue

1

The Seduction of American Youth

"Nothing is of more importance for the public well-being, than to form and train up youth in wisdom and virtue."

Benjamin Franklin

Insight #1
Knowledge helps us to accurately see the world around us, but understanding helps us to choose wisely, live abundantly and happily.

When I was fifteen, I worked in a doughnut shop with an older man who was easy to talk with. One night I asked, "What do you think about sex before marriage?"

His answer was short and simple, "There's nothing wrong with having sex before you're married, but there is something wrong with getting pregnant."

The American youth—for decades—have been seduced by the idea that there is nothing wrong with premarital sex except the physical consequences: pregnancy, abortion, sexually transmitted diseases, AIDS. They've been taught how to keep from getting pregnant and what to do if they do get pregnant. They have been taught the sex drive cannot be controlled, and that there's such a thing as "safe sex". They have been taught anatomy, various sexual practices, every sexual lifestyle imaginable, and assorted contraceptive devices. But they have *not* been taught the emotional and spiritual hazards of sex, or the reasons and rewards for postponing sexual relations until a loving, loyal and legal relationship is established. How can we criticize the youth for the off-the-charts teenage pregnancy rate when they have not been properly informed?

The seduction came from all sides: movies, music, books. Some schools—even churches—would not consider teaching abstinence because they believed it to be unachievable. Hollywood would not consider it because it was not profitable. The sexual revolution and the free love movement tossed traditional values to the wind. The idea of waiting until marriage changed to waiting for the next consenting relationship. Fidelity in marriage was altered to fidelity as long as everything was going okay. Being "engaged" was replaced by "living together".

Our happiness is determined by the ideas that we believe. Ideas form attitudes, and attitudes determine behavior or actions. Bad ideas produce unhappy and unfulfilling lives; good ideas produce happy and fulfilled lives. The idea "if it feels good, do it" was a bad idea that seeded bad behavior. The idea that sex is simply a biological urge was another bad idea that seeded more bad—irresponsible, exploitive—behavior.

The sexual revolution was a national temper tantrum to avoid honor, loyalty and commitment in sexual relations. It reminds me of the spoiled girl, Veruca Salt, in the movie, "Willy Wonka and the Chocolate Factory." Remember when she throws a temper tantrum and demands to get what she wants, when she wants it? Such an attitude with a child is irritating, but with a whole society it's scary. The sexual revolution created widespread deception, distrust, disloyalty, divorce, abortion, and off-the-charts illegitimacy.

The free love movement had nothing to do with love and even less to do with freedom. Where's the freedom when the "every man for himself" game makes us all feel threatened and scared? Where's the love when men prey upon women, and women prey upon men?

The Counter Sexual Revolution

Lately, however, there's an awakening in the air. A new revolution is brewing—the Counter sexual revolution. The value of abstinence before marriage and fidelity after is being reconsidered. One study shows that Americans are more worried about the loss of morals in their society than anything else. They are worried about the high illegitimacy rate—the highest in the world. They are worried about the lack of human tenderness and respect. They are worried about AIDS. They are worried about tax dollars spent on single mothers and their children. They are worried about how children will fare growing up without fathers. They are worried about the high divorce rate. They are worried that things have gone too far.

There are more than just the physical consequences of casual sex; there are emotional and spiritual consequences as well. Casual sex can inflict the deepest kind of pain and suffering for the human soul—children robbed of childhood, girls who cry in the night over boys who never loved them, boys who must put aside skateboards to grow up too soon and too fast. The real tragedy of casual sex isn't the cost to the government, or the pregnancies, or the AIDS threat—it's the broken hearts and broken lives.

As a fifteen-year-old, I didn't really know what I was searching for when I asked about having sex before marriage, but as a fifty-year-old I realize I was searching for knowledge that would help me to make responsible sexual decisions. I wanted more than just the facts of life, I wanted understanding. Factual knowledge helps us to accurately see the world around us, but understanding helps us to choose wisely, live abundantly and happily.

I believe that there are universal and natural laws—self-evident truths—for human success. Some things do not work; other things work every time. Values may change from culture to culture, but natural laws for human happiness and success are always the same. Cooperation, service, compassion, sacrifice, understanding, honor, and integrity will always enhance the harmony in any heart, in any home, in any nation. On the other hand, selfishness, callousness, insensitivity, dishonor, and deception will always tear at the peace and harmony of any heart, of any home, of any nation.

"Consider the freedom of chastity."

Recently, a young man told me his sad story. Two years ago Hank was in high school, a star football player with several college scholarships lined-up. Then a series of events turned it all around: his sometime-girlfriend got pregnant. They moved in together for the sake of the child, but it didn't work out. Eventually, she started going out with someone else. Hank got jealous, hunted the guy down, jumped him and beat him up. Now Hank was being charged for assault and battery.

He looked old for his young age—haggard, worn and shell shocked. He said, "You never think these things are going to happen to you. I thought I had my future all sewed up; I had everything. Now I have nothing."

"You might want to consider the freedom of chastity." As I said these words I could tell it was a major revelation to him. I added, "Think of it this way—you'll know exactly where your seed is at all times."

It was obvious that Hank had never before considered the possibility of waiting to engage in sex until marriage. He thought for a moment, and then said, "It sure is, isn't it? It's the ultimate freedom!"

"If we have no values to transmit to our young, we need not be surprised that we live in an increasingly valueless age."

George Roche III

Most youth, like Hank, were never taught a better way.

"Surely, these young people cannot be blamed," wrote George Roche III, president of Hillsdale College, "for the direction of our society. Surely, a system which produces young people, some of whom cannot read, many of whom cannot think, and most of whom lack knowledge of their own heritage and the moral values which underlie it, is a system which needs serious attention." (Education in America, p.5)

Decisions that Bring Lasting Joy

Often I use this demonstration in teaching: I put a candy bar, a handful of various coins, a dollar, and a hundred-dollar bill on the table. I then ask the youth, "If I were to give you a choice of these items which one would you choose?"

The answer is always, "The hundred-dollar bill."

Then I ask, "Who has a three-year-old brother or sister?"

When someone raises their hand, I ask, "What do you think he or she would choose?"

The answer, "The candy bar."

"But a hundred candy bars could be purchased with the hundred-dollar bill, right? What could you do to help him make a wiser decision?" I ask.

The usual response, "I could advise him to pick the hundred-dollar bill and we could go to the store and buy all the candy bars he ever wanted."

I then say, "There are lots of choices in this life. Every day we make choices based upon what we think is the most valuable, and what will bring us the most happiness. Wouldn't it be a shame if we, like the little child, choose what will bring immediate gratification over what could bring lasting joy?"

Politicians have recently said to the youth, "Just say no to sex." Parents have always been saying, "Just say no to sex," but the children are asking, "Why?" As a youth, I deserved more information, and our children deserve more *now*.

The youth of America have a right to know their options. They have a right to know what ideas have seduced them into thinking that the only down sides to premarital sex are pregnancy and sexually transmitted diseases. They have a right to a wider view. They have a right to know the rewards of self-control and moral virtue: self-respect, freedom to be a friend and have friends, spiritual strength, honorable love and marriage, sexual fulfillment (intimacy of mind, heart, soul and body), children's respect and confidence.

They have a right to know the clear difference between having sex and making love. They have a right to know that there are other sexually transmitted diseases that affect the heart, mind and soul. They have a right to be warned of abusive relationships masquerading as love, and of the dark side of passion that seems titillatingly exciting on the surface, but leaves a deadly hangover. They need to know that pretending love for selfish conquests may lead to being unable to love at all. They need to know that they cannot use and abuse another human being without first abusing themselves. They need to understand that when conscience is shut down in order to feel good about doing bad, eventually it does just that—shuts down—leaving them without an inner guide. They need to know that there's a force that would twist the powers to love, honor and cherish into powers to hate, dishonor and despise. They need to know that the monsters who use their sexual powers to inflict pain were never born that way; monsters become monsters one step at a time.

This book is the result of a forty-year search for the answers to the question, "Why?" It answers the questions that, as a youth, I never knew to ask. It exposes the dangers of casual and exploitive sex, and explores the wealth of enlightened chastity—for the individual, friendships, marriages, families and society. It's a journey to explore insights that will assist in making responsible and ethical sexual decisions.

Ultimately, each one of us must make the decision of how we will use the God-given gift of sexuality. This decision—one of the most important decisions of our lives—deserves the journey to understanding. This book is dedicated to every curious teenager who wants to hear more than "no" and for every parent, teacher or youth leader who must answer the question, "Why?"

The Forgotten Virtue 2

"Chastity is a wealth; it comes from an abundance of love."

Tagore

Insight #2
Loving and loyal relationships naturally lead to commitment because sexual desire is not just a physical need; it's also an emotional, intellectual and even spiritual need.

No question about it, chastity—sex only in marriage—has become the forgotten virtue. The words, *morality* and *chastity* have become politically incorrect, generating anger like the use of profanity used to in the old days, "Whose morality? How dare you impose your morality upon me! How dare you attempt to tell me what I ought to be doing? Chastity? You can't be serious; no one believes in that anymore."

I recall a stimulating talk with a bright, energetic businessman. During our conversation, he asked,"What are you writing about?"

"It's a book on the value of chastity," I said. After a brief silence, he said, "I thought that went out with the dark ages."

A few days later I was having lunch with a very successful career woman, discovering how little we had in common. She was career first/ family second—which never happened. I was family first/career second. We did have a few things in common: a love of nature, horses, and meaningful films. We had both lived through the raging propaganda of the sexual revolution. She converted, and I probably would have if not for a stroke of fate that changed my life. I met my future husband and overnight the idea of love and marriage was in fashion.

The conversation was clipping along when she asked, "What are you writing?"

Despite our differences we'd managed to disagree agreeably; I wanted to keep it that way. To tell the truth, I was a little bit intimidated by this woman and desperately wanted to answer, "Oh, the need for recycling and other environmental concerns," but my integrity was at stake.

"Actually," I stammered, "right now I'm researching for a book on healthy and unhealthy love relationships. . ."

"Sounds good," she responded, "we certainly need that."

"Well. . .specifically, it will show the difference between having sex and making love, or the value of moral discipline in promoting healthy love relationships. The bottom line is that it's a case for chastity."

She smiled that look big sisters give to their little know-nothing siblings, and asked, "You're joking, right? Why would anyone be against sex?"

"Who said anything about being against sex?" I asked.

"I thought chastity meant celibacy, and celibacy means no sex. I've always thought it was a part of the whole religious self-deprivation thing—you know like those who eat mush, work all day in the hot sun, and sleep on boards."

"Well," I began, "there will always be extremists, but chastity isn't celibacy. Celibacy means no sex while chastity means holding out for the best."

"You make it sound like chastity can actually mean better sex."

"Chastity can mean better everything—especially better sex. For instance, you could pig out on junk food all day long if you wanted to, so why wait for something better?"

"The anticipation of a great meal?"

"Right. That's what they didn't tell us in the seventies—discipline of the passions can increase sexual fulfillment. There's been a high price for free love."

"So you're saying that people should wait for what—marriage?"

"Well, technically, chastity means sex only-in-marriage, but my point is to promote loving and loyal relationships that naturally lead to commitment, and yes, a legal relationship. Sexual desire is not just a physical need; it's also an emotional, intellectual and even spiritual need. We've bought into the idea that it's all just biological, but it's so much more than that. Making love isn't just a physical workout; it's the whole purpose of life—to make love to one another! The physical act is only part of it. True lovers are making love the whole day through, whether they are washing clothes, preparing dinner, or listening to music together—it's all making love. Those who reduce it down to a romp will never know such a symphony of love making. You could say it's holistic intimacy, not simply intercourse of body, but intercourse of mind, heart, and soul. That's why the one night stands aren't fulfilling—they never fulfill all the desires."

She looked confused, then asked, "How can it be wrong to love?"

"Casual sex isn't love; it's usually exploitation," I answered.

"Well, we would disagree on that one," she argued. "The way I see it, it's wonderful to have the ultimate closeness with someone you care about."

"That's the problem," I said, "it usually begins with a warm feeling of closeness and ends with a cold feeling of separateness. Are you still friends with any of these lovers you've had?"

"One," she said. "He's living at my apartment right now—we're still great friends, but we've learned to leave the sex out."

"Precisely my point," I said, "fulfillment doesn't come with lovers. It comes with love."

"Come on! I can't imagine anything else. Why would anyone choose anything else? Is it because you think that you'll go to hell if you have a good time with someone besides your husband?"

"No," I answered. "I think it would create a hell for both of us right here. Some things just don't work."

This is how the conversation went till the shadows of evening began to work their way across our table. Then with a sigh, she said, "I'd give anything to have what you have. I've had some great lovers, but it never lasts. I've always wanted to have a couple of kids, but it doesn't look like that's going to happen either. In some ways my life has been a fantastic success. After all, I actually produce and direct movies—who wouldn't want to do what I do? But when the day's over I go home to an empty apartment. Your life sounds like a fairy tale. I didn't think love lasted anymore. You've been lucky."

"Luck? I don't think so. I remember a cartoon that read, 'Some people think marriages are made in heaven; I think they come in a kit and you have to put them together yourselves.' This is more in line with reality; at least this is the way it has worked for us."

"Okay," she said. "So what you're saying is that you don't just stumble onto a good thing, you create it?"

"Right, you can buy a great car, then trash it and have it break down. Same thing happens in relationships. Love relationships are very fragile. They can start out right and good, but if not cared for properly, they can go sour.

"Statistically, our marriage didn't have a chance, but we have been able to keep our love growing and renewing through the years. It hasn't been easy, but the truth is I just keep falling in love with the same man over and over—my husband."

"Tell me about it."

"Well, we were very young. I was only fifteen when I met my husband; he was nineteen. It seemed like one day I was in high school carrying a load of books, and the next day I was out of high school carrying a baby. The slap into motherhood—and adulthood—was painful. I was haunted by the thought, 'This isn't where I belong. This isn't where I belong.'

"The experience was so traumatic that for years I had nightmares about going back to high school and not remembering where my locker was. Then when I finally found it, I had forgotten the combination. Oh, how I wanted to go back—to again be leading a cheer at a football game! To just walk through the hallways and see everyone. It was so difficult to accept that I would never be with my friends again. Sometimes my girlfriends would come over to see me, but it wasn't the same anymore; our worlds were different.

"I recall one night; it was late, but I couldn't sleep. I had turned off all the lights, and was pacing the floor like a caged lion. Everywhere I looked I saw gray. The walls were gray, the junk furniture that we purchased at a garage sale was dirty gray, the cold tile floor was sprinkled gray, the rain running down the windows was silver gray.

"Questions kept racing through my mind, 'What am I suppose to do now? Who's going to tell me what to do? What are my goals now? What do mothers do? What do mothers look forward to? Why didn't someone tell me this would happen? Why didn't someone warn me? I don't know this life; I only know being a teenager and high school.'

"I wanted to run—but where? I wanted to hide—but where? I never felt so lost. I found myself doing something I never thought that I would do—praying. I didn't know if I even believed in anything like a God, but there was nowhere else to turn. My heart screamed out in silence, Let me go back. Please let me go back; I promise I'll do better. Let me go back home. Let me be with my family. Just let me be a kid again.

"I figured if there was a God, He ought to be powerful enough to take me back in time. For hours and hours I sobbed and prayed. Then at the point that it seemed I would be swallowed up in complete despair, a thought formed in my mind: 'You have the power to change your life. You can't go back, but you *can* go forward.'

"I realized then and there, I had a choice—I could either continue to grieve over my lost life, or I could begin to build a new one. I decided to begin building.

"In my longing to go back, I had been unwilling to go forward. Even though I was going to be a mom, I still had myself. I loved learning, so I began taking classes at the local college. I stopped reading romance magazines and began reading classical literature. I enrolled in ballet classes. I kept growing—learning, becoming, meeting new people. I stayed alive. Years later, when I was expecting my tenth baby, I graduated with a Bachelor's Degree in English and American Studies.

"No, I never regained my carefree teen years, and I'll always feel a nostalgic longing at football games and formal weddings. I will never know what I lost, but I do know what I gained, and I am grateful. Looking back I realize that however painful this experience was, it was that moment in time when I formed resolves that would last my whole life."

Then she asked, "So that's the reason you're writing this book, because of the mistakes you have made?"

"Not really," I said, "I think my experience has helped me to have understanding and compassion for others, but the real reason is because I think those who settle for promiscuous sex are missing out, and they don't even know what they're missing out on. My search for answers has been rewarding. There are solid reasons, rational reasons that support chastity. I just want to share them."

We parted friends. When I arrived home the younger children were outside making a slide in the snow. The teenagers were listening to music and dancing wildly in their room. Our son, Adam, was composing music with his synthesizer. I began to pull food from the refrigerator for dinner—grateful for the noise of family, and the life that surrounded me.

3

The Power of Enlightened Chastity

"One of the most striking characteristics of a man who is really in love is that his conversation is chaste. He is willing to analyze sentiment, not sensation."

Ernest Dimnet, French Priest

Insight #3

Enlightened chastity protects the fragile but powerful capacity to love and to bond until it fulfills its destiny—a wholesome, loving, loyal and legal relationship.

Looking out the bedroom window, when I was little, I was fascinated that I couldn't see the screen and the view of the backyard at the same time. If I looked at the screen, my eyes focused on the screen and the landscape was blurred; if I looked at the landscape, the screen disappeared. There's a short-range and long-range perspective on human sexuality—immediate gratification versus soul-bonding. The secular view focuses on the short-range perspective: simply a biological urge, while the traditional view focuses on the long-range perspective; that intimacy is a desire of heart, mind, soul and body to be bonded together in a "one flesh" relationship. Focusing on the short-range perspective can obscure the vision of the bigger picture. The human spirit longs for more, and deserves more.

The long-range view sees making love, not simply as a physical act, but the purpose and meaning of life—to build a circle of love together, a circle of beauty, a circle of children, a circle of happy memories, a circle of growing and learning together. Going for my evening walk, I'm always impressed by the way in which our neighbors show love and care for their yards. There seems to be a natural spilling-over of love into the gardens. Husbands, wanting to make love to their wives, mow lawns, plant trees, paint fences. Wives, wanting to make love to their husbands, create beautiful flower gardens, and decorated homes. Adam and Eve were given the garden of Eden, but we must sweat for it.

Circles of Love

Let's stand back and scan the need for love. Babies are born with the need to be loved and nurtured, but within just a few months they show the need to give love as well. Watch a baby cuddle a doll and clothe and feed it. Watch their tender hearts break when their ripped-up and worn teddy bear is lost. Watch a mother cuddling her baby—while her baby cuddles a teddy bear. Children—and grown-ups—need to give love, and to receive it.

The Creator planned for every baby to be born into a circle of love where they can bloom and grow physically, mentally, emotionally, and spiritually. And just as night follows the day, as children pass through puberty and then mature, a new longing takes place—the longing to create their own circle of love. The longing is not simply sexual; it's a whole-souled longing to become one—one in heart, one in mind, one in spirit, and one in body with another person.

Enlightened chastity protects the fragile but powerful capacity to love and to bond until it fulfills its destiny—a wholesome, loving, loyal and legal relationship. Casual sex, on the other hand, based upon a short-range perspective detours this natural process away from its destination, and creates circles of distrust, alienation, separation, even hatred.

Circles of wholesome love cannot be mandated by the state, enforced by the justice system, or manipulated by false and contrived motives. They are built only upon sincere love, loyalty, and commitment. Just as houses built on shaky foundations eventually collapse, relationships built without honor and commitment are likely to collapse as well. The living-together-to-see-if-it-works-out approach is like building with tacky materials in preparation for the tear down.

The heart seems to have a delicate compass that guides us to our soul-mates, and tampering with this delicate mechanism can be damaging. Insincere "I love you's" can prevent us from ever knowing what is sincere and what is not. Using the feelings of the heart as a tool for seduction can eventually seduce the heart into feeling nothing at all. (More on this in the chapter titled, Betrayal Against the Heart).

Like all virtues, enlightened chastity is a manifestation of love for oneself and others. All virtues are love in action: self-discipline, compassion, responsibility, friendship, work, courage, honesty and loyalty. The virtuous envision in their minds and feel in their hearts that all human life, including their own, is worthy of love, respect, and protection. Our society is currently scrambling for these virtues, but many have forgotten chastity. Maybe chastity has been overlooked because no one wants to go back to the old version that shrouded sexual intimacy with shame even in marriage. No one wants to lose the free social interaction between men and women that used to be *inappropriate* . Certainly, no one wants the chastity that created less love for everyone.

A New Look at an Old Idea: Enlightened Chastity

Enlightened chastity is "for such a time as this" when we're ready for a new look at an old idea. "Enlightened" is added because it's lived by love and goodwill rather than as a restrictive law, with the focus on the rewards rather than the restrictions. The rewards are great: self-respect and other-respect, spiritual strength, peace of conscience, confidence, free social interaction without the suspicion of hidden motives, wholesome brother-sister friendships, equality of the sexes, interdependence rather than crippling dependence, enhancing personal growth rather than stagnation.

Enlightened chastity calls into play every other virtue: self-discipline, integrity, honesty, responsibility, compassion, friendship, courage, loyalty. It's the immortal virtue because it effects our children's lives and their children's lives forever. It's the most important virtue because honorable love is the main source of human happiness, and dishonorable love the main source of human misery.

Living chastity by law might have a tendency to keep us distant from others, but living enlightened chastity never will. It comes from a vision of the sacredness of human life and sincere feelings of love that inspire compassion, sympathy, friendliness, goodwill and a sense of humor. On the other hand, living the letter of the law without the feelings of love and respect defeats the whole purpose.

Chastity is the immortal virtue because it effects our children's lives and their children's lives forever. It's the most important virtue because honorable love is the main source of human happiness, and dishonorable love the main source of human misery.

Chastity by Love, not by Law

One of the themes of the New Testament is the contrasting perspectives on living the counsels of God. There were those who exalted the law as the highest virtue, but Jesus taught that love was the highest virtue.

When asked by a lawyer, "Master, which is the great commandment in the law?" He answered, "Thou shalt love the Lord thy God with all thy heart, and with all thy soul, and with all thy mind. This is the first and great commandment. And the second is like unto it, Thou shalt love thy neighbour as thyself." (Matt. 22: 36-39)

We often hear of loving our fellow man, but only through loving God first can we have the ability to love His children, and know how best to help them. Jesus Christ emphasized that genuine goodness, or virtue, must come from the inside out, not the outside in. He criticized those who looked to the law, but were without life and love when he said, "Woe unto you, scribes and Pharisees, hypocrites! For ye are like unto whited sepulchres (burial tombs) which indeed appear beautiful outward, but are within full of dead men's bones, and of all uncleanliness. Even so ye also outwardly appear righteous unto men, but within ye are full of hypocrisy and iniquity." (Matthew 23:27,28)

The idea of sepulchres—burial tombs— suggests that there was no *life* in them. The glorious power of chastity to change hearts and lives does not come from a law. It comes from staying connected to the God who gives life and the ability to love "more abundantly".

Remember the story of the Prodigal son? He leaves his home, spends his inheritance on riotous living, then having spent all returns home to his family. His father realizes his son's folly, but welcomes him back home with open arms and a grand welcome home dinner. The elder son, who has been dutiful his whole life, is bitter, resentful and jealous. He will not attend the dinner, sulks, and complains to his father that having been good and righteous all his life he has never received such attention. Christian philosopher, Henry Drummond, used this story to illustrate that there are two kinds of sins—the sins of the body and the sins of the disposition. The Prodigal son was guilty of the first—the sins of the body—while the elder brother was guilty of the second—the sins of disposition.

The elder son had been obedient, but he erred in his feelings of jealousy, bitterness and resentment. Those who use their obedience to the principle of chastity to love their fellow men less, are like the elder brother—looking good to themselves, but contributing to the cold indifference of this world. They may be true in body to the law, but not in disposition. "If you love," said Henry Drummond, "you will unconsciously fulfill the whole law."

"I hope to add a measure of grace to the world."

The power of enlightened chastity is beautifully portrayed in the screenplay, Man of La Mancha by Dale Wasserman, based upon the classic novel, Don Quixote, by Miguel de Cervantes y Saavedra. There are two main characters in the play: Don Quixote, a man of honor and virtue, and Aldonza, a prostitute. Quixote, after reading and despairing over man's inhumanity to man, resolves to go forth and begin a quest to right wrongs and bring justice into the world. Believing himself to be a gallant knight, he seeks out a virtuous lady to whom he can dedicate his good deeds.

He travels to a distant inn and discovers the "lady" he is seeking, Aldonza. She is only a lady in his eyes, to others she is nothing more than a common whore. She has long ago surrendered to the forces of vulgarity and vice, and having known only men without honor, she distrusts them all. She spends her days serving and fighting off the dirty-minded men who are constantly pawing and taunting her.

Quixote sees her with a mind that captures her true worth, and a heart overflowing with tenderness and respect. He says to her, "Sweet lady. . .fair virgin. . .I dare not gaze full upon thy countenance lest I be blinded by beauty. I see heaven when I see thee. . .thy name is like a prayer an angel whispers. . .Now I've found thee, and the world shall know thy glory."

She is skeptical and cynical, "What do you want of me?" she says.

"Nothing," he replies.

"Liar!" she shouts.

"I deserved the rebuke," He responds. "I ask of my lady."

"Now we get to it," she accuses.

"That I may be allowed to serve her," he answers. "That I may hold her in my heart. That I may dedicate each victory and call upon her in defeat. And if at last I give my life I give it in her sacred name."

"Why do you do these things?" she shouts.

"I hope to add some measure of grace to the world."

He then sings, "The Impossible Dream."

> To dream the impossible dream
> To fight the unbeatable foe,

To bear with unbearable sorrow,
To run where the brave dare not go.
To right the unrightable wrong,
To love, pure and chaste, from afar,
To try, when your arms are too weary,
To reach the unreachable star!

Eventually the power of his love and respect transforms her life and her vision of herself. After his untimely death, she continues his quest to "add a measure of grace to the world." The relationship between Quixote and Aldonza is totally platonic; there are no signs of romantic inclination. This is an example of one of the rewards of chaste love. It allows the freedom to love as brother or sister in this world that is starving for love.

This topic is explored in depth in the chapter titled, "The Wealth of Chastity." We can be confident that all virtues counseled by God are to help us to love, not to hinder us.

One who lives *chastity by law* would be inclined to say to an attractive person of the opposite sex, "I must ignore you to be chaste—stay away. If we must interact, then we must do so in a businesslike way without personality or charm." One who lives *chastity by love*— a wellspring of warmth and goodwill—would be inclined to say, "I delight in you and I would love to become friends. I love you too much to use you in any way. I will treasure your mind, heart and soul as I do my own. I would not, I could not, take advantage of you for my own pride, vanity or gratification. I want to watch you bloom in my presence, not wither and die."

Loving More

It was a hot, summer afternoon so a friend and I went for a walk and an ice cream. The young man at the ice cream counter seemed stressed, so I was friendly with him. As we walked away, my friend chided, "You are always so flirtatious."

"What do you mean by flirtatious?" I asked.

"As if you don't know." She responded. "It means coming on to someone."

"Actually, I was just being playful and friendly. I would have acted the same whether it was a man or a woman. That's how I know it's being friendly, not flirting."

"I've always considered it being flirtatious," she said.

"I just wanted to be friendly and help his day go a little better. Life would get pretty dull if people weren't friendly with one another, don't you think?"

"I think you're just rationalizing. That young man might misinterpret your motives and think you want something more than ice cream," she warned.

"I can't control what he thinks, but I *can* control what I think. Besides, I trust myself well enough to know my motives."

She looked confused. "But you have to admit that you let your feminine charm play a part in your friendliness."

"I guess you're right," I said. "It's a part of my nature though; I wouldn't want to leave it out."

"Well, you should," she said. "After all, do I need to remind you that you're a married woman?"

"That's true, but I *am* still a woman," I said. "And my love for my husband inspires me to love others more not less."

Some think that friendly interaction is being flirtatious and unchaste. Again, living chastity by law might have a tendency to keep us distant from others, but living enlightened chastity never will. It comes from sincere feelings of love that inspire friendliness, goodwill and a sense of humor.

The topic of chastity is laden with misunderstandings; there are others.

Enlightened Chastity is NOT:

1. Simply a legal issue

Chastity means to show such respect for human intimacy that it is reserved only for a loving, loyal and legal relationship. All three are necessary. Loving (in the intimate sense) without also being loyal and legal, is usually a masquerade—to be discussed later. Merely being legal without love and loyalty is a farce. Even marriage relationships can be legally right, but morally wrong, specifically in cases of spousal abuse.

Like young colts in a pasture, teenagers are full of life, adventure, and curiosity. They constantly test the limits of their enclosure by leaning against the fence. Teens go to their clergy and ask, "How far can I go?" They want to explore their sexuality without violating the letter of the law. Some couples, in their cunning to get around the law, travel over a state line, get married, have sex for a weekend, then have the marriage annulled before they go home. Legally right, morally wrong—a loophole. There is always a way to slip through a loophole when chastity is lived by the "law"; but there is never a way when it's lived by love.

2. Denying masculinity and femininity

The physical, mental, emotional, and sexual differences are an endowment of God, to deny them is to deny a part of God's creation. Children are naturally feminine or masculine. There are outside and inside differences between men and women; they complement one another physically, mentally, emotionally and spiritually. If we have to deny a part of ourselves in order to live a virtuous life, something's wrong! It stands to reason that the Creator never intended to eliminate the differences between men and women in personality and mannerisms, but to liberate them to flourish in a community of trust and goodwill.

3. Merely consent

There is the idea floating around that if two people consent to indulge in sex without commitment it is somehow morally right, or at least according to the Popular Opinion. The term "consenting adults" is one of many expressions that translate down to sex without honor and commitment. It is used to suspend conscience for an experiment—to see if it works out. The reality is, if I consent to let the man of the night steal from me, I am still left robbed!

The "consentors" plan to jump ship when the honeymoon is over or when problems arise, but even in healthy bonding, there will always be problems. Deeper, more resistant-to-disease love comes by working out the problems, not running from them. Real love inspires commitment, not merely consent. The smoke screen of passions has been known to cloud clear thinking. Being willing to wait for the right time to ignite sexual bonding is a sign that it's the real thing; true love inspires restraint—not recklessness.

Being willing to wait for the right time to ignite sexual bonding is a sign that it's the real thing; true love inspires restraint —not recklessness.

"This is it. This is the real thing," a young man said. "You know, before her, I would have just gone to bed without even thinking it over. But with her I am so afraid of losing what we have that I am willing to wait until it's totally right. I don't want any regrets—it's too important to me. She's too important." This attitude shows the key element in all healthy relationships: the willingness to sacrifice! Dimnet wrote, "One of the most striking characteristics of a man who is really in love is that his conversation is chaste. He is willing to analyze sentiment, not sensation."

4. Celibacy

"I was surprised to find the scriptures so candid about sex," said a friend who read the Bible for the first time.

"Surprised?" I said, "Why would you be surprised? The Bible is about life—and sex is life."

"I know, but *sex*. It just doesn't seem right to have such a Holy Book mentioning such an earthy thing. It just doesn't fit."

"Maybe sex is holy," I said.

"Holy?" she said with a raised eyebrow.

"It's the most holy—sacred—act of all. Two humans locked together as one in an act of love. That's holy. Giving birth to a sweet baby that is created in their image. That's holy. Growing and becoming more than they could apart—that's holy, too."

I was surprised that she was surprised—scriptural references to sex show a candidness, a wholesomeness, a sure evidence it is not dark, sinful, and evil. The Bible places restrictions on sexual practices; it does not condemn sexual pleasures. Let's look at a few scriptural passages: "And they shall be one flesh." Genesis 2:24 "And Adam knew Eve, his wife; and she conceived. . ." Genesis 4:1 "Neither is the man without the woman. . .in the Lord." 1 Cor 11:11 "Let thy fountain be blessed: and rejoice with the wife of thy youth. Let her be as the loving hind and pleasant roe; let her breasts satisfy thee at all times; and be thou ravished always with her love." Proverbs 5:18-19. This is my favorite: "There be three things which are too wonderful for me, yea, four. . .the way of an eagle in the air; the way of a serpent upon a rock; the way of a ship in the midst of the sea; and the way of a man with a maid." Proverbs 30:18-19

Taste buds were created to celebrate eating, eyes were given to celebrate the beauties of the earth, and the delights of sexual passion were created to celebrate marital intimacy.

Popular evangelist, Billy Graham, said the Bible

> "...celebrates sex and its proper use, presenting it as God-created, God-ordained, God-blessed. It makes plain that God himself implanted the physical magnetism between the sexes for two reasons: for the propagation of the human race, and for the expression of that kind of love between man and wife that makes for true oneness. His command to the first man and woman to be 'one flesh' was as important as his command to 'be fruitful and multiply.'
>
> "The Bible makes plain that evil, when related to sex, means not the use of something inherently corrupt but the misuse of something pure and good.
>
> "The Bible teaches clearly that sex can be a wonderful servant but a terrible master: that it can be a creative force more powerful than any other in the fostering of love, companionship, and happiness or can be the most destructive of all of life's forces." (Billy Graham, "What The Bible Says About Sex,"

Reader's Digest, May 1970 p.118)

Despite the clear message of the Bible, there have been those who have advocated celibacy—no sex at all, that anything that has to do with the body was sinful. Some have isolated themselves from the opposite sex, living lives of extreme deprivation of the flesh—eating only enough to stave off starvation, sleeping on hard bunks, laboring in the heat of the day in chores designed to keep the body exhausted and spent.

Pope Gregory said, "Sexual pleasure can never be without sins." St. Augustine taught that sexual intercourse is the way that original sin is transmitted from one generation to another. Then there's the "if-you-can't-hack-it" interpretation of Apostle Paul's writings.

It is recorded that he said, "If they cannot contain, let them marry: for it is better to marry than to burn." (1 Corinthians 7:9) However he also taught, "Neither is the man without the woman, neither the woman without the man, in the Lord." (1 Corinthians 11:11) Some have apologized for Paul, saying that he was speaking specifically to missionaries while they are in missionary service. After all, Paul was married himself. In any case, since the interpretation of some of Paul's writings on sexual relations seem to conflict with the overall message of the Bible, we can conclude that the final word on the matter must be left to the overall theme, and to God himself, who summed it up simply, "It is not good for man to be alone." (Genesis 2:18)

Make no mistake. Chastity does not mean celibacy. I

visited what had been a flourishing Quaker community in Pennsylvania. They believed in absolute celibacy. The buildings were vacant, empty. There were empty dorms for the men and empty dorms for the women. For awhile, they attempted to keep their congregation replenished by adopting children, but most of these children grew up and left. Men and women were separated and alone in order to better serve a God who said that "it is not good to be alone." Celibacy is not progress; it is not growth; it is not life.

Summary

Our family just watched a Disney movie titled, "Hunchback of Notre Dame," based on the novel by Victor Hugo. Quasimoto sings, "So many times out there I've watched a happy pair of lovers walking in the night. They had a kind of glow around them. It almost looked like heaven's light." Quasimoto's longing to love, and be loved, is a part of being human. Again, enlightened chastity protects the fragile but powerful capacity to love and to bond until it fulfills its destiny—a wholesome, loving, loyal and legal relationship. It also allows social interaction without hidden motives. Each one of us has the ability to add a measure of grace to this dreary, depressing world when we reach for the power of loving "pure and chaste from afar!"

4 What Happened to Chastity?

"ye are all the children of light, and the children of the day; we are not of the night, nor of darkness."

1Thess 5:5

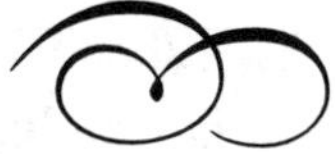

Insight #4
Free love never was freedom; sex without honor and commitment leaves a bitter aftertaste—feeling less loved and more lonely.

I was visiting my parents and laughing at old family photos. We came across their wedding portrait—sixty years old! They looked so handsome. Oh, Mother! The classic porcelain face and strawberry-blond curly hair. Daddy! A Clark Gable look-alike, with moustache and black wavy hair. There was a moment of silence, then Daddy said, "Those were the days when couples fell in love and got married. That doesn't seem to happen too often anymore; things are different now."

Mother added, "Our favorite song was 'When I Fall In Love It Will Be Forever.' The song is still popular, but no one believes in it anymore. Things *are* different now."

"Things are different now"—these words were haunting. My generation watched as the idea of romantic love and "living happily ever after" was discarded.

I recall one of my college teachers saying, "Romantic love is a myth. It is an illusion of a desperate and irrational mind, and no one lives happily ever after."

No one lives happily ever after; but romantic love, the type that continues to bloom and grow through the years is not a myth. I watched such love growing up, and I have lived it in my own life, but it is, however, in danger of becoming extinct. Soul-bonding love is fragile; it dies a natural death when the soil is too acid to survive. Without love, honor and cherish—without honesty, integrity and loyalty—it's in soil too acid to survive.

Our society has contributed to its extinction by becoming too acid with the idea that sexual desire is merely an itch to be scratched. Too acid with the idea that life is nothing more than a journey from sea to dust. Too acid with the idea that repressing sexual urges is unhealthy. Too acid with the idea that there are no moral values—only societal conditioning. Too acid with the idea that the highest value is self-fulfillment. Too acid with the lie perpetrated by some therapists that an extra marital relationship could actually help a troubled marriage.

There's been a terrible price—a devastating price—for buying into the lies, especially the one that says, "If it feels good, do it and to hell with the consequences." Unfortunately, *hell* usually is the consequence.

Romantic love that continues to bloom and grow can and does exist, but it's dying a natural death in soil too acid to survive.

When I was growing up, romantic love and waiting till marriage were still in style. The movie industry had strict rules on sexual conduct. The most suggestive scene in the movies those days was Donna Reed losing her bathrobe and hiding in the bushes in "It's a Wonderful Life." Couples could only kiss for so many seconds, married couples were not shown in bed together, and the plot of the movie had to have some redeeming social value.

Music glorified love and marriage: I remember walking to school singing, "Love and marriage, love and marriage, go together like a horse and carriage. Ask the local gentry and they will say, 'It's elementary'," or, "When I fall in love, it will be forever, or I'll never fall in love. And the moment that I feel that you feel that way too, is when I'll fall in love with you."

The Smokescreen of the Sexual Revolution

Then came the Sixties, when ideas such as lasting romantic love and morality were dismantled piece by piece and tossed to the wind. By the time the Seventies were upon us, the raging nonsense of the sexual revolution, as it was called, was in full swing. It reminded me—then and now—of carnivals and I hate carnivals. Barkers yelling at you, gaudy colored lights, cheap prizes, and giant stuffed animals. You spend every cent in your pocket in an attempt to win the grand prize. Then when you do, you find yourself walking through the crowd carrying a giant bright lemon-colored dinosaur, heavy in your hands, and heavy with the thoughts, "Why? What will I ever do with this?" In the morning light—you wake up, look across the room at the yellow monster cluttering up your room and again wonder, "Why?"

The barkers for free love were on every side, luring the youth into casual sex. I watched as friend after friend succumbed and gave their childhoods for the prize, which was only an illusion that sex was better than chocolate, movies or slumber parties. Only later did they wake up with heavy hearts, and shame and confusion cluttering up their lives. Some said that there was no reason for shame, that it was all a result of false religious and societal traditions, but for some reason the shame was still there all the same.

It was a unique period of American history. Rebellion and resentment were in the air; you could feel it. Some were resentful of everything—they burned the flag, spit upon the cross, and scorned their mothers and their apple pie. All traditions—particularly moral traditions—were challenged. Everything was up for debate.

It was the season for lots of questions, and few answers: Why go to school? Why get married? Why live in houses when a VW bus will do? Why live in single unit families when you can live in communal groups? Why are women supposed to be a certain way and men another—is it because they have been conditioned by society? Why is there a double standard? Why is there any moral standard at all? Whose morals? Whose values? Like being given a problem to solve in a mathematics class and arguing with the teacher: Why this particular problem? Why these numbers? Why numbers at all? Why mathematics at all? Why life?

The flower children of San Francisco emerged in the midst of all of this unresolved contention and confusion. I remember going to the city and watching the young men and women as they stood on corners, handing out flowers to the people as they passed by. They carried placards with a simple message: "Make Love, Not War."

It seemed reasonable—just reduce all of life's problems down to the religion of love. After all, it was noncontroversial at a time when everything was controversial! Almost overnight, love was enthroned: if it's love, it's right; if it feels good, do it. Anything that even came close to resembling love was accepted.

With the philosophical climate in such a vacuum, and almost everyone grappling for something—anything—to believe in, it was a hit. Magazines, movies and music hailed the message: "All ya gotta have is love. . .It can't be wrong, when it feels so right. . .Let's slip away into the night. . .I'm a woman in love, so I'll do anything. . .You're a woman now; you've learned how to love. . .My virgin child. " A middle-age man singing to a young teenager, "Leave the boys behind and come live with me," would have outraged the previous generation, but no longer.

Gradually, the movies that glorified chastity were replaced by movies that portrayed virginity as the plague of the naive and innocent. Young men and women who had not been initiated were considered to be "out of it"—uncool—unsophisticated.

New technology contributed to acceptance of the sexual revolution. Contraceptives were available at the corner market or even distributed free at the local high school. Unwanted pregnancies could be avoided by "the pill." If that failed, after 1973 there was always legalized abortion. The problem of venereal disease had been worked out with condoms and miracle medicines, until AIDS came onto the scene.

We knew the sexual revolution was in full swing when we heard ourselves or others saying, "It's okay because we're really in love. . .It's okay; we plan to get married someday. . .I know he's married, but we're in love. . .He's young enough to be my son, but we're in love. . .We're mature enough to make our own decisions. . . How else can we find out if we're really in love?. . .If you really loved me, you would. . .I love you so much that I just can't help myself. . ."

Seeing Through the Smokescreen

Some instinctively saw through the hoax of it all, surprisingly I saw it among the youth. Through the years, several youth have told me their sad stories. Some children suffered the heartache of watching their parents immorality. They could have told their parents that marriage needs total and absolute fidelity to survive, but who would have listened to the children?

Charlene was quite a tomboy—always in pants, short haircut, low voice—in fact, we didn't realize until she had been coming around for over a year, that she was a girl. She loved our family, and hated to go home after their playtime together. Sometime later I discovered why.

Her parents lived in different homes with seasonal mates. I recall the first time our son Aaron went to her house to play for the afternoon. She said that their family owned the two homes on the property; her Mom lived in one house with her boyfriend, and her father lived in the other with his girlfriend. As a little girl, she was too young to realize, but later that would all change. Her innocent acceptance turned to bitterness. Listening to her mother moan when once again a lover had deserted her, she said, "What can you expect? Why should anyone marry you when you give yourself so cheaply? Why are you so surprised when they leave when there was no commitment in the first place?"

This daughter's plea to her mother reminded me of the moment in Shakespeare's play when Hamlet pleads with his mother,

> "Nay, but to live in the rank sweat of an enseamed bed, stewed in corruption, honeying and making love over the nasty sty. . .confess yourself to heaven. Repent of what's past, avoid what is to come, and do not spread the compost on the weeds to make them ranker." (<u>Hamlet</u>, Shakespeare, p. 119.)

I love the expression, "do not spread compost on the weeds to make them ranker." In other words, don't keep feeding a bad relationship that reeks.

"I have seen so much unhappiness," she said, "come from my parents' affairs that I have determined this will never happen to me. I am going to stay virgin until I'm married and if the guy doesn't like it, he can go find someone else. I have hated what my Mom and Dad have done to our family and what they've done to themselves—it won't happen to me. I don't want my children to go through what I've gone through." True to her word, she now lives happily with her husband and three little daughters. Her mother lives alone; her father has remarried.

Infidelity in marriage can create a cesspool of hurt feelings and bitterness. I have observed fathers cunningly strive to turn the hearts of their children away from their mothers, and mothers turn the hearts of their children away from their fathers. Seeding such hatred always backfires; the children become embittered toward both!

Often Lyn, fourteen, would ask if she could spend the weekend with our family. Her mother was either away with a boyfriend for the weekend, or having one over. So she inevitably told Lyn to "find someplace to stay." There is no child who feels as unwanted as one who is a third wheel in their parents' love affair. Lyn determined that her life would be different, but lessons had been taught and absorbed; a few years later she became imprisoned in an abusive relationship with a young man.

Sex outside of a loving, loyal and legal relationship usually has little to do with love and a whole lot to do with selfishness and exploitation.

The Awakening

Those of my generation watched as the idea of waiting until marriage and fidelity afterwards was tossed to the wind. The devastating hurricane force of the sexual revolution has taken it's toll and changed the landscape, but the good news is that there's an awakening occurring. We're beginning to realize that sex without honor and commitment leaves an aftertaste that's bitter to the very soul. Loveless sex leaves us feeling less loved and more lonely. Free love never was freedom. It's inflicted society with a disease more deadly than AIDS, more devastating than any natural disaster. It's inflicted diseases of the heart and soul.

Young women who celebrated their freedom from the double standard found themselves mothering all alone. Young men who said the magic word "love" to get sex found that after awhile neither mattered anymore—like the song, "When I was young, I never needed anyone; making love was just for fun. I don't want to be all by myself anymore." They found that the more they surrendered to, "if it feels good, do it," the less they could feel anything at all—like the bulemic who in a mad frenzy for food loses all sense of taste.

Men still hunger and hope for more meaningful relationships, like they had with the girl next door who had a good, kind heart and feminine charm—the sisterly type— "coloured all through with that golden light of reverence and naturalness." (C.S. Lewis) They realize they need a soul-mate who offers that glorious challenge—the challenge to be at their best. Men without women of virtue are prone to complacency, and women without men of virtue are prone to complacency.

Women still long for the knight in shinning armor, the man of virtue and honor who will love and protect them. They want a relationship that is built upon "love, honor and cherish." They want to be able to trust, in order to give their all—emotionally, spiritually, and physically. They want a lover who is also a friend, someone to make a life together. They want someone who is genuinely interested, someone to share the little daily happenings like when they couldn't find a parking space, or how long they waited at the doctor's office. They want someone who will light up when they enter the room.

Men and women still long for a soul-bonding love. They want the best of both the old and the new. They want the kind of love that they saw in the old photos—the kind that grandparents talked about—the kind that lasts, and they also want the glorious freedom to enjoy sexual marital intimacy to its fullest without the unfounded taboos of the Victorian period.

By restoring the forgotten virtue, romantic love and striving to "live happily ever after" just may have a chance.

Recently, my fifteen year old daughter Mary, and I were

arranging family photos when I came across a picture of my husband. He looked extremely attractive. While I was putting it in a frame to set on the mantle, I said, "Oh, Mary, what a lucky woman I am; I've been in love with the same man all these years—your Daddy."

She answered, "Wow, that's great Mom. That doesn't happen anymore; things are different now."

is the principle thesis of this book." (People of The Lie, p.10)

We will never begin to understand man's inhumanity to man, or the dangers of exploitive sex until we recognize the undercurrents or the "brutal force" as Leo Tolstoy calls it.

The Clash of Ideas

Now we turn to the leaves of the clash of ideas between the sexual revolution and traditional American values. My studies were enlightening:

1. Finally, I understood why "abstinence" was scoffed at—it conflicted with the idea that sex is a biological need—like food, air, and water.

Recently I watched a talk show. Teenagers were being asked very personal and intimate questions regarding their sexual practices and values. One girl stood up and said, "I think that sex should be reserved for special relationships. You should be really in love. You shouldn't have sex with just anyone."

Almost immediately a young man shot up to refute, "I don't agree. Our bodies need it, so why not do it whenever we get the chance?" The crowd applauded in approval.

This idea is the most dangerous of all. It gives an excuse to take advantage of others for a supposed bodily need, but the truth is, those who live a celibate life—without sexual intercourse—do not die. The sex drive is however, a stimulus/response control area of our identity. Like a dimmer on a light switch—we have the power to either increase or decrease these passions. With stimulation—either physically or mentally, it is increased, without stimulation it decreases and can go into somewhat of a dormant state. We have the power to control sexual expression, but we can give it the power to control us.

What a clash of ideas: that the powers of procreation are merely an itch to be scratched, or that these powers are to guide us to our soul-mates in a "one flesh" partnership!

2. I understood why the word "morality" was always rebuffed with, "Whose morality?" It conflicted with the belief that there are no absolute values—only societal conditioning and situational ethics.

I recall one conversation; the subject of "abstinence" came up. One woman said, "You're talking a moral issue; we do not have the right to impose our values on the youth; we're only supposed to educate them."

I responded, "But isn't education teaching all the alternatives? What's wrong with teaching abstinence as an alternative?"

She said, "Oh, wake up, we can't stop these kids from having sex! In order for them to feel good about themselves we've got to make them feel okay about what they're doing—not worse. We want to stop the guilt trips."

I countered, "They also have a right to know all their options, and abstinence is the safest and surest option of avoiding pregnancy, disease, and heartache."

"It's an option that no ones chooses to take," she said.

The idea that what's popular determines what's right can tamper with the delicate mechanism called conscience. Larry

McQuay, a school bus driver who molested more than two hundred children said, "Sometimes I wish I was born a hundred years ago when you could marry a twelve-year-old girl and nobody would think twice about it. Or back in the Greek culture when they had sex with boys. But in today's society that's not acceptable and I'm not a time traveler, so I can't go back into another society or another culture."

3. I finally understood why the "guilt" word had to be stamped out at all costs. Guilt was merely an inconvenience standing in the way of free sexual expression, besides it created mental disorders.

Throughout my studies of "family life" curriculum guides there was a persistent effort to make the kids feel all right with whatever sexual behavior they chose. Now I realized why—the motive was to eliminate the guilt or the pain of conscience. Students were taught, "Guilt is a negative emotion that is self-induced by rigid moral indoctrination. In order to eliminate guilt—which causes so much mental distress—you must eradicate the idea of moral absolutes. Values should be based upon what is socially acceptable."

This idea came from Jeremy Bentham who in an attempt to discard God's commandments said that what is moral is that which brings pleasure, and what is not moral is that which brings pain. Therefore, good and bad, or right and wrong are to be determined by what brings pleasure, thus the expression, "If it feels good, do it."

In his book, <u>Principles of Morals and Legislation</u>, Benthan wrote, "Nature has placed mankind under the governance of two sovereign masters, *pain* and *pleasure*. It is for them alone to point out what we ought to do, as well as to determine what we should do. On the one hand the standard of right and wrong, the other the chain of causes and effects, are fastened to their throne."

In the discussion of guilt, the traditionalist would say, "In order to reduce guilt, you must stop doing whatever you are doing to cause guilt, and be grateful for the fact that you have these guiding feelings." The secularist would say, "Guilt comes from the idea of sin—or absolute values—get rid of that idea, and you get rid of the guilt. Besides, it gets in the way of the pleasure."

4. I understood why all sexual behaviors were considered "preferences." When there are no absolute values, anything goes.

Dr. Chisholm, past president of the World Federation of Mental Health said, "The only psychological force capable of producing these perversions (inferiority, guilt and fear) is morality, the concept of right and wrong. . .Freedom from moralities means freedom to observe, to think and behave sensibly, to the advantage of the person and of the group, free from outmoded types of loyalties and from the magic fears of our ancestors. If the race is to be freed from its crippling burden of good and evil, it must be psychiatrists who take the original responsibility."

However, Dr. O. Hobart Mower, president of the American Psychological Association admitted, "By abolishing sin, the psychologists have also abolished moral restraint. As a result, personality disorders are more pervasive and baffling today."

5. I understood "It's the way I am, I can never change" thinking. It was a part of the idea that man is a product of hereditary and environmental conditioning—he cannot master himself; he does not choose his destiny.

This is one of the hefty issues of the debate, and again the two ideas clash. The American view is that men and women have been endowed by their Creator with free will or the right of life, and to direct that life "in the pursuit of happiness." If the opposing view is accurate, then the case for moral discipline, or any other kind of discipline is closed. This idea has contributed to the pitty-partiers of our generation who say, "This is the way I am; I can't change. It is all Mother's fault, after all. . ." The idea is: how can we be held responsible for our actions if we cannot overcome a dysfunctional family?

I was listening to one of our children's friends tell the story again. I had heard it before. "My Dad was a dentist, but as soon as he came through the door at the end of the day he started drinking. He was so abusive when he was drunk! My Mom escaped the nightmare by having one affair after another. That's why I left home when I was only fourteen; I couldn't stand it any longer. Then I started drinking, and..."

"John," I said, "I know that your childhood was bad, and I don't mean to be insensitive, but it seems to me that you're so busy looking back that you can't look forward. You don't live there anymore. You're not a child; you're almost thirty.

You can create the kind of life that you always wished for. What a waste it would be if you are so busy looking back that you never look forward. We have the power to create ourselves—to become whatever we want. We have the power to take charge of our own lives, and to make up for an unhappy childhood."

"It's not that easy," he said. "You wouldn't understand. You never lived through it."

We have been given the right to life, and the power to direct that life. We have the power to create our own heaven or hell, and to choose what will or will not condition us. With Divine help, we can take control of our own lives, and create the home that we wished we had as a child. The idea that we are conditioned to be something our family and environment has mapped out for us, has created the "I can't help it," syndrome that is crippling lives.

6. I understood why our justice system has difficulty punishing certain sex crimes. No-control means no responsibility, and no responsibility means "all punishment is cruel and unusual."

Take the case of Westly Dodd. He was a child molester who admitted over and over to the police that he could not control his behavior—yet was set free again and again. After he killed a three-year-old boy, the courts ruled for the maximum penalty—death. But some thought this was cruel and unusual punishment for a man who had no control over his behavior; they tried to block the execution. Dodd announced that he would sue anyone who tried to stop it, and was put to death.

7. I finally understood—after debating this issue for hours— why the terms "normal" and "common" and "majority" were so popular, in some minds, what is popular or common determines what's moral.

For a time I taught classes in philosophy at a nearby prison facility. It was an interesting experience; I was locked in a room with over sixty inmates and a couple of security guards. The inmates were serving terms for various reasons—some were rapists and murderers—but I actually felt fairly safe and protected. The discussion of ethics, or morals came up.

One man said, "It's all a matter of where you live. I'm in here for spousal abuse, and I admit it—I did beat on my wife, but she deserved it. If I were in another country where wife beating was considered a husband's right, there's no way I would be jailed. I just happen to live in the wrong country."

I asked, "So what you're saying is that what's socially right is what's morally right?"

"What I'm saying," he said, obviously frustrated with me, "is that there's nothing wrong with a man keeping his wife in line."

"The bottom line of your argument," I said, "is that right and wrong is determined by the society. Have you ever considered that while dehumanizing Jews was socially acceptable in Germany, it was still morally wrong? Wrong will always be wrong even if the law permits it and people praise it."

Recently Time Magazine noted that the 2.9 million

member Presbyterian church asked the denomination's General Assembly to consider abandoning traditional sanctions against sex outside of marriage. Other churches—Episcopal, Evangelical and Methodist—are also considering abandoning God's strict moral code. As one professor of Christian ethics said, "The problem is that what was thought unthinkable and even unmentionable a short time ago is now commonplace." (U.S. News and World Report, June 10, 1991, p. 60) When the voice of authority from the church joined ranks with the majority, moral virtue took a nose dive.

Interestingly, studies indicate that what people do does not necessarily reflect what they think they ought to do. According to many surveys, most Americans still believe the best way is total abstinence before marriage and absolute fidelity after. This could explain why the only churches that are gaining members are those churches that are sticking to traditional values.

8. I understood why teaching human sexuality needed to begin in kindergarten and go through high school; it takes a few hours to teach reproductive processes, but it takes years to replace family values.

In the curriculum guides that I studied, I found myself wondering why sex education instruction needed to take place from kindergarten through high school. Some concepts were repeated over and over. Now I finally understood.

Summary

I find it fascinating that we are always alarmed when children scoff at moral values, when in fact, they have been taught to do just that—scoff at moral values. The skeletal structure of ideas that have replaced God, commandments and the idea of sin, are very simple: there is no God, there are no moral absolutes, there is no sin, there is only bodily needs.

The American republic was founded upon a few philosophical ideas: the central one is that man is a child of the "Supreme Creator." It seems only fair that this idea be represented in our schools as it is in the pledge of allegiance and on our currency. How strange that some have "debunked" traditional values only to establish values of their own.

"Those who 'debunk' traditional, or (as they would say) 'sentimental' values have in the background values of their own which they believe to be immune from the debunking process. They claim to be cutting away the parasitic growth of emotion, religious sanction, and inherited taboos, in order that 'real' or 'basic' values may emerge. . .Every appeal to pride, honour, shame or love is excluded. . .the modern situation permits and demands a new sexual morality." (C.S. Lewis, The Abolition of Man, p.41)

Just as the sexual revolution grew out of ideas and an identity crises, so the case for enlightened chastity begins with understanding our true identity. Only by knowing who we are can we capture the glorious potential of human sexuality, and the tragedy of casual sex. The next two chapters explore this view.

Notes on chapter six:

1. Thomas Jefferson wrote, God "has made us moral agents. . .that we may promote the happiness of those with whom he has placed us in society, by acting honestly towards all, their rights, bodily and mental, and cherishing especially their freedom of conscience as we value our own." (Dewey, Living Thoughts of Thomas Jefferson, p.104)

2. "We find ourselves faced with the same questions always faced. . .What view of man and human nature and the universe should we espouse? Should we base our view of man on the assumption that he is a mere material animal? Or should we endow him with a soul? If we give him a soul, we have to give him a Creator, and we have to give him certain fixed rules to live by, a framework within which he may exercise his reason. . .Either man has a heritage from his God, his experience, his tradition, with which he can find standards, or he does not. If he does, he should begin to order his world and his goals to such a system. . .If he truly does not believe that man has such a heritage, then he should continue to place his values in materialism, collectivism, centralization of power in the state, and secularism. . .Thus, the problem always remains the same after these thousands of years. Does God exist? What is man? What is man's nature? What standards should man adhere to in this world? In the final analysis, the answer to these questions dominates our political and social thought, as well as our very existence." (George Charles Roche III, Legacy of Freedom p. 327)

Life As It Should Be 7

"When life itself seems lunatic, who knows where madness lies? Perhaps to be too practical is madness. To surrender dreams—this may be madness. To seek treasure where there is only trash. Too much sanity may be madness. And maddest of all, to see life as it is and not as it should be!"

Dale Wasserman, Man of La Mancha

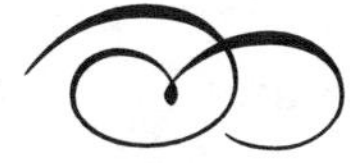

Insight #7

We will never know what life is all about, or what human sexuality is all about—unless we come to know what being human is all about. If we listen to our hearts and our souls we will come to know our true identity and the true purpose of sexual desire.

The real "facts of life" begin with a correct understanding of human life—as it is or as it should be. The duck story illustrates this idea.

When our family numbered eight children, we bought an old farm house with eight acres—an acre apiece for the Sorensen kids to run, skip, hop, hoop and holler on. It wasn't much of a farm, and we were not much at farming, but we wanted our family to have some of the enriching experiences of farm life. We acquired chickens, turkeys, horses, dogs, and one lonely little duck given to us by some friends. Rather than make a whole pen for one measly duck we put him in the pen with the chickens.

It wasn't long until the little guy became convinced that he was also a chicken. He fell right in line behind all the chicks as they followed their mother around the chicken pen.

It was cute and we all laughed watching the duck who thought he was a chicken, until he became a teenage duck and his hormones kicked into gear. It was then that all the trouble started. Those geared-up hormones caused him to chase the chickens all around the yard. It seems that he was ready to start his own little family. The chickens, on the other hand, would have nothing to do with him. Nature never intended for ducks and chickens to mate. The faster he chased a chicken, the faster she would run, until both dropped from exhaustion. After a few minutes' rest, the duck would get up and begin the chase again.

The chickens quit laying eggs, and our neighbors started calling with complaints: "What is going on over there? Can't you keep those chickens quiet?"

"The problem is not the chickens," I would attempt to explain. "It's the duck that's chasing the chickens."

"Well, do something! We can't hear ourselves think!"

We had a family counsel and discussed the problem. Someone suggested, "Get a female duck for the male." Good idea—or so we thought. We asked our friends who owned a whole pond of ducks if they would provide a "bride" for the hormonally deranged duck.

We were all excited when we placed her in the pen with the male; we were certain it would be love at first sight. No chance! He didn't even give her a second look. My husband joked that, "She just didn't look like the 'chicks' that he had been hang'n around with."

Now visualize this. The lonely duck is going crazy chasing a dozen chickens around. The female duck is chasing him with equal determination, but he is totally ignoring her, and the neighbors keep calling with complaints. Now they have cackling and quackling!

The story is not over, yet. While we were thinking seriously of doing something—anything—Miss Duck did. She decided—like a smart woman—to stop chasing and start building her own life. All day long—while he chased the chickens—she gathered bits of this and pieces of that to build a nest. Then one day, finally satisfied, she sat down right in the middle of the nest. From then on, she laid one egg a day, and faithfully sat on them. Obviously, she resolved that if she could not have a man, she would at least have a family.

There was a serious problem, however. She, evidently, didn't understand the facts of life; her eggs had not been fertilized. No matter how faithfully she sat upon them, they would never hatch.

Finally our sons Aaron and Shiloh (then about eight and ten) took pity on her, and put some fertilized chicken eggs in her nest. After awhile the baby chicks hatched out and adopted the duck as their mother. Now all of nature was turned topsy-turvy. We had a duck that thought he was a chicken, and baby chicks that thought they were ducks. Talk about identity crises!

After the chicks were grown and the problem still had not resolved itself, Aaron and Shiloh decided to help the ducks discover their true identities. They gathered them up in their arms, carried them to the top of our four story water tower, and tossed them off. The two ducks hollered a protest at such cruel treatment, spread their wings and flew away—together. For a few days they were seen honeymooning in the creek. Then they eventually flew away—we hoped to live happily ever after. About once or twice a year the children would come running and shouting, "They're back; they're in the creek floating around!"

Once in awhile I would follow the children down to the creek to see our old friends-the male duck that thought he was a chicken, and the female duck that was rejected. Finally they had discovered their divine destinies and ultimate happiness!

We learn so much from this duck story! (The obvious is that happiness doesn't come with chasing chicks around.) They lived happily ever after only after discovering the "real" thing—marital bliss. But marital bliss could not have taken place had the male duck not discovered his true identity. *Likewise, we will never know what life is all about, or what human sexuality is all about—unless we come to know what being human is all about.*

Discovering our True Identity

Let's begin this exploration into our true identity with a simple question: who am I? Let's discover our true identities. Close your eyes and ask the question, "Who am I? What am I?" Pause and allow your identity to surface in your thinking. What makes you the person that you are? Begin with your physical body. Pay attention to your legs, feet, arms and hands. There's definite feeling in them, but they do not have the power to think or reason, and there's certainly no emotional feelings radiating from them. They respond or follow orders from a master control center. That's what we're looking for, the "control centers" of our being. If a leg or an arm were to be amputated, there would be no less of your identity. What then does compose the real you?

Think about the *stomach.* Even though it doesn't think, it has the ability to let us know when it needs attention. It can become a major control center if we allow it. Like a spoiled brat, it can shout within, "I want the whole bowl of chocolate chip cookie batter! I've had a hard day, I deserve to eat it! Besides, who even cares what I do? There isn't a single soul in this whole universe who even cares whether or not I eat this batter.. umm, good." The stomach is definitely a control center and it can become a master control center if we let it.

Now take note of what's below the stomach, the *genital area*; there is definite sensation there. The "electricity" can be increased or decreased according to the stimulus—either physical or mental. A romantic movie may increase it, while a sweaty game of basketball decreases it. Over-stimulated and under-disciplined, this control center can take over to become a terrifying master of our whole being.

Now let's turn to another part of our being—*the mind.* Even as we read these words we can discern the thought waves as they radiate from this control center—it creates thoughts and pictures, it analyzes and draws conclusions. Obviously this is a major control center of our identity.

Some would stop right here and say that humans are composed of a body with an advanced computer—the "trousered ape." But there's another control center that's very alive and very much a part of our uniqueness. We call it *the heart*, or the center of emotion. It swells with feelings of love or happiness, and it seems to break with feelings of despair. While the mind handles the reasoning process, the heart responds to stimuli that trigger emotions.

Besides these control centers there's still more to our identity.

The Spirit which Gives Life to the Body

This control center is widely accepted by those of faith, but questioned by those without faith—it is the *soul or the spirit.* In Christian theology, the spirit is that which gives life to the body—like a hand in a glove. The glove looks as if it has life when the hand is inside, but when the hand is removed, the glove is lifeless. In this same way the spirit gives life to the body.

The New Testament speaks of the soul. "Thou shalt love the Lord thy God with all thy heart, and with all thy soul, and with all thy mind," said Jesus recorded by Matthew (22:37). Recently, evidence has come to light which documents the reality of the soul, especially with the many "after life" experiences. Dr. Raymond Moody noticed that many of his patients—who had "died" for a few minutes, but come back to life—had similar experiences while their spirits were out of the body. He sums up their stories with this experience:

> "A man is dying and, as he reaches the point of greatest physical distress, he. . .begins to hear an uncomfortable noise, a loud ringing or buzzing, and at the same time feels himself moving very rapidly through a long tunnel. After this, he suddenly finds himself outside of his own physical body, but still in the immediate physical environment, and he sees his own body from a distance, as though he is a spectator. . .He notices that he still has a body but one of a very different nature and with very different powers from the physical body he has left behind. . .a being of light appears before him. This being non-verbally asks him a question to make him evaluate his life and helps him along by showing him a panoramic, instantaneous playback of the major events of his life. . ." (Reflections on Life After Life, p. 6)

My favorite "after-life" experience is recorded by George Ritchie, a psychiatrist. As a young soldier during World War II, he was confined to a hospital with a case of pneumonia. During the night his body dies and his spirit leaves the hospital. He writes,

"Looking down I was astonished to see not the ground but the tops of mesquite trees beneath me. . My mind kept telling me that what I was doing was impossible, and yet. . .it was happening. A town flashed by beneath me, caution lights blinking at the intersections. This was ridiculous! A human being couldn't fly without an airplane!"

"Gradually I began to notice something else. All of the living people we were watching were surrounded by a faint luminous glow, almost like an electrical field over the surface of their bodies. This luminosity moved as they moved, like a second skin made out of pale, scarcely visible light. . .(I realized) that my own unsolid body was without this glowing sheath."

"God is busy building a race of men who know how to love," he wrote at the end of his book, "I believe that the fate of the earth itself depends on the progress we make—and that the time now is very short. As for what we'll find in the next world, I believe that what we'll discover there depends on how well we get on with the business of loving, here and now." (George G. Ritchie, Return From Tomorrow, pages 38, 59, 124).

Free Will and Conscience

There are two other attributes of human nature that were

recognized by the American view: free will and conscience. With the gift of life comes the gift to direct that life; in other words, we are not merely programmed or conditioned to think and act a certain way. Regardless of dysfunctional families, we have the power to direct our own lives, and regardless of society's values, we have an inner guide that senses right from wrong.

This is not to say that we are not affected by hereditary and environmental factors, but, despite these factors and with Divine assistance, we can choose to change, choose to break away from negative patterns, choose to form new ideas, choose to create new habits. We are "endowed by (our) Creator with certain unalienable Rights, that among these are Life, Liberty and the pursuit of Happiness."

In the next chapter we will explore these two attributes; both are important in the discussion of sexual responsibility and ethics.

To Be or Not To Be 8

"The individual's entire life is nothing but a process of giving birth to himself."

Erich Fromm

Insight #8

We have been given the gift of life, and the ability to direct life; we can choose which control centers will be developed and which will be neglected to atrophy and stagnation—which to make the master of our being and which to make the servants.

It has long been a Sorensen tradition to enjoy fresh corn on the cob. The corn is purchased from local growers and hand-picked to insure the ears have young, tiny kernels. The corn is cooked immediately after picking to retain the sugar content. The rule is only the best or none at all.

One summer our family decided that we were wasting a lot of money buying corn when we had eight acres to raise our own. With great anticipation and energy, everyone grabbed for the rakes and shovels and dug the long furrows. We followed the planting instructions on the seed envelope exactly—except for a couple of minor details. We didn't fertilize the soil first, and we didn't thin the weaker seedlings as they grew.

We had good reasons for leaving these two little items out. We were so excited to get started with the project that we didn't want to go to the store for fertilizer, and we were so pleased when the little stalks began to grow that we didn't have the heart to uproot the "extras." It seemed so cruel.

Well, the plants grew vigorously for two weeks, then they seemed to stop growing. They stayed the same size for over a month. The children kept asking, "What did we do wrong? My friend's corn is over six feet high, and they planted their corn at the same time we did."

I answered, "We didn't do anything wrong; they're just having a hard time getting started. Any day now they'll take off."

They didn't take off, in fact after a few days the stalks started to turn yellow. The children kept asking, "How come the corn is not growing? It's turning yellow!" I responded, "They're not turning yellow; that's just the sunlight on the leaves."

I was into denial; pride was obscuring the view. There's fierce competition between gardeners—egos are always on the line. "You call these tomatoes? You should see ours. Why the vines are over six feet high and the tomatoes are three pounds apiece! You call that corn? Those puny ears! That's the way ours looked when they were a couple weeks old. What? You're still on that old drip system? Haven't you heard about. . ."

Finally, I had to admit, maybe we *did* need to fertilize and to thin away the smaller plants after all. One day I walked up and down the rows of corn and thinned away the inferior seedlings—leaving only two of the stalks—the heartiest—every foot or so, then I retraced my steps and scattered chemical fertilizer at the roots.

Within just a few days the leaves began turning green again. Then the stalks started to grow. I was thrilled and amazed what a little chemical fertilizer and thinning would do. We had a hearty crop of corn that fall—tiny but delicious ears.

The instructions on the seed package were clear: fertilize and thin corn seedlings as they begin to grow so that the healthier ones can prosper, but I didn't want to take the time to fertilize and it seemed so cruel to rip out the tiny plants just when they started to grow, but in neglecting these two steps I stunted the growth of all of the stalks and the ears. Feeding and pruning is a process that increases the quality of the harvest— in gardens and in people. (Does anyone notice that this story began with "we" and ended with "I"? Are other families like mine? The gardens begin as a family project and end up Mother's project.)

Just as I had the choice to either follow instructions or to ignore them, so each of us has the choice of how to direct our own lives—whether to nourish or to neglect, whether to prune away negative attitudes and actions or to grow wild—both work together in the "pursuit of Happiness" or in the "pursuit of Hell."

"Self-love, my liege, is not so vile a sin as self-neglecting."
(William Shakespeare, Henry V. Act II.Sc. 4)

The gift of free will

We are given two lives: the life we were born with, and the life we create for ourselves. The great Russian novelist Leo Tolstoy wrote, in the novel, Anna Karenina, "My whole life (apart from anything that can happen to me every minute of it) is no more meaningless, as it was before, but it has the positive meaning of goodness, which I have the power to put into it."

Henry Weaver, explores this idea in his book, The Mainspring of Human Progress.

> "Insects and animals follow certain patterns of action. Honeybees, for example, all make the same hexagonal cells of wax. Beavers all build the same form of dam, and the same kinds of birds make the same kinds of nests. Generation after generation, they continue to follow their changeless routines—always doing the same things in the same ways. But a man is different because he is a human being; and as a human being, he has the power of reason, the power of imagination, the ability to capitalize on the experiences of the past and the present bearing on the problems of the future. He has the ability to change

himself as well as his environment. He has the ability to progress and to keep on progressing. Plants occupy space and contend with each other for it. Animals defend their possession of places and things. But man has enormous powers, of unknown extent, to make new things and to change old things into new forms. He not only owns property, but he also actually creates property. Through foresight, imagination, and individual initiative, man develops tools and facilities, which expand his efforts and enable him to produce things which would not otherwise be possible. This is an outstanding difference between man and animal..." (pp 20-22)

Philosopher Jean-Paul Sartre said, "Man is nothing else but that which he makes of himself." Henry Bars said, "I must win and pay dearly for my personality as for my freedom."

Nourish or Neglect

We were endowed with hearts that feel, minds that think, spirits that aspire, but it is our choice to either give more life—by nourishing—or less life to each of these attributes. When we volunteer to help at the local hospital, we develop the attributes of the heart: compassion, sympathy and service. Listening to great music nourishes the heart. Playing with little children, the angels of the earth—feeling their tenderness and sensitivity, nourishes the heart. Joining with friends to clean up a widow's yard nourishes and gives life to the heart. Learning a new idea or reasoning through a problem nourishes the mind. Every time we create a landscape in our yards, compose a piece of music, or express our feelings on paper we are about the business of taking charge. Every time we venture out to meet someone new, to share ourselves, to risk rejection, we are becoming.

My nephew Garrett captured this vision at the age of eight, when he wrote:

> I used to be dumb, but now I'm rad.
> I used to read little books, now I read big books.
> I used to not be able to know times tables, but now I do.
> I used to draw bad, but now I draw good.
> I used to be in preschool, but now I'm in second grade.
> I used to watch Sesame Street, but now I don't.
> I used to have hardly any money, but now I have thirty or more dollars.
> I used to be rad, but now I'm awesome.

Master, Servants and the Upside-down Man

We also have the choice which control centers will be masters and which will be the servants. There's the football star who neglects development of the mind in order to excel at the sport. The woman who spends hours applying makeup with no thought to inner beauty. There's the scholar who spends hour after hour hovering over books—giving life to the mind—but is socially inept. There's the doctor who knows human anatomy, but has little human empathy. There's the woman who feeds upon cheap romantic novels hour after hour until tweaked emotions of the heart take control over clear reasoning of the mind.

There's the man who nourishes the sexual passions with pornography and allows this center to become the master, to rule and reign over heart, mind and soul. In neglecting the heart, mind and spirit, and allowing what's below the waist to take control over what's above the waist, he becomes the *upside down man*—ruled by his genitals.

The endowment of free will—or free agency—allows us to choose whether to nourish or neglect. If we stop giving life to our mind, it becomes dull. If we stop giving life—or blood—to muscles, they atrophy. If we stop giving life to the heart, it hardens like wax. If we refuse to be connected to the life-force of God, souls droop into a comatose state of dormancy. Piece by piece the control centers deteriorate, surrendering to the forces of stagnation.

The Conscience and the Principle of Pruning

The principle of pruning in order to produce a quality crop is not only an important part of gardening, it is an important part of directing our own lives successfully and happily. Pruning back some corn stalks produces heartier, healthier corn. Pruning the rose bush produces more roses, and better quality roses. Pruning the apple tree produces more apples, bigger apples and tastier apples.

In humans, pruning gluttony allows the freedom of enjoying a great meal; pruning disorganization sets us free to find what we want when we want it; pruning out false ideas allows us freedom to think clearly; pruning the powers to love and mate, to keep them from becoming powers to use and hate, gives us the freedom to love ourselves as well as others. Pruning works for corn, apples, and people, but only people have the choice whether to prune or to grow wild.

How do we know what needs to be pruned away from our lives? The Creator provided counsel through prophets and scriptures and an inner light—the conscience—that's a guide in the "pursuit of happiness." This is a control center that's designed to be *the* control center. It's a protection to the spirit. It's the peace/sorrow mechanism in the same way the pleasure/pain mechanism is a protection for the body. It's a sense, a feeling of fairness and direction, a guide to know what is wrong, and it is also a guide to what is right and good. The conscience or still small voice acts like a compass leading us to truth, integrity and happiness. It whispers counsel to our souls—what needs to be pruned away and what needs to be nourished. If we use the guide merely to gauge what is ethically right and wrong, we will miss out on the glorious higher purpose leading towards our best selves, our unique selves!

By being honest with ourselves, and staying in tune to our inner guide we instinctively know what is right—not just what is morally right but what is personally right. In this sense, our conscience guides us to ourselves—our divine selves. This is all so natural. We are children of God, when we stay connected to that life and strength we naturally grow and become more and more what we were created to become; we instinctively sense our unique gifts and talents. Following his destiny, Mozart created masterpieces of music. Martha Stewart inspires beauty in creating beautiful homes and gardens. The immortal Bob Hope shares his gift of humor in this dark and dreary world. Abraham Lincoln broke the chains of slavery with his gift of leadership. These are men and women who were right to themselves and right for the world. I believe, this is the higher purpose of the ever-so-gentle inner guide! This is my religion, short and simple: stay connected with the Creator and bloom and grow forever.

Staying true to ourselves generates a self-respect that stands above any other honor that this world can bestow. Self-mastery—whether in diet, exercise, study, sexual passions—creates self-respect. A commitment to love and honor one's fellow men creates self-respect. A clear conscience is the very center of self-respect.

It's not easy to prune back those parts of ourselves that are stifling our growth and freedom—especially when we are disconnected from the Creator and spiritually weak. There's the tendency to go with the flow, to take the road most traveled. If the gardener were to tell the rose bush as he approached it with the shears, "O.K. Today's the day you're going to be cut back," the bush would cry out, "No, no, leave me alone. I'm growing just fine."

The Gardener Within might whisper, "Maybe you ought

to quit smoking; it's damaging your lungs. You can hardly walk anymore, let alone run." We might be inclined to say, "Hey, I'm not hurting anyone but myself. Besides, I've been doing it for so long that I've already wasted my lungs. It's not going to make any difference. . .My friends won't want to hang out with me anymore if I quit. . .What will I do with my hands when everyone else is smoking? I'll be a total loner. . . Everyone's going to die of something. Why not lung cancer?"

When the Gardener Within says, "No, don't do it. Don't take advantage of her in that way. You'll feel bad about yourself and she'll feel bad about you and herself. She needs your love and protection. Protect her, dear son. Choose to love in this world that has forgotten how to love. Above all, don't use the word love to penetrate her heart simply to penetrate her body. It is a mockery. You were created to love, remember?"

There might be the tendency to respond, "What makes me think I could give up what I've been doing for years? Hey! She wants what I want too, she just doesn't want to admit it. I refuse to be disciplined! I want my way now! I want what I want now!"

Sexual exploitation, using other humans for sexual gratification, is self-destructive, other-destructive and socially destructive.

Refusing to be pruned produces a bad crop—for corn and people. It's not easy to maintain a healthy self-respect when you're licking the last of the chocolate chip cookie dough, but it's impossible when you are stalking a warm body purely for a night's entertainment. There will never be a way to hurt others without hurting oneself in the process. On the other hand, there will never be a way to give respect and honor to others without also bringing respect and honor to oneself.

Summary

What a tremendous power we have over ourselves! We can choose which control centers will be developed and which will be neglected to atrophy and stagnation—which to make the master of our being and which to make the servants. Every day we face this choice: to nourish or to neglect, to become more what we were created to be, or to become less.

These control areas to satisfy (stomach), to bond in intimacy (sex), to reason (mind), to feel (heart), to aspire (spirit or soul), to be empowered (agency), and to guide (conscience) offer a bright contrast to the idea that man is simply animal and that life is nothing more than an experience in time.

Roots of a tree go deep into the earth and pull water and nutrients that sustain life. We, too need to be connected to the source of life—the Creator. We can feel the rejuvenation when the soul feeds and fills with spiritual strength—hearts become full and overflowing with love, tenderness, sympathy, goodwill, confidence, self-love, peace. Praying and meditation nourish the soul, and keep us connected with God and the divinity within ourselves. Minds are quickened and enlightened. Souls are magnified with inner strength, integrity, and courage. Staying connected with the Creator provides us with the power to overcome our tendency to hurt ourselves and to hurt others.

Plants that are hearty and healthy are disease-resistant; humans that are spiritually healthy are also more disease-resistant. Women who are happy with themselves and are about the business of becoming are not as likely to fall for love at any price. Men who are alive emotionally and spiritually are not likely to fall into the dead mans' disease of exploiting women. Next, we journey to the vision of soul-bonding love.

Notes on chapter eight:

1. A.C. Green, a basketball star with the Dallas Mavericks, is 33 and has never married. He promote the cause of abstinence. He said in a recent magazine article, "I am still a virgin. Abstaining from extramarital sex is one of the most unpopular things a person can do, much less talk about. From a sheer numbers standpoint, it can be a lonely cause—but that doesn't mean it's not right.

"I abstain as an adult for the same reasons I did as a teen—the principle doesn't change, or the feeling of self-respect I get. My fellow ballplayers do not tell me, "You are crazy"—it's more that they think I'm being unrealistic. It's ironic, but the guys who are parents—and especially the guys who have daughters—tend to look at sex before marriage a lot more carefully now." U.S. News & World Report May 1997

9

The Power of Majestic Love

"The mentally healthy person is the person who lives by love, reason and faith, who respects life—his own and that of fellow man."

Erich Fromm

Insight #9

Majestic love is part of a rich tapestry of life building together; it is spiritual, emotional, and physical. Bonded together in mutual respect and friendship, sparked by sexual attraction, a circle of love is created with catalytic power for inspiring ambition, progress and advancement.

A wise man said that the best thing a father could do for his children is to love their mother. It was always obvious in our home: Daddy loved Mother; and Mother loved Daddy. In my mind and heart, there's a chest full of memories. What a legacy of love! Mother is standing at the kitchen counter—preoccupied with a task, Daddy sneaks up behind her. He winks and then enfolds her in his arms, and with the accent of Dracula says, "Ahh. I've got you. You're mine—all mine."

Mother pretends to resist, and with a smile, says, "Oh,

Harry, leave me alone!"

They married during the Great Depression and began their married life in a cold-water flat complete with cockroaches. They stood in lines together to buy a loaf of bread, or to buy coal for the stove—they could never afford both, but as they have often said, "We were so in love, we didn't know how miserable we were. It seemed as if we were the only two people in the world."

Several years ago, while mother was undergoing surgery, Daddy and I waited together for hours. Of course, I was concerned for Mother, but at the same time I was looking forward to the conversation with my Daddy. He's a wonderful conversationalist, educated in politics, history, religion and philosophy. He was already in the waiting room when I arrived. He stood to greet me, but forced a smile. He's a small man, but has always been robust until the last few years. Now I keep saying, "Daddy, eat more; eat more." He eats, but still grows more and more frail. His black hair is now almost completely white; his moustache, too. He's a private man, quiet to strangers but completely open to family.

I sat down next to him, and as usual began asking questions to get the conversation going. Soon enough I realized that Daddy can't talk while his other half is in surgery. We sat in almost complete silence.

As she was wheeled through the double doors, he jumped up and ran to her, touching her legs and arms to reassure himself that she was all right. When the surgery was over, the conversation began.

Last week Mother and Daddy celebrated their sixty-first wedding anniversary. One of the grandchildren sent an anniversary card and wrote, "Thank you for your example to us—that it can work! That marriages can last."

My Daddy always smiles, then says, "I remember when you were just a gleam in your daddy's eye." That gleam—the wondrous attraction between a man and a woman—is like a crackling warm fire on a cold winter's night. It creates a circle of love and warmth that radiates to thousands within a few generations. If anything is good, it is good. Good for the body, yes, but good for the heart, good for the mind, good for the soul, good for the individual, good for the couple, good for the children, good for society.

The Goodness and Glory of Intimate Love

Napoleon Hill, in his famous book titled, Think and Grow Rich interviewed hundreds of men who had become peak performers in their lives and discovered that "practically every great leader, whom he had the privilege of analyzing was a man whose achievements were largely inspired by a woman." He wrote:

> "Love, romance, and sex are all emotions capable of driving men (and women) to heights of super achievement. Love is the emotion which serves as a safety value, and insures balance, poise and constructive efforts. When combined, these three emotions may lift one to an altitude of a genius. . .Sex alone is a mighty urge to action, but its forces are like

a cyclone—they are often uncontrollable. When the emotion of love begins to mix itself with the emotions of sex, the result is calmness of purpose, poise, accuracy of judgment, and balance. . .(However) when driven by his desire to please a woman, based solely upon the emotion of sex, a man may be, and usually is, capable of great achievement, but his actions may be disorganized, distorted, and totally destructive. When driven by his desire to please a woman, based upon the motive of sex alone, a man may steal, cheat, and even commit murder. . .A sex-mad man is not essentially different from a dope-mad man! Both have lost control over their faculties of reason and will-power. . . But when the emotion of love is mixed with the emotion of sex, that same man will guide his actions with more sanity, balance, and reason." (p.191)

Recently our son Aaron fell in love and married beautiful Kaia. He wrote this poem for the wedding invitation:

Thoughts of you eclipse my stupor
You are beautiful
You are kind
You are comfort
A mother, a lover and a friend, a companion
You inspire me to greatness!

"You inspire me to greatness" is the key to all healthy relationships—they inspire devotion, dedication, sacrifice, consistency, compassion, tender service. "The greatest happiness of life is the conviction that we are loved," said Victor Hugo, "loved for ourselves, or rather in spite of ourselves."

"The highest goal to which men can aspire."

This highest form of love inspires "to greatness" but sometimes it is the only motivation to live at all. The beautiful but tragic experience of Viktor Frankl is an example. He suffered through the nightmare of living in a Nazi concentration camp. In moments of deep despair he found the strength to persevere in his love for his wife. He records an instance one day that gives us a glimpse of this magnificent love. He, along with other prisoners, walking to their labor assignment one cold, predawn winter morning:

> "We stumbled on in the darkness, over big stones and through large puddles, along the one road leading from the camp. The accompanying guards kept shouting at us and driving us with the butts of their rifles. Hardly a word was spoken; the icy wind did not encourage talk. Hiding his mouth behind upturned collar, the man marching next to me whispered suddenly: 'If our wives could see us now! I do hope they are better off in their camps and don't know what is happening to us.'

"That brought thoughts of my own wife to mind. And as we stumbled on for miles, slipping on icy spots, supporting each other time and again, dragging one another up and onward, nothing was said, but we both knew: each of us was thinking of his wife. Occasionally I looked at the sky, where the stars were fading and the pink light of the morning was beginning to spread behind a dark band of clouds. But my mind clung to my wife's image, imagining it with an uncanny acuteness. I heard her assuring me, saw her smile, her frank and encouraging look. Real or not, her look was then more luminous than the sun which was beginning to rise.

"A thought transfixed me: for the first time in my life I saw the truth as it is set into song by so many poets, proclaimed as the final wisdom by so many thinkers. The truth—that love is the ultimate and the highest goal to which men can aspire. Then I grasped the meaning of the greatest secret that human poetry and human thought and belief have to impart: the salvation of man is through love and in love. I understood how a man who has nothing left in this world still may know bliss, be it only for a moment, in the contemplation of his beloved. In a position of utter desolation, when man cannot express himself in positive action, when his only achievement may consist in enduring his sufferings in the right way—an honorable way—in such a position a man can, through loving contemplation of the image he carries of his beloved, achieve fulfillment. I did not know whether my wife was alive, (she was not) and I had no means of finding out. . .but at that moment it ceased to matter. There was no need for me to know; nothing could touch the strength of my love, my thoughts, and the image of my beloved."

(Man's Search For Meaning)

Love, Honor and Cherish

Majestic relationships are built upon the three magic words: love, honor and cherish. They begin when each one develops these attributes in his or her character; and they continue to bloom and grow because of these qualities. They have little to do with luck, and everything to do with preparation. It is the creation of two who are dedicated to building it together.

Let's explore these three simple but extremely important words: love, honor and cherish. Together they set the climate for human happiness and total sexual joy. **Love** is that passion—magnetic connection—that brings a man and woman together. It means genuine caring, warm affection, sexual attraction, goodwill and friendship. **Honor** is the virtuous attribute of a healthy love relationship. It includes loyalty, honesty, integrity, fairness, goodness, morality, decency, faithfulness, constancy and sincere commitment. The third, **cherish** is different from the first two, it means to treat tenderly or affectionately, to treasure or prize a loved one. Those who cherish would be willing to sacrifice for their loved one, to protect, to defend, to cradle, to nurture, to assist in their growth, etc.

Majestic love inspires all three and creates a circle of love that warms and inspires and creates a place of security, safety, and refuge. Visualize this circle with the words love, honor and cherish written on the circumference. While all three are active in a healthy relationship, as life rolls on, one takes prominence over the others and rises to the top. There are times when the love passion is on top of the wheel and the excitement of honeymoon intimacy eclipses everything else. There are times when the stresses of life demand that love passion gives way to honor, and honor nobly holds the marriage together. In difficult times, cherish rises to take over. We see this when a husband and father sacrifices the desire for sexual intimacy to care for his pregnant wife or when life-spent couples nurse and nurture each other. The magnetism continues, even when love passions are quiet. Cherish holds the circle together long after physical passions are quiet.

Love, honor and cherish lead the way to majestic love relationships and enhance the chances that such love will continue to bloom and grow through the years. Let's begin with honor because honor sets the stage for majestic love.

Honor Before and After Marriage

Honor is the foundation upon which all healthy and wholesome relationships are based. Honor is being true to oneself and God. Visualize a three layer-cake. The first layer is having honor, respect, and goodwill toward oneself and others—everyone. The second is having honor, respect, and goodwill to close friends and family. The third layer is having these same basic qualities with the addition of electricity or sexual magnetism. The top layer—the most sublime of all human relationships—must have the same foundation as the others. Otherwise it will topple over.

Honor provides the love relationship with the best chance to last because it's based upon the virtues of honesty, integrity, friendship, goodwill, morality, responsibility, commitment. Honorable people create the basic motives that lead to majestic love. This is why the idea that "we'll live together to see if it will work" rarely does. Without commitment, there is no foundation of honor to work through problems.

Men and women of integrity, by their very nature, set the foundation for successful marriages. Those who have focused their vision on the short-range picture of sexual intimacy—as a game, a sport, a hunt, a pride boost, etc.—miss out on the greater view. To those who see it from the wide-angled view—love, honesty, honor, partnership for life, children—the short-range picture seems so selfish, immature, and detoured away.

"I want to get married and have a family."

Recently, I was visiting with a neighbor, Kathy, who had come over with her baby girl to see our chickens and ducks. She had had three children in three years and was loving every minute of it. She said, "I used to play the game like everyone else, but then I came to the point in my life that I saw what a farce it all was. You pretend you're falling in love and live together. Then it all falls apart. Everyone knows from the beginning that it's all just a game, but no one will admit it. Well, I realized that I was too smart for that. When you're a kid you might have the time to mess around with your life and others like that, but I was getting old and my chance for having a family was passing me by. I told Todd (her husband) on the first date, 'I want to get married and have a family; if that's not what you're looking for there's no sense in our dating.' He was shocked by my honesty, but I didn't care—what did I have to lose? Nothing. He said, 'Hey, no one has quite put it to me like that, but that's just what I want, too.' Within three months we were married and expecting our first baby. We love our little family so much. We feel like we missed out on the best years of our lives playing games."

She had her first baby at the age of thirty-nine. She added, "If I hadn't started so late, we would have had more children. Todd is the best father they could have; we totally love each other and our little family."

Kathy was able to bring the real thing into her life when she became honest with herself, and honorable enough to tell her date exactly what she wanted and exactly what she didn't want. Men and women with similar ambitions naturally gravitate to one another.

Immortal Love

In a sense the love between a man and woman is immortal not only when, but especially when, there are children. Its radiance permeates through the generations, forever and ever. What greater power can be given to human kind than the gift to create life and to guide that life? Little ones patterned after your own image. Little ones that naturally—at least in the early years—think of Mom and Dad as gods and goddesses. Little ones whose hearts will bond with yours forever and ever. Little ones that can ultimately become your closest and dearest friends.

Some have looked at us with a squinted eye when they see the tribe of children trailing behind the Sorensens, but craziness or not, we have enjoyed having a large family. One time our family went to the California state fair together; we had ten children at the time, and in order to keep them together we all wore matching tee-shirts. The children's were numbered on the back, ten, nine, eight, seven, six, five, four, etc. according to their birth order. What seemed like a simple, practical plan to prevent a child from becoming lost ended up creating more interest than most of the fair attractions. We never expected such attention. As we passed, people parted to make way, and then stood gaping at our family—as if we were celebrities. Most of them seemed pleasantly amused, but some seemed critical. Then we entered a exposition building that housed a booth titled, Zero Population Growth. There were three women behind the table, with literature piled high in front of them. Instantly we caught each other's eyes, and then we all—interestingly—laughed. As the children dispersed to see the exhibits, I ventured over to the women at the booth. We talked briefly. One of them said, "I'm for population control, but let's face it, you have a beautiful family."

I answered, "Each one of them was invited into our family; there are no unwanted children. Oh, maybe they came earlier than we planned, but they were all planned." Although we were coming from two quite opposing views on having children, there was a mutual respect between us. We agreed to disagree.

The Willingness to Wait

Honor also inspires the willingness to sacrifice for the loved one, the willingness to wait for marriage. "Carnal men who can get what they want from any woman are not likely to die for one. But true men in true love will do anything necessary to protect and to prove worthy of their loved one." (C.S. Lewis)

An honorable person shows an attitude of love and respect towards the opposite sex and the sex act itself. Living by principle rather than undisciplined passion, they are willing to wait for sexual intercourse until a loving, loyal and legal relationship. Those married would respect and honor their spouse and the sexual intimacy they share together—to keep it sacred and above the vulgarity of the world. He or she would be warm and friendly to other members of the opposite sex in a brotherly or sisterly manner. Most of all, an honorable person prepares the way for majestic love by having the crucial basic ingredient: integrity.

"True to each other our whole lives."

Ed, a struggling music student, husband and father of three sons, delighted our family when he sang for our son Adam and his bride Daniell's wedding. Our spirits later bonded when we had a chance to converse, and he told me, "Whenever I sing a love song, I think of the love I have for my wife, Lilly. Then the deep passion comes. She's the only one who would ever be right for me. We both knew it for years before we married. We were both virgins and we feel that has made all the difference in our marriage. We hear others talk about the sexual relationships that they had before they were married, and they always seem to be wondering. We don't have it to deal with. In fact, it seems that Lilly and I were true to each other our whole lives. There are no ghosts in the closets."

Virtue before marriage contributes to the appreciation of intimacy after marriage. Those who cherish the life of their Beloved feel honored to even hold hands. Consequently sexual intimacy is a banquet of delight—physically, emotionally and spiritually. On the other hand, coarse, vulgar men or women leave their mates feeling cold and unloved—even in marriage. Marriage contracts don't change attitudes, they merely change marital status. Disrespect for sex before marriage dulls the sensations after marriage. Unfortunately, men and women who are promiscuous, loose, undisciplined, sexually flirtatious or inviting, do not change their nature with marriage. Actions may be changed, but attitudes stay the same. Sowing wild oats before marriage contributes to the same craving for oats after marriage.

"I'm too busy becoming myself."

"People ask me why I'm not willing to just sleep around," said Ann, a young college student. "I tell them that I'm being faithful to my husband, and they always laugh about that, but I'm serious. I know that I don't know him yet, but I want to be faithful to him now. I didn't always feel this way. I used to think that if you're really in love that you should have the right to go to bed together, but what fourteen-year-old girl doesn't think she's in love with the guy that's taking her to bed? I was the same way. I have thought I was in love over and over—about twenty or thirty guys so far. Love can't be the issue—the issue is a legal commitment of marriage. That's what I'm waiting for, but actually, I'm not waiting for marriage to happen, I'm too busy becoming myself. I know that if I just stay on track I'll know when the time is right. Till then I'm staying faithful to my future husband, and I hope that he's doing the same thing."

This young woman was willing to pay the price for romance that is built on honorable love by being honorable to herself.

Genuine Love and Sexual Passion

Passion is the fruit of a healthy relationship, but not the center and core of it. Such passion continues to bloom to greater heights through the years, and creates a love circle that radiates outward warmth, goodwill, family gatherings and sweet memories.

Making love is based upon a wholeness of bonding—physical, spiritual and mental. The husband who gets up at five in the morning to go to work, or repairs the toaster, or builds a playhouse for his daughter, *is* making love. The wife, who diapers the baby, prepares meals, helps with the children's homework, *is* making love. Making love is the very purpose and meaning of their lives.

True lovers have the greatest sexual stimulator of all: they treasure the whole life of their loved one—not simply the body of their loved one, or the face of their loved one, or the muscles of their loved one, but the wholeness of life. Consequently, love making becomes a multi-colored tapestry as rich as life itself. Sometimes the body leads the way. Sometimes the emotions lead the way. Other times the depth of the soul leads to bonding. Sexual intimacy inspires life, ambition, purpose, direction, security, comfort, safety.

C.S. Lewis, Christian philosopher, was a bachelor and professor until he met and married a woman named Joy—a woman who brought him complete joy. After a few brief years together, she died of cancer. He tells of the banquet of love-making that they had together,

> "For those few years (we) feasted on love; every mode of it—solemn and merry, romantic and realistic, sometimes as dramatic as a thunderstorm, sometimes as comfortable and unemphatic as putting on your soft slippers. No cranny of heart or body remained unsatisfied."

Fragmented sex—physical only—will never know such majesty of intimacy. This is why the idea that various partners, techniques, or positions to enhance the thrill of it all doesn't work—at least for long. They are all stimulators for the body only. It's like pouring hot salsa on everything to bring taste. In time the taste buds become so seared they taste nothing at all. The answer is to restore the ability to taste again, or the ability to love again.

Fragmented sex is me-first, selfish, turns inward, and rides high on sexual passion until it becomes burned out, then succumbs to dullness, even numbness. While making love has everything to do with real life, fragmented sex has nothing to do with real life. It's usually to escape loneliness, or for vanity, pride, power, to conquer, to hurt even to destroy. The tail-spin continues downward. Cheap intimacy leads to emotional and spiritual poverty and the poverty creates a craziness for more cheap intimacy. The less they feel, the more they crave to feel again. Some get caught in the swinger's cycle: fall in love, a passionate romp, a cooling-down, a dullness, irritation, separation, loneliness, change of partners, fall in love, passionate romp, etc. From the beginning it's a game of pretense.

This holistic idea of love making and the dangers of exploitive sex was beautifully expressed by university president, Jeffrey Holland:

> "Human intimacy. . .was ordained to be a symbol of total union: union of their hearts, their hopes, their lives, their loves, their families, their futures, their everything. . . In this ultimate physical expression of one man and one woman they are as nearly and as literally 'one' as two separate physical bodies can ever be. . .but such a total, virtually unbreakable union. . can only come with the proximity and permanence afforded in a marriage covenant, with the union of all that they possess—their very hearts and minds, all their days and all their dreams.
>
> They work together, they cry together, they enjoy Brahms and Beethoven and breakfast together, they sacrifice and save and live together for all the abundance that such a totally intimate life provides such a couple. And the external symbol of that union, the physical manifestation of what is a far deeper spiritual and metaphysical bonding, is the physical blending that is part of—indeed, a most beautiful and gratifying expression of that larger, more complete union of eternal purpose and promise. . .(Such) symbolism of 'one flesh' (Genesis 2:24) cannot be preserved if we hastily and guiltily and surreptitiously share intimacy in a darkened corner of a darkened hour, then just as hastily and guiltily and surreptitiously

retreat to our separate worlds—not to eat or live or cry or laugh together, not to do the laundry and the dishes and the homework, not to manage a budget and pay the bills and tend the children and plan together for the future. No, we cannot do that until we are truly one—united, bound, linked, tied, welded, . . .married.

"You must wait until you can give everything, and you cannot give everything until you are legally pronounced as one. If you persist in sharing part without the whole, in giving parts and pieces and inflamed fragments only, you run the terrible risk of such spiritual, psychic damage that you may undermine both your physical intimacy and your wholehearted devotion to a truer, later love."

Cherish

Making love/life together by its very nature continues to bloom and grow because of this attribute of cherishing. To cherish is the deeper part of love that sets one person above everyone else; it inspires appreciation, gentleness, tenderness, protection and affection that come from the depths of one's heart. To cherish is to reverence the totality of another. Those who cherish another might say, "I am in awe over you. I treasure every thing about you, your hair, your hands, your pigeon-toed walk. Being your love and life's partner is the greatest honor to which I aspire."

Elizabeth Barrett-Browning composed this poem that best describes the cherishing quality:

"How do I love thee? Let me count the ways.
I love thee to the depth and breadth and height
My soul can reach, when feeling out of sight
For the ends of Being and ideal Grace.
I love thee to the level of every day's
Most quiet need, by sun and candle-light.
I love thee freely, as men strive for Right;
I love thee purely, as they turn from Praise.
I love thee with the passion put to use
In my old griefs, and with my childhood's faith.
I love thee with a love I seemed to lose
With my lost saints—I love thee with the breath,
Smiles, tears, of all my life!—and, if God choose,
I shall but love thee better after death."

You Discover the Power of Majestic Love When:

You want not to possess, but to bless the life of your loved one.

You find yourself becoming more alive in your loved one's presence.

You are motivated to do better and be better when you are around him or her.

You find yourself more sensitive to children and the elderly.

If a child comes from the union, he or she will bask in the

wealth of your love.

You become a child yourself.

You find your soul magnifying, your love multiplying, your intellect quickening, your compassion enlarging, your integrity growing, your life beginning.

You begin to notice sunsets and sunrises.

You wonder about mysteries of life that never occurred to you before.

Trivial things—walking in the park together, having an ice cream cone together—become grand events.

Moments alone are precious, but moments with others are great as well.

You're anxious to introduce him or her to your family.

You're more free, not less.

Your personality begins to bloom into areas you never knew.

You feel you're in a creation process of building a mansion of happy moments together.

Summary

The rewards of moral virtue span from self-respect to the prosperity of freely loving others without hidden motives. The most precious of all is the quality of love that's possible only for men and women of virtue who love, honor and cherish one another—majestic love. Bonded together in mutual respect and friendship, sparked by sexual attraction, a circle of love is created with catalytic power for inspiring ambition, progress and advancement.

By its very nature, majestic relationships continue to grow.

Relationships that are without honor and cherishing eventually die out because by their very nature, they do not grow. If the motive is to capture another heart, once it is captured the relationship dies. If the motive is to entice into a romantic romp, eventually the fascination leaves. If the motive is to escape oneself in another, there will be a nagging reminder to be born unto oneself. If the motive is simply to scratch a sexual itch, once the itch is scratched, it's over. Like the popular song, "the feeling's gone, and I just can't get it back."

When a man cherishes a woman, or a woman cherishes a man, they are filled with inspiration, ambition to grow, to do, to become more worthy of their "Beloved." Women of honor and virtue inspire men to greatness. Women without honor lead men to complacency. Men of honor and virtue inspire women to greatness to become all that they can become. Men without honor cause women to feel less, lower, used, abused, unappreciated, unhonored, unloved.

Notes on chapter nine:

1. In her book, Women Who Love Too Much, which I highly recommend for all men and women, Robin Norwood writes of a healthy love relationship,

> "(It) is a partnership to which two caring people are deeply committed . . .(they) share many basic values, interests, and goals, and tolerate good

naturedly their individual differences. The depth of love is measured by the mutual trust and respect they feel toward each other. Their relationship allows each to be more fully expressive, creative, and productive in the world. There is much joy in shared experiences both past and present, as well as those that are anticipated. Each views the other as his/her dearest and most cherished friend. (They have a) willingness to look honestly at oneself in order to promote the growth of the relationship and the deepening of intimacy. Associated with real love are feelings of serenity, security, devotion, understanding, companionship, mutual support, and comfort. . .I once heard a recovering alcoholic put it so simply and so beautifully. He said, 'When I was drinking I went to bed with lots of women, and basically I had the same experience many times. Since I've been sober I've only been to bed with my wife, but each time we're together it's a new experience.' The thrill and excitement that comes not from arousing and being aroused but from knowing and being known is all too rare." (pp.44, 46)

A Time and A Season

10

"The inventor of the human machine was telling us that its two halves, the male and the female, were made to be combined together in pairs, not simply on the sexual level, but totally combined.

The monstrosity of sexual intercourse outside marriage is that those who indulge in it are trying to isolate one kind of union (the sexual) from all the other kinds of union which were intended to go along with it and make up the total union. There is (not) anything wrong about sexual pleasure, any more than about the pleasure of eating. . . (but) you must not isolate that pleasure and try to get it by itself, any more than you ought to try to get the pleasures of taste without swallowing and digesting, by chewing things and spitting them out again."

C.S. Lewis

Insight #10

Sexual intercourse creates a magnetic bond in the relationship—for better or worse. If the relationship is mature, loving, loyal and legal, the added dimension of sexual intimacy will be for the better, but if the relationship is founded upon immature and unhealthy motives, adding the "super-glue" of sex will be for the worse.

Ron and Christina, a young teenage couple, had come to me, hoping for the acceptance they were not getting from their parents. Christina was fifteen, but looked twelve. She had long curly red hair, and soft, delicate features. Ron towered over her in height, had short cropped hair, and a great smile. He hardly said a word; Christina did the talking, while holding onto his arm. After telling their story, how they fell in love, began to have sexual relations together, and planned to marry *someday*, Christina smiled and said, "Our parents just don't understand. They want us to break up until after high school; can you believe that? I figured that you would understand because you got married so young, right?"

"Right and wrong," I said.

"I do understand what's it's like to love someone with that passion, but frankly, you've bought into some bad ideas. I know because I used to believe in the same ideas. I don't want to offend you, but I believe that the reason that you have come to me is because I have a message for you that you need to hear. You're going to ultimately make your own decision, but I would be doing a disservice to you, and to myself, if I didn't help you with some insights.

Here are some of the ideas that I think are playing into the picture. You seem to think that love and sex have to go together, but they don't. In fact, the more sincere and healthy the love is, the more willingness there is to wait until marriage. True love means to bless each other's lives, not possess each other. Somehow you've bought into the idea that because you love each other you no longer need to care about your parents and their hopes for you, but true love will cause you to love your families more, not less. You have used your 'love' to stifle your other ambitions—your education, goals, and plans—but true love creates more ambition, not less. You've used your love to escape life, friends, family, and school social activities, but true love isn't an escape from life, it is the spark that inspires life. Having sex is meant to be part of making love and making life together, but you're not ready for that. Christina, have you ever thought of how a woman needs security in order to fully enjoy sexual relations? Fear blocks sexual fulfillment, and pre-marital sex is full of fears.

"There's a time and a season for all phases of our lives; you're attempting to jump over the self-discovery phase of life. *You can't know who is right for you until you know who you are yourself.* Think of it, who were you in love with last year? Who was it in grade school? Usually, who you choose to be with in high school is not the person you would choose after college. As you mature, you change. You change who you are, and whom you fall in love with. There's a time to be single, and a time to be married. There's a time to surround yourself with friends, guys and girls, to develop socially. Too often teenagers jump into marriage-type relationships because they want to hide together, to avoid the challenge of developing personally and socially. It's not the time or the season; I encourage you to reconsider what you're doing, and why you're doing it."

"I thought you would understand," Christina whimpered, holding tightly on Ron's arm. "We can't help ourselves; we're in *love.*"

"Where there is real love, there is a real willingness to sacrifice—to do without, to wait," I continued. "When it's really, really important, you don't want to risk losing it."

"But we know that we're going to get married someday; we've both agreed to that," Ron said. "It's just not right to be married now; we're too young."

"Then stop playing married together," I said. "There's no substitute for time and commitment to test a relationship! If it's right, it'll last; if it's not right, you're creating pain for both of you. The pain of breaking up. The pain of a possible pregnancy. The pain of guilt. The pain of bad memories. The pain of getting sidetracked away from personal development. The pain of self-betrayal."

"Wait, a minute," he said angrily, "Are you saying that we shouldn't have sex until marriage? That will be years. Besides, sex is a need; it's a physical need."

"Sex is not a physical need, like food, air and water. That's another bad idea that you've bought into. We can control it, and for our own happiness and the happiness of those we love, we must control it.

"We can choose to activate this power, or to keep it somewhat dormant. The soul was designed to rule over the body; otherwise we're at the mercy of every appetite and passion that carries us away. But keep in mind that passions are definitely stimulus/response. In other words, don't tease the passions like a feather tickles an itch, then try to stop the itch. Don't sneak off in the dark together and expect to keep the thermostat of passions at a controled level. Remember, there's not any more important decision in your life than choosing how, and with whom, to use your sexual powers. It can create the greatest heavens or the most miserable hells. It deserves the wait until a loving, loyal and legal relationship."

They left upset, but a few weeks later, they came by again with a new resolve: they decided to take a time out on the relationship to discover themselves. He later went into military service; she's now attending college.

A Time and a Season

Puberty awakens a whole new control center—the sexual center—with hormones kicking in, it's no wonder that we are clumsy with it all for awhile. It's also no wonder that the best way to avoid broken hearts and lost childhoods is to avoid all sexual encounters until an honorable marriage. There's so much to lose and so little to gain by becoming sexually active before adulthood and emotional maturity!

Nature has a way of taking us from one phase of our lives to another. There's a time for childhood and a time for adolescence, a time to be alone, a time to be with friends, and a time to be married. If we attempt to leap over a phase of our life to the next one, something inside warns, "Not yet, too soon. Wait." Adolescence is the time and season for self-discovery, development and casual friendships. We cannot be right for someone else until we are right for ourselves—and it takes time to discover ourselves.

Mature and honorable love has the potential to create human happiness like nothing else; immature and dishonorable love has the potential to create human misery like nothing else. Especially if for one it's an investment of heart and soul, and for the other it's merely an investment of temporary play time. Young, immature women are prone towards obsessive love relationships—worshiping, rather than loving. Young, immature men, on the other hand, are prone to feign love relationships for sexual gratification.

The Fear Factor

By its very nature mature marriage provides a love nest of commitment and security that allows sexual feelings to bloom freely. The absence of the fear factor is a strong reason to wait for marriage. Dishonor, disloyalty, deceit and disrespect create fear whether in friends, family or loved ones. Remember the last time you were in the presence of someone who was critical and cold. Did you find yourself being careful and tongue-tied? Now think of the last time you were with that friend who enjoys you and what you have to say. Remember feeling free to be yourself, to joke around, to be quick and spontaneous? Fear causes us to tense up emotionally, and fear causes men and women, but especially women, to tense up sexually as well.

Casual sexual relationships, by their very nature, create fear: fear of pregnancy, fear of venereal disease, fear of being found out, fear of being caught, fear of hidden motives, fear of abandonment, fear of the lover's husband or wife, fear of lost self-respect.

Sexual fulfillment requires that we freely give, and freely receive. Such freedom is impossible with fear. *That's why the sexually promiscuous may know sexual pleasure, but they'll never know sexual joy—an ecstatic burst of body delight, emotional completeness, spiritual wholeness, and internal peace.*

Relationships that are founded upon love, honor and cherishing set the foundation for sexual fulfillment; they provide an emotional love nest that's warm, cozy, safe, free of fear, and free of false motives.

In an article titled, "What Sex Means In A Happy Marriage," Dr. Alexander Lowen explained this idea:

> "Tension makes the body contract and prepares a person for action; the absence of tension permits the body to expand. When you relax, your heart slows its beat, blood surges to your skin, you feel warm and outgoing and you are particularly sensitive to touch. When you tense up, however, your heart beats faster, blood leaves the surface and goes to the interior of your body, you feel chilled and withdrawn and you are comparatively insensitive to touch. You are defending yourself against pain. It is important to realize that these physical reactions are beyond conscious control. This means that the body acts as a silent witness to feelings we hide from ourselves. For example, a woman may deceive herself into thinking that she loves a man or that he loves her; yet when she is with him, her responses are those of a person on

guard—her body is tight with tension. She may be totally unaware of this or may confuse it with sexual excitement, but the blood is not flowing freely to her skin, and when the man touches her, she feels little physical pleasure. . .She can will sex, but not sexual joy. . .for like all living organisms, we move away from pain and toward joy.

"*There is nothing complete about genital pleasure alone. It is a fragment of our total capacity for joy—powerful, crucially important, but a fragment all the same. The joy we seek, the completion we long for must fill all the dimensions of our being: sensual, sexual, emotional and spiritual. Love is commitment, and with commitment, with faith in the belief that today's happiness will return tomorrow, the body opens to joy.* Without commitment, the body holds back, anticipating disappointment and pain. It remains tense and on guard and cannot fully respond to another's touch.

"With love, however, with the feeling of total commitment that extends from the present into the future, the body willingly, eagerly surrenders itself to the pleasures of the moment. Thus love liberates our sexuality. . .Here is the completed circle of joy that lets the lover tell his beloved how much he loves her: more than yesterday, less than tomorrow. . .When a man and a woman live together, openly pledged in heart, body, and mind and accepting full responsibility for each other. . .they are married. And despite the clear change in public attitudes towards sex today, most young women, and more young men than is commonly believed, require the security of marriage for the full unfolding of their sexual responses. . .Long after the joy of sex has subsided, the joy of love floods the entire being with a feeling of harmony, tranquility and completion..."

Natural Stages of Attraction

Everywhere I go I sense this longing in the eyes of the youth. They want desperately to believe that romantic love has a chance to survive. They hope against hope that one day they will find their love, marry and stay in love. The pessimism is all around them, but still they have that hope. Usually they do not realize that playing house before maturity can damage their chances for the real thing.

Ron and Christina did not realize that being really in love inspires sacrifice and self-discipline. They did not know that you can have a love friendship without sex. They did not know the difference between having sex and making love. They did not know that all human relationships—whether friends, family or loved ones—succeed only when they have a foundation of genuine loving, honoring, and cherishing. They did not know that there are natural stages of attraction that eventually lead to a wholesome relationship.

Through the years, I have observed a natural process of attraction between the sexes that gradually advances with independence and maturity. The first stage could be called **fascination**—it is the natural admiration and attraction between the sexes. We see this fascination stage at its height in early adolescence when the young men are standing at one end of the dance floor with the young women at the other—their attention towards one another. They're admiring, watching, and giggling—but at a distance.

Men are intrigued by a woman's attractiveness, her softness, curves, sensitivity, beauty. Women are fascinated by the differences in men—their masculinity, their angles, their confidence, sense of humor, and tenderness of heart.

The next stage of natural attraction begins when **friendship** occurs with conversation and shared interests. I noticed that when our sons passed through this stage (later teens) they were more comfortable with young women who were open, friendly and confident, but who did not press for heavy involvement. This has also been the case with our daughters. Our daughter, Mary, now fifteen, is surrounded by young men friends who want a brother-sister relationship—and nothing more.

The third stage occurs when the fascination and friendship turn to **infatuation** or "puppy love"—when one man or woman stands out above the rest. An infatuation naturally comes and goes, but if it is magnetized by sexual bonding it may last longer than either party wants it to last. (This is one of the dangers of early sexual experiences.)

The final phase of attraction between men and women takes place when wide-angled fascination with universal femininity and masculinity advances through friendship, infatuation, then true, mature love: intimacy of mind, heart, and soul. This mature love naturally leads to loyalty and commitment; the main focus is upon the whole person—the "Beloved" as Lewis defines it.

> "What comes first," says C.S. Lewis, regarding healthy attraction, "is simply a delighted preoccupation with her in her totality. A man in this state really hasn't leisure to think of sex. He is too busy thinking of a person. The fact that she is a woman is far less important than the fact that she is herself. (Healthy love) makes a man really want, not a woman, but one particular woman. In some mysterious fashion, the lover desires the Beloved herself, not the pleasure she can give." (Four Loves, p. 135, 133.)

Sex with honor intensifies natural passion because it springs from an inner reverence for the loved one.

Summary

Giving someone the power to stimulate and activate the sexual bond is like giving them a key to your very soul—maybe even your sanity. It deserves serious and mature consideration, and time to test the relationship.

If the key holder is one who would use, abuse, neglect, or

control, it's misery of the worst kind. Crimes to the heart inflict the deepest of human suffering. That's why it's smart to hold onto the key until a loving, loyal and legal relationship.

Sexual intercourse creates a magnetic bond in the relationship; it's meant to create circles of love that last forever—for better or worse. If the relationship is founded upon loving, honoring and cherishing and has reached the time and season for a marriage commitment, the added dimension of sexual intimacy will be for the better. If, on the other hand, the relationship is founded upon immature and unhealthy motives adding the "super-glue" will be for the worse!

"The truth is," wrote C.S. Lewis, "that wherever a man lies with a woman. . .whether they like it or not, a transcendental relation is set up between them which must be eternally enjoyed or eternally endured."

Notes and factors to be considered:

1. "Only when we truly reveal ourselves can we ever be truly loved. When we relate as we genuinely are, from our essence, then if we are loved it is our essence that is loved. Nothing is more validating on a personal level and more freeing in a relationship. It must be noted, however, that this kind of behavior on our part is only possible in a climate that is free of fear, so we must not only conquer our own fears of being genuine but also avoid people whose attitudes and behaviors towards us produce fear. No matter how

willing to be genuine you become with recovery, there will still be people whose anger, hostility, and aggression will inhibit you from being honest. To be vulnerable with them is to be masochistic. Therefore, lowering our boundaries and eventually eliminating them should happen only with those people—friends, relatives, or lovers—with whom we have a relationship bathed in trust, love, respect, and reverence for our shared, tender humanity." (Robin Norwood, Women Who Love Too Much, p. 275)

The Masquerade of Love *Especially for Women 11

"How could I be expected to know? I was a child when I left this house four months ago. Why didn't you tell me there was danger in men folk? Why didn't you warn me? Ladies know what to fend hands against, because they read novels that tell them of these tricks, but I never had the chance o' learning in that way, and you did not help me!"

Young Tess of the novel, Tess of the D'Urbervilles,
Thomas Hardy

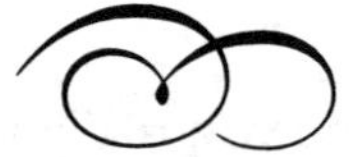

Insight #11
Young women, in their desire for love and affection are inclined towards unhealthy love relationships masquerading as love.

A mother pleads with her daughter, "I don't know why you stay with him; he's broken your nose three times, he's blackened your eyes more times than I can remember."

"You wouldn't understand," her daughter replies. "You don't know what it's like to be *in love.*"

"I deserved the beatings."

Who would believe that she had ever been abused? She was beautiful, slender with dark, brown hair cut to her shoulders. She had a soft, childlike voice that was easy to listen to. She was renting the apartment next to ours, and upon our first visit we immediately became friends. After awhile she told me that her first marriage was a nightmare of physical abuse. Despite the abuse, she stayed with him for several years.

"Why did you stay with him?" I asked.

"Well, with the first few beatings I was enraged," she said, "and threatened to leave him. After awhile I grew kinda numb to the whole thing; I thought maybe all wives get beat up. It was my only marriage—how was I to know? Besides, I thought maybe I deserved the beatings."

"Deserved?"

"Well, when someone you really love is abusive, your self-esteem is shattered to the point that you begin to believe that maybe you deserve such treatment. After awhile, you just don't have the will to fight it."

"How did you finally get away?"

"One day I looked at myself in the mirror after a beating the night before. My face was all puffy and I had a black eye. As I stood staring at myself in the mirror, I began thinking to myself, 'I used to be pretty; I'm not pretty anymore. I'm ugly.' Then something dawned on me. I realized that the reason that I wasn't pretty anymore wasn't because of the beatings; the ugliness was coming from within—deep within.

And it wasn't really that I was ugly, I was dying! Not physically dying, but dying emotionally, dying spiritually. I knew then that I had to get out—to save my life, or what was left of it.

"When he came home that night I said, 'If you ever hit me again, I'm walking out. I'll never come back.' Two weeks later he hit me; I walked out."

When Unhealthy Relationships Masquerade as Love

Long after this conversation, and others like it, the difficult questions kept coming back. What happens to the instinct for self-preservation? What happens to clear thinking? What keeps women or men stuck in relationships that are emotionally and physically abusive? What leads to the tragic loss of conscience?

We have all heard the reasons: "He really loves me; he just can't control his temper. . .She didn't mean to do it. . .He just needs someone to love him enough, then he won't do those things. . .She likes to control me, but then that's the way she is. . .That's just the way he is, but we're really in love."

On the outside looking in, we can see clearly these relationships are unhealthy relationships masquerading as love, but for those caught in the smokescreen it's not so clear. Some go along with the abuse because abusive relationships are all they've ever known—having grown up in an abusive family. Others, like the song, "Some of them want to use you, some of them want to get used by you, some of them want to abuse you, some of them want to be abused," actually *want* the abuse. Some fall victim to masquerades—especially the immature—because they like the dramatics of it all! With hormones raging, they choose relationships to match their youthful nature: wildly emotional. The rifts, and tears, and passion make it all so much more colorful, exciting—and often painful.

"It's all a part of the game," said C.S. Lewis, "a game of catch-as-catch-can, and the scrapes and tumbles and head-on-collisions are to be treated as a romp."

Masquerades can range from simple unhealthy and stagnating relationships to abusive relationships, either physically, sexually, or emotionally. Since young women are prone to enter into a masquerade, and surrender virginity in the name of love, they need to be prepared to recognize unhealthy relationships masquerading as love and the motives that lead into them.

The Men Women Difference

Women's strong emotional side, unchecked by reason and spiritual strength, can lead them into masquerades—unhealthy relationships masquerading as love—or to fantasies of romantic love. Men's strong physical side, unchecked by reason and spiritual strength, can lead into what I call the *mystique*—sex divorced from love, affection, emotions, courtship, friendship, honor, honesty, commitment.

Men seem to be drawn towards the fascination of naked bodies—panting together, while women are fascinated with naked emotions—weeping together. Men fall for the fantasy of lust (sex for power), while women fall for the fantasy of obsessive love.

This man/woman difference shows up in studies. While women are inclined towards romance novels and magazines that stimulate emotionally, men are inclined towards pornography, that stimulates sexually—one study reported that 94% of those addicted to pornography are men.

The old expression that women give sex to get love is still true. In a survey conducted by Mark Clements Research, Inc. "More than four in five (83%) said girls engage in sex because boys pressure them or they think they will lose their boyfriends if they don't have sex. 'Girls often trade sex for love, just as they always have,' maintains Deborah Tolman, director of the Adolescent Sexuality Project at the Center for Research on Women at Wellesley College. 'Society teaches girls that love is what should matter to them, and we teach boys that what they should want most is sex. We end up shortchanging both genders.' "(San Francisco Chronicle, Feb. 2, 1997)

Intent of the Heart

Masquerades are all unhealthy, but some are more unhealthy than others. Some are immature, or frustrating, or stagnating, but others can be abusive! The intent of the heart makes all the difference. The darker the motives of the heart the more diseased the relationships will be. When the heart is cold and hard—without compassion, without respect—the abuse can be ruthless.

When a crime is committed, the judge and jury weigh the evidence carefully to determine both the crime itself and the premeditation—or intent of the heart—that proceeded the crime. In this same way, masquerades are unhealthy or diseased depending upon the intent of the heart and the behavior. There are those who inflict intentional harm, and those who do harm without malice. There's a difference between the man who accidentally runs down a pedestrian and one who kills "in cold blood" with calculated and premeditated intent. Yet, each took a life. A woman who steals a loaf of bread to feed her starving, sick child, could be considered a thief, but the intent of her heart would not be in question.

A young girl who gives into her boyfriend's demands and surrenders to an immature relationship may be acting out of the craving to be loved and fear of abandonment. The man who cunningly plots to win a young girl's love and affection in order to score another virgin is motivated by self-centered power and vanity. A woman who stalks another woman's husband in a spirit of competition and jealousy may be acting on selfish pride. The husband who gives in to the affair may be acting out of pride and vanity. The intent of the heart makes the difference—but all are a self-betrayal. All lead to unfulfilling relationships.

There's a *definite* difference between adolescent curiosity about sexuality and a cold-hearted craving for sexual conquest. Even so, such child-like playing with so powerful-of-forces produces immature and usually short-lived relationships; there's a time and season for all things, and something within gently reminds us that it's too soon for something so important. These immature masquerades lead to broken hearts, premature parenthood and aborted childhoods.

Motives for Human Bonding

Another attribute of masquerades is that they are collusive—there's a loss of conscience. Healthy relationships heighten conscience; unhealthy relationships diminish conscience. This idea needs developing.

People bond together for various reasons. Some gather together with common beliefs and goals like garden groups, political groups, church groups, save the environment groups, etc. These collective groups form for the common good, to *contribute* to society. Joining together increases their power to do good like a rope becomes stronger with more strands.

The rope idea also works for opposite motives. It increases the power for *crime*, such as gangs, terrorist groups, mafia, etc. The goals that bond them together determine whether the group is bonded for the greater good, or bonded for the greater bad.

In healthy groups, consciences are enhanced. In fact

that's one reason that they have frequent meetings and lectures, to remind each other of their common interests, and to take action based upon those interests. Bird watching groups gather to share their love and appreciation of birds, and to plan trips together to act upon that love. They may form lobby groups to influence legislation to protect and preserve birds that are threatened with extinction.

Our family attends a wonderful church group where each week we gather together to discuss our common belief system. Through the talking, and the teaching and the discussions we keep our beliefs alive and the motivation to act according to those beliefs. We humans are a forgetful lot; we need constant reminders that "the things that matter most should not be at the mercy of the things that matter least."

Now contrast this with unhealthy bonding. Consciences are silenced, human sympathy is shut down and gang spirit reigns. Think of the gangs in which the initiation process demands that the new comer must commit murder. Think even of the elite groups that band together in wealth and shut out the poor. Think of religious groups who profess to be followers of Christ, but love the family of God less, not more. This list could go on and on; the idea is simple: people bond together for various reasons, and couples bond together for various reasons. If the bonding leads to progression, peace of conscience and more love it is healthy, but if that bonding leads to stagnation, anxiety of conscience, and indifference or hate, it is unhealthy. Preventing masquerades and preparing for healthy love relationships begins with oneself and understanding the difference between heater problems and engine problems in relationships.

Heater and Engine Problems

Imagine you're flying all alone in a small plane—it's late at night, in the middle of winter. The moon's light is reflected off the snow-capped mountains, and you marvel at the beauty of it all. The air is biting cold, but you're comfortable inside, enjoying the sights. Then all of a sudden, the heater stops working—that's bad. Gradually the air inside the cockpit turns cool, then cold. You think to yourself, Why? Why me? Why this? Why now? This is about the worst thing that could happen. I'm going to freeze. Why do things always happen to me?

As you reach over to grab the jacket in the back seat, the engine sputters and stops. Suddenly irritation turns to terror. In a flash of a second the heater problem is no problem at all. Now there's a real problem—a life and death problem. There are heater problems and there are engine problems in relationships. Heater problems are: leaving the toothpaste out, forgetting to put gas in the car, friendly disputes and disagreements about disciplining the children. They are frustrating, but hardly cause for divorce or separation. Fine-tuning heater problems—the process that naturally goes on in relationships like two musicians trying to get the harmony right are normal and even productive. This needs a bit more explanation.

While love and marriage is a refuge from the prickles of the world, it is still a refining process. The day-to-day intimacy of marriage enables us to see quirks of character of the other—and family traits—that hinder growth and happiness. Young couples, beginning their new circles of love, naturally discuss and determine what family traits and traditions they want to hold onto from their original families and which ones to discard. By this process of natural selection, each new family builds upon the good of the previous family. This is the heater refining process.

There's the old line that women marry men they want to change, but marriage, by its very nature prompts growth and change for both. This is one of the greatest challenges and *rewards* of a marriage—together they become more than they ever could alone—more in marriage, but more personally, as well. Men need women to help them become better men, and women need men to help them become better women. It's the, "Did you realize that you. . ." factor, that I recently used when I told my husband that he needs to balance Saturday chores so that there's more time for the family. There will always be heater problems in relationships—not because one is the victim and the other is the enemy—but simply because both are human and still maturing.

Now let's turn to engine problems. Whenever there's a deliberate abuse—emotional, physical, or sexual—it's an engine problem. Engine problems are stagnating, demoralizing, and even enslaving. Whenever there is a craving to escape oneself, it's an engine problem. Whenever conscience must be silenced, it's an engine problem. Whenever there is indifference, dishonor, and despise, it's an engine problem. Engine problems mean an eventual collusion, they require immediate attention and immediate action.

Preventing the masquerades begins with understanding and recognizing the difference between heater problems, engine problmes and the signs and symptoms of healthy and unhealthy love relationships. Simple self-evaluations like the following may help detect a masquerade. Once again the key words for mature and wholesome love are: love, honor and cherish.

Signs of Healthy Love and Symptoms of Unhealthy Relationships: Three Keys

1. Love—adore, passion, fascination, magnetism.

Healthy Signs:

He/She wants to meet out in the open—with friends and family.

He/She is anxious to learn what you think and what you feel.

Being with him/her makes you feel more alive.

You feel like you've found your other half—your better half.

Exciting warmth, tenderness and joy flows between you.

Intimate feelings of mind, heart, and soul are shared.

You share the same dreams and aspirations.

Unhealthy symptoms: Hate—enmity, hostility, rancor.

The relationship incites a reckless passion that shuts out rational thinking.

The relationship leads to a dead end—no commitment, no future, no chance of building together.

Love-making is physical only, without tender conversation or spiritual bonding.

No one can understand why you're together—especially family and those who love you.

In the worst case your partner wants you to view pornography.

2. Honor—willingness to sacrifice, high motives and morals, responsibility.

Healthy Signs:

He/She assists you to become your better self.

He/She shows willingness to make sacrifices for the good of the relationship, including abstaining from sexual relations.

He/She encourages you to develop yourself, intellectually, spiritually, emotionally and physically.

He/She helps you to attain your noble goals and aspirations.

He/She sharpens your conscience and desires that you be a person of integrity.

He/She desires to build life a life together.

Unhealthy symptoms: Dishonor—contempt, scorn, humiliate.

He/She criticizes you with a hostile nature that includes

cursing, vulgarity, ugly names.

He/She cuts you off from family and friends.

He/She shows intense jealousy and mistrust.

He/She dulls your conscience and confidence.

He/She causes you to feel alone and misunderstood.

He/She blames others for his/her faults, weaknesses, problems.

He/She rants and raves about things that cannot be changed.

He/She has mood swings that lead to out-of-control temper tantrums.

He/She demands control of your time and your life; wants to know where you've been, who you talked with, what you talked about, why you didn't do this or that.

3. Cherish—treasure, reverence, prize

Healthy signs:

He/She shows goodwill and respect towards others.

He/She is kind, considerate, thoughtful.

He/She is thoughtful of your time, your independence.

He/She treasures your time alone together, but enjoys being with others, as well.

He/She places a high value on your feelings, thoughts, happiness.

Unhealthy symptoms: Indifference, neglect, vulgarity

He/She tells you that you are the only woman that he respects.

He/She seems ashamed introducing you to family or friends.

He/She shows meanness, ill spirited nature, "I hate the way you. . ."

Beware if:

You find yourself being someone you're not.

You have to ignore certain characteristics that are offensive.

You become confused.

You feel used.

You feel less motivated to do the right thing.

You become alienated from everyone else.

You feel bound and stifled.

You know that goals will be harder to attain.

Life will be harder to live.

There's nothing to talk about before or after the sex.

Childhood is lost.

You hate to be alone.

You dislike each other's families.

You feel less alive after being in his or her presence.

You feel you're in a state of bondage, stagnation, even deterioration.

You feel unsafe, threatened.

The question is, "Do I feel loved, honored and cherished in my relationship?"

After understanding the signs and symptoms of healthy and unhealthy love relationships, we need to understand ourselves well enough to detect the motives that lead to an unhealthy relationship in the first place.

Tolstoy wrote, "Happy families are all alike; every unhappy family is unhappy in its own way." The same is true in romance; the healthy are all alike, the unhealthy are each unhealthy in a particular way. In the next chapter we will explore unhealthy motives that lead to the masquerades.

Notes and Factors to Consider:

1. "Nationwide, the number of girls ages 15 to 19 who reported having sex increased from 29% in 1970 to 52% in 1988. Nearly one million teenagers become pregnant every year, and of these about 400,00 have abortions. " This article was exciting. A group calling itself Best Friends was formed to assist young woman to choose sexual abstinence. It cited that in one survey, 85% of young women polled wanted to belong to a Best Friends support group. One young woman wrote, "peer pressure and lack of direction and guidance from adults leads to early sexual intercourse." (Reader's Digest, "These Teens Know How to Say No", Mona Charen, March 1977)

2. "Middle class girls, even more than those raised in poverty, begin sexual experimentation with *romantic myths*—that they'll marry their boyfriend, finish school, raise a loving family and get a good job. . .Every year some 350,000 teenage girls have babies out of wedlock—a figure that has dramatically increased over the last several decades. . .more

than half of all teenagers—boys and girls—have had sex by the age of 18." (Suzanne Chazin, "Teen Pregnancy", Reader's Digest, September 1996)

3. "It would be unfair to blame teenagers for the epidemic of out-of-wedlock births; only 30 % of the children born outside marriage every year are born to teenage mothers, but the problem of children conceived by unmarried teenage girls is more debilitating than the numbers suggest: children of teenage mothers are more likely to be born into poverty, family instability and welfare dependency, forever locked outside the American mainstream." (Journalist Cynthia Tucker, San Francisco Chronicle, Jan. 27, 1996)

4. "Fewer than half the teens who give birth out of wedlock marry within the next few years. Those who do marry are twice as likely to divorce in five years as women who marry in their 20s. . .fatherless children are more likely to take drugs, drop out of school, turn to crime and become teen parents themselves.

"According to Child Trends, a Washington, D.C., research organization, more than half of teenage mothers are not residing with their child's father by the time that child reaches grade school. More than one-quarter never lived with the father. Nor will the father offer much help. . .only 20% of never-married mothers receive formal child support. By contrast, four out of five women who wait until age 24 to give birth are still residing with the child's father when the child reaches grade school—and two out of three of those children have never lived in poverty."(Suzanne Chazin, "Teen Pregnancy, Let's Get Real", Reader's Digest, September 1996)

12
The Motives That Lead To Masquerades

"Sexual desire can be stimulated by the anxiety of aloneness, by the wish to conquer or to be conquered, by vanity, by the wish to hurt and even to destroy, as much as it can be stimulated by love. . .(but) if the desire for physical union is not stimulated by love, if erotic love is not also brotherly love, it never leads to union in more than an orgiastic, transitory sense."

The Art of Loving, Erich Fromm

Insight #12

Masquerades, unhealthy relationships masquerading as love, begin with unhealthy motives. Just as we are attracted to individuals with complimentary interests, so are we attracted to those with complimentary weaknesses.

It has become popular to advertise for companionship. I have decided that this is a great way to show—in a concise and clear way—the contrast between healthy and unhealthy motives. Keep in mind, though, that this is all in enlightening fun. In other words, don't take it too seriously. The hope here is that we'll be better able to see through the smoke-screen of the masquerades.

Healthy Motives

HONEST and FRIENDLY, seeking companion to love, honor and cherish, to share life, dreams, ambition. Permanent position.

Unhealthy Motives

OWNER/OPERATOR: looking for someone to own and operate. Must be docile.

PRETTY ONE: seeking someone to compliment my good looks, must be attractive and in excellent condition.

PARASITE: shy, insecure, and confused seeks someone to escape in. Must be domineering and controlling.

OUT-TO-LUNCH: in love with fantasy love and looking for a romance like in the cheap novels. Extremely temporary position.

SWINGER: sexy buffed male looking for a warm body for the night. Must be female, no other requirements. Temporary help only. Advancement not possible.

PARTNER-IN-CRIME: looking for someone to join me in a fantasy love affair—preferably married. High risk; high adventure. Temporary.

EXTREMELY SWEET AND SUBMISSIVE IDOLATER: desperately craving an addictive and obsessive relationship—someone to put on pedestal. No possibility of advancement.

FIX-R-UPPER: seeking father substitute; hoping to

resolve the unresolvables of childhood. Must have same dysfunctional behavior.

LIFEGUARD: anxious to save someone's life—addicts, alcoholics, drug abusers please apply. No job too difficult.

Extremely Unhealthy Motives

THE GREAT AND ALMIGHTY ONE: looking for someone who will center their life, their thoughts, their desires, their heart, might, mind and strength on ME, ONLY ME AND ME ALONE !

PREDATOR: seeking another trophy to add to my collection; must make it interesting, challenging; temporary position.

POWERFUL BRUTE: interested in someone to release pent-up aggression and hostilities upon. Must be submissive and silent. No other requirements necessary.

BRUISED AND BATTERED: but willing to take more. Looking for someone to punish me for past mistakes. Must be abusive. Whip provided.

Interlocking Motives

This is just a sampling of the unhealthy motives that lead to unhealthy relationships—either friendships or romance. Some are based on the craving to be loved. Some are founded upon the desire to control, others the desire to be controlled. Some are based upon the need to hurt; others on the need to be hurt. Some motives are uncomplicated: simple sex.

Notice the motives interlock—like a puzzle—with each other; the unhealthy needs of one are attracted to the unhealthy needs of another.

"I need someone to escape myself," matches with, "I need someone who wants to be controlled."

"I need love, but I'll accept sex," goes with, "I need sex, but I'm willing to fake love."

"I need someone who will punish me," interlocks with, "I need someone to punish."

"I am looking for someone I can save," goes with, "I'm looking for someone who will save me, then I won't have to take responsibility for my own life."

"I am looking for someone who will treat me coldly and indifferently like my father did; I didn't solve the problem with him, but maybe I'll succeed with someone else," naturally fits with, "I am cold and indifferent: I am looking for someone who will try to change me."

"I want someone who will compliment my good looks," matches up with the motives of someone looking for a beautiful trophy to impress friends with.

Like two pieces of a puzzle, they fit together because they fit each other's wants. Just as we are attracted to individuals with complementary interests, so are we attracted to those with complementary weaknesses.

Now let's discuss a sampling of these motives.

Parasite: Escaping Oneself

Some years ago, I had this conversation; the young woman was bright, beautiful but without purpose. "So, are you interested in going to college?"

"No," she said, "I don't have any desire to go to college. I just want to get married and have children."

"Well," I responded, "you might like to take some classes in the homemaking arts—like sewing and cooking."

"No," she said, "I don't care about that either; I just want to get married and have a family."

This conversation went along like this for awhile, then I got the point: she didn't want to talk about life's options. For her, marriage was the only option. It *was* life. Parasitic love occurs when one attempts to escape oneself in another. The parasite is likely to say things like, "I feel so insignificant; I need someone to make me somebody. . .I don't want to go to college; isn't there someone around here to take care of me?. . I'm just an old-fashioned girl; you know the kid who just wants to give herself totally to someone. . . .Life's just too hard; I hate making all these decisions. Isn't there someone who will tell me what to think and what to do?. . I don't want to grow up."

The desire to escape into another may just be a hangover of false traditions. Women, throughout history, were not considered whole—or even a member of society—without a man. The Biblical definition that man and wife become one flesh and the head of the flesh is the man has influenced some women to believe that without a man they are incomplete. Society has upheld this view of women by depriving them of the right to vote (women only received the right to vote in 1920), not allowing them to own property or conduct a business, etc. These attitudes carry over through the generations, even though the laws themselves have changed. I recall when we first saw a female newscaster on television, and it seemed so strange. We're still working through all this.

The way to avoid the parasite motive is to accept the challenge of giving birth to oneself. More on this in the next chapter.

Idolater: Looking for the Almighty One

Parasites form passive, lethargic, and stagnant relationships, but Idolaters take a leap into more compulsive/obsessive relationships. The Idolater wants more than just someone to escape into, the Idolater wants someone to worship. They sacrifice mind, heart, body and soul for their love. The Idolater and the Almighty One, who is craving to be worshipped, form an unbreakable bond. Notice the interlocking motives: craving to worship, craving to be worshipped; craving to be controlled, craving to dominate.

Watching young women at rock concerts, we see this principle in action. They are screaming, crying, waving their arms in a display of "worshiping" their "Gods." Young women who give their all to their boyfriends—in the name of love—are the Idolaters seeking what only God can provide for his children.

The fury of the Idolater is portrayed in the anguish of Anna for her lover Vronsky in the classic novel Anna Karenina by Leo Tolstoy. Actually, Anna displays characteristics of both—the Idolater, craving to worship, and The Almighty One, in her craving to be worshipped. She wants to both engulf and be engulfed by her lover.

> "My love keeps growing more passionate and egoistic, while his is waning and waning, and that's why we're drifting apart. . .and there's no hope for it. He is everything for me, and I want him more and more to give himself up to me entirely. And he wants more and more to get away from me. We walked to meet each other up to the time of our love, and then we have been irresistibly drifting in different directions. And there's no altering that. He tells me I'm insanely jealous, and I have told myself that I am insanely jealous; but it's not true. I'm not jealous, but I'm unsatisfied. . .if I could be anything but a mistress, passionately caring for nothing but his caresses; but I can't and I don't care to be anything else.. . And by that desire I rouse aversion in him, and he rouses fury in me, and it cannot be different." (p. 1240)

Realizing "how miserably she loved and hated him" she resolves, "I will punish him and escape from everyone and from myself," and she throws herself in front of a train. She dies in the insanity of a masquerade.

The Sadie Syndrome—Craving to be Loved

One woman said, "I know a few women who think that when a man's pawing them they're loved. It never occurs to them that these guys are just looking for a good time." They are like Sadie, our family beagle. Sadie acts so desperate for love that she makes herself a pest to everyone who would love her if she were not so desperate. She is not allowed in the house, but she runs in whenever a door is left open, then attacks the first person she finds with her wet licks and cold nose. Her obnoxious behavior and insatiable craving for love make it impossible to love her.

If, in a moment of pity, you pat her or acknowledge her with, "Hi, Sadie," she translates it—in desperate dog language—to mean, "I love you, Sadie, come and jump all over me and lick my face forever and ever." (We are mere mortals, and all this adoration and face licking just doesn't seem right—whether from dogs or people.)

Everyone has learned that the best way to deal with Sadie is to keep their distance. Those who display the behavior of Sadie would likely say, "I feel so lonely and weak, I need to be loved even if it isn't the real thing. I know it isn't love, but it resembles it just a little. Well, not at all, but, hey, it beats coming home to an empty house. . .Sure, he's married, but he really loves me. She doesn't understand him like I do. . She's controlling, sure, but that's the way women are who are madly in love with a guy. . .Why do I dress like this? Cause, the guys like it. They look at me and I love to get their attention."

> "(Those individuals with) ravenous love," said C.S. Lewis, ". . work to their own misery and everyone else's. The situation becomes suffocating. If people are already unlovable, a continual demand on their part to be loved—their manifest sense of injury, their reproaches, whether loud and clamorous or merely implicit in every look and gesture of resentful self-pity—produce in us a sense of guilt (they are intended to do so) for a fault we could not have avoided and cannot cease to commit.
>
> "They seal up the very fountain for which they are thirsty. If ever, at some favored moment, any germ of affection for them stirs in us, their demand for more and still more petrifies us again." (Four Loves, p. 65)

Notice that we are not talking about loving too much, but rather craving to be loved—at any price. It's a matter of self-consciousness, a stumbling block to becoming other-conscious.

The Owner/Operator—Looking For Someone To Own And Operate

My friend and I were visiting in the living room of her home when her husband came through the door, returning after a day at the dental office. She did not say "hello" but—like a sergeant—began yelling orders: "First I want you to bathe the boys, then you need to go out and look what they did to the flower garden. And be sure and get dinner started." He did not say a word, showed no emotion, but turned and walked away. Two years later, he left. She cried, "How could he do this to me? After all I did for him?"

Loyalty and faithfulness is promised at the altar—not ownership. Love is fragile; it cannot be forced or mandated. Love is won by tender courtship and recaptured in the same way. When we attempt to reign and rule in a relationship it backfires. Love is founded upon those ever-eternal principles of all solid relationships: respect, loyalty, patience, freedom, kindness, and love.

One spring I labored with the decision whether to attend the university or stay home. My husband said, "You have always enjoyed your summer studies; it's important for you, and I want you to go." Later one of my husband's friends said, "I don't know why you put up with that: I wouldn't let my wife do that for a second—let alone a whole summer." My husband answered, "Let? We don't do that in our marriage." Our reunion is always sweet; he's anxious to show off his gift of love in decorating our home, and I'm always anxious to share the knowledge I've gained. It's a "Win-Win" situation.

Such comments always amaze me; I've heard wives say something like, "I won't let George go fishing this weekend." And I've heard husbands say something like, "Martha wanted to take a class out at the college, but I put my foot down on the whole idea. Who's going to get my dinner if she's off taking classes?"

"Wishing that it would crash."

A young, fairly attractive woman, but worn-looking after two divorces, told me her story of being married to an Owner/Operator. "He was so tight. I had to sneak money to the children because he did not want them to have more than a few dollars a week. We lived under stress knowing that he would hold us accountable for every penny. One time I had to buy a poster board for Tommy's science class project. My husband told me to go clear across town to a store where I could buy it cheaper. We got into an argument because I tried to reason that while we would save fifty cents, we would burn more than that in gas. But he wouldn't listen, so I did it. Also, he wouldn't let anyone disagree with his opinion; he seemed to feel that since he was head of the house, he was to do the thinking for all of us. It was a nightmare. At first I tried to fight it, but eventually I gave in and let him have his way on every issue.

"Then last year, while flying home in a commercial airline, I found myself wishing that it would crash so that I would die. It was only then that I realized how horrible the situation was. I knew that I had to get out. As soon as I got home from the airport, I told him I wanted a divorce."

Her spirit was not longing to die; it was longing for freedom. I found myself wondering, however, if the relationship could have been changed and the marriage saved. Our spouses need to know what we stand for and what we will not stand for. To leap from co-dependency to total independence seems hardly fair to either one.

"I will serve as will and conscience both to you."

In the classic play A Doll's House by Henrik Ibsen we see a case of the Owner/Operator. To Helmer, his wife Nora is little more than a beloved pet. He gives her everything except equality and respect.

Helmer says to Nora, "Try to calm yourself, and make your mind easy again, my frightened little singing-bird. Be at rest and feel secure. I have broad wings to shelter you under. How warm and cozy our home is, Nora. Here is shelter for you; here I will protect you like a hunted dove that I have saved. . ."

"There is something so indescribably sweet and satisfying, to a man, in the knowledge that he has forgiven his wife—forgiven her freely and with all his heart. It seems as if that had made her, as it were, doubly his own. She has in a way become both wife and child to him. So you shall be for me after this, my little sacred helpless darling. Have no anxiety about anything, Nora; only be frank and open with me, and I will serve as will and conscience both to you."

Nora explains to Helmer that she is tired of not being consulted in the serious matters of their marriage. Helmer wonders why she would be concerned with such matters. When she tells him that she plans to leave, he asks, "It's shocking. This is how you would neglect your most sacred duties?"

Nora answers, "What do you consider my most sacred duties?"

He answers, "Do I need to tell you that? Are they not your duties to your husband and your children?"

She replies, "I have other duties just as sacred."

Helmer retorts, "That you have not. What duties could those be?"

Nora's answer was not only shocking to Helmer, and audiences, but sent ripples of change throughout America.

She answers firmly, "Duties to myself."

Helmer commands, "Before all else, you are a wife and a mother."

Nora answers, "I don't believe that any longer. I believe that before all else I am a reasonable human being, just as you are—or, at all events, that I must try and become one."

When Helmer asks if there's a possibility that she might change her mind, she tells him that the "most wonderful thing of all would have to happen." When he asks, "What would that be?" she answers, "That our life together would be a real wedlock."

The Lifeguard—Looking for Someone to Save or Control

The Lifeguard is looking to find someone to heal, in order to feel loved and needed. Little boys seem to have a natural inclination to fix things, and some little girls—and big girls—are inclined to fix people. The Lifeguard would say,

"Where is someone I can save? He's a drug addict? Perfect; he'll do. Through my love, my power, I can save him. No one else has been able to do it, but I will." There's pride in this motive, but there is also compassion, as well.

In her book, Women Who Love Too Much, Robin Norwood describes this situation:

"Since suffering has to be in the picture in order for it to be *love* these women look for a man who is different, mysterious and elusive. The depth of love is measured by the intensity of obsession with the loved one. There is little time or attention for other interests or pursuits, because so much energy is focused on . . .the great obstacles to overcome. . .another indication of the depth of love are the feelings of excitement, rapture, drama, anxiety, tension, mystery, and yearning. . .The woman who loves too much feels for the man who is impossible. Indeed, it is because he is impossible that there is so much passion." (Robin Norwood, Women Who Love Too Much, p. 44)

The Almighty Luv-God Motive

This masquerade may be more dangerous than all the others. Its root lie is that love itself is the great and almighty power that just has its way with us. It can takes us whenever, wherever and with whomever it will. There's nothing we can do but give in, give up and go with it. The Idolater wants a person to worship, now we turn to worshipping the Luv-God itself—the person is not as important as the feeling. This false

God has the power to sweep us into a love and marriage, and then to an affair, and then to a divorce, but the attitude is—who can fight it? It's *Almighty Luv.*

The headlines: *He's 14, She's 44, They're Married.* The story, Janet, who is divorced, has five children ranging in age from 7 to 23. She hired John as her babysitter and spent a lot of time talking with him. After they realized that they were in love and decided to get married, they had many problems. First, John's parents would not consent to the marriage, but almighty love prevails.

This is but one of many such articles prevalent today, newsworthy because it's bizarre. The overt message is that a woman and boy thirty years apart are getting married. The underlying message is that "love" struck and there was nothing they could do but accept it. "They realized that they were in love and decided to get married." Who can fight it? It's more powerful than the both of them.

In reality, they choose to enter the smokescreen of a masquerade. They believed the lie: love is the almighty; no mortal can fight it—why try? I found myself wondering why they did not see their relationship as a wonderful and rare friendship? In this sex-saturated society have we forgotten how to love "pure and chaste from afar"?

Those caught into the Luv-God motive might say things like, "Did you hear? I'm in love again. I thought that John and I would last forever, but then I saw Ted. Actually I met him in the laundromat—it was love at first sight. He was loading his washer while I was loading mine. He looked over at me; I looked at him, and that was it. We're going to be together forever. I can feel it. Well. . .I. . .just. . .wait! Who's that over there! That man with the blond hair and rippling muscles. It's him, I can feel it. This is it—the one! See you later."

Our teenage son, Micah, asked, "What if you fall in love with someone? Then there's no choice. Is there?"

"You can love many individuals throughout your life," I answered, "but only your inner compass can guide you to your soul-mate."

The Creator endowed us with the gift to love and the gift to *choose* whom to love romantically. Throughout life we may find ourselves more attracted to certain people over others—this is natural and normal, but sexual intimacy is reserved only for loving, loyal and legal relationships. The sacred nature and power of sexuality is too great to surrender it to every infatuation that comes along. Romantic love by its very nature, seeks an eternal partnership of intimacy, two becoming one in heart, mind, soul and body. It does not flit from one to another, like bees foraging in the flowers.

However, with the wonderful freedom of chastity there's always a place for warm platonic friendships. Those whose hearts are filled and overflowing with the wondrous awe of humanity, cannot stop themselves from falling in love—daily.

Sometimes the fascination and mystery of it all isn't upon a person at all, but a fantasy love that's impossible to ever obtain.

Fantasy Love—the Mirage

Love is only fascinating and exciting to those in the fantasy mode when it's out there in Never-Never Land. Real life stuff like making oatmeal together or washing the car together, doesn't fit into the picture—it's all too dull, too mundane, too real. They want the mirage, but it disappears the closer it comes to reality. This, though, is the attraction and makes it all even more mysterious, fascinating and exciting.

I could feel the sadness radiating from Bob every time I saw him at church. I knew that he and his wife had just divorced, but knew nothing of the circumstances. He was grief-stricken, pale and without life. I wanted to comfort him, to say something, anything, but didn't find the opportunity until one day he happened to be shopping at the same store.

We began to talk, and it poured out, "I love my ex-wife with all my heart. We were very happy together until she started reading romance novels. She read them by the hundreds. They were all over the place—in the kitchen cabinets, everywhere. Then one day she said, 'I want a divorce. This isn't what I call love.' Don't get me wrong, we had our share of problems, but we were a very happy family until she started reading those books; we have five children together. I guess I just couldn't compete with the men in the novels."

"I doubt that it's the men in the novels that you're competing with, but the type of love in the novels. Marital love seems dull when compared with the emotional hype in romance novels. It has occurred to me that these books can be dangerous for women in the same way that pornography is for men," I said.

"What do you mean? How could they be?"

"When men become addicted to the type of sex portrayed in pornography, it breaks down their desire for marital sex. When women are addicted to the type of love in romance novels, it dulls their sensitivity to marital love. Both of them present a fantasy world—a sexual fantasy for men, and an emotional fantasy for women. Women don't get why some men go for the raw stuff and men don't get why some women go for the mushy stuff. Pornography strips intimacy down to an animalistic romp—without love, warmth, caring, or conversation. Silly romance novels separate love and passion away from real life: paying bills, cleaning the garage and changing diapers. About a year later, Bob found another love and they've been gloriously married ever since; his ex-wife remains alone with her novels and fantasies.

The escape into the fantasy can prevent the real joys of marital love and intimacy from ever happening.

"Hidden in the Mist"

An example of fantasy love is vividly shown in the great American classic novel, Gone With The Wind, by Margaret Mitchell. The setting is the Grand Old South before, during and after the Civil War. The main character is Scarlett

O'Hara, a beautiful southern belle who has everything a woman could ask for, except the man she thinks she wants. Men clamor for her attention, but her heart is fixed upon the man who is beyond her grasp: Ashley Wilkes.

Ashley marries Melanie, his cousin and soul-mate, but Scarlett convinces herself that he has done this horrible thing out of a sense of duty and family tradition. Through the novel, and three husbands, she still longs for Ashley. She is never able to enjoy what *is* because she is focused on what *isn't* . Rhett Butler, her third husband and match in mind and spirit, tolerates her fantasy love with Ashley until one night:

"Rhett kept her too busy to think of Ashley often. Ashley was hardly ever in her thoughts during the day but at night when she was tired from dancing or her head was spinning from too much champagne—then she thought of Ashley. Frequently when she lay drowsily in Rhett's arms with the moonlight streaming over the bed, she thought how perfect life would be if it were only Ashley's arms which held her so closely, if it were only Ashley who drew her black hair across his face and wrapped it about his throat.

"Once when she was thinking this, she sighed and turned her head toward the window, and after a moment she felt the heavy arm beneath her neck become like iron, and Rhett's voice spoke in the stillness: 'May God damn your cheating little soul for all eternity!"

The next night while Scarlett sleeps she has a nightmare that "something terrifying was pursuing her and she was running, running till her heart was bursting, running in a thick swimming fog, crying out, blindly seeking that nameless, unknown heaven of safety that was somewhere in the mist about her."

Rhett takes her into his arms and soothes her terrified heart, "his hard muscles comforting, his wordless murmuring soothing, until her sobbing ceased."

She tells him, "Oh, Rhett, I just run and run and hunt and I can't ever find what it is I'm hunting for. It's always hidden in the mist. . ."

At the novel's closing, Rhett leaves Scarlett, realizing that he will never be the one to make her feel safe, or the one to help her overcome her nightmare fantasy with Ashley. Scarlett missed out on the love that she could have for the love that she would never have. She continues to go on running and running toward whatever it is that's "hidden in the mist".

Healthy love is founded upon love, honor and cherish; masquerades are founded on such motives as escaping life's challenges, the craving to be loved, to control, to be controlled, worshipping the Luv-God or to fantasize a love that can never be. In the next chapter, we discuss the five joys of healing unhealthy motives and unhealthy relationships.

Summary

We cannot be right for someone else until we are right for and with ourselves. We cannot be together happily in a romance until we have first learned to be together in honorable friendships—without gossip, without envy, without deception, without manipulation, without bursts of temper tantrums, etc. We cannot expect someone to want to travel with us unless we're going somewhere, doing something, have something to talk about. Love and romance cannot be an escape, a detour, or a dead-end.

Preventing the masquerades begins with avoiding or healing unhealthy motives; in the next chapter, we'll show how.

13

The Four Joys of Togetherness

"Oh, Rhett, I just run and run and hunt and I can't ever find what it is I'm hunting for. . . It's always hidden in the mist. . ."

Gone With the Wind, Margaret Mitchell

Insight #13

Healthy love relationship begin with emotionally and spiritually healthy individuals.

After my husband and I married, our relationship limped along for years, neither of us was quite sure what was wrong, but we both knew that *something* was wrong. By the time I turned thirty, illnesses kept occurring; what my conscious mind refused to see, my body could not ignore. Eventually the pressure began to seep out here and there—failing health, flash temper, and depression. I was into denial, denying that there could be bad parts to an otherwise good relationship.

In her book to help women overcome destructive love relationships, Robin Norwood noted, "All of us unconsciously employ defense mechanisms such as denial throughout our lives, sometimes about rather trivial matters and at other times about major issues and events. Otherwise, we would have to face facts about who we are and what we think and feel that do not fit with our idealized image of ourselves or others and our circumstances."

(Women Who Love Too Much, p. 139-141)

The "idealized image of ourselves and others" described my attitude—I wanted to believe that I had the perfect marriage, the perfect family. Little did I realize then, that facing problems and progressing *is* the perfect state for individuals, marriages and families.

Our heater problems included my inclination to practice Idolatry—my love for my husband bordered, even slipped over the edge into—worship. It took years for me to realize that humans aren't meant to be worshipped—only loved. Gradually, I learned that love means giving one's heart to another—but our souls belong only to God. I learned that the greatest contribution I could make to our marriage was not to become him, but to become *me*. I learned that he needed me to help him overcome his weaknesses—not to slide into them, too. I learned that my ability to love in a healthy way was directly connected with self-respect. I learned that leaning too much on my husband caused both of us to stumble.

Changing the Dance

When I began my quest to heal, I found help everywhere. It seemed that I was somehow guided to read certain books, to realize certain insights that would bring freedom and release, and to listen to other's stories—one belonged to Patty. I met Patty when she arranged a community women's conference and asked me to be the keynote speaker. One word described her: alive. She talked fast, moved fast, and told me that the last conference she organized had over five hundred women in attendance—with only one month's preparation. I was impressed; obviously she was a woman who gets things done.

After the meetings, we went out for a frozen yogurt and she shared some of the struggles in her marriage, "I used to have a real problem with my husband trying to control me. He would call me several times a day to see what I was doing; I hated feeling like I was being spied on constantly. His former wife had an affair on him, and I guess, he hasn't gotten over it. We had to change the dance of the relationship; now we've worked it through, and we're happier than we've ever been."

I loved the phrase "changing the dance." Unhealthy people bond together because needs attract, but as one heals, both can heal—if there's a sincere desire to change the dance. Changing the "dance" in relationships—becoming more in harmony, more respectful of one another, more loving is the glorious quest of all healthy loves, and can heal heater-problem relationships.

Marriage is filled with life and life is filled with highs and lows, but when there's commitment, and a willingness to work through, to wait, to reason, to try, to pray, to go on all things are possible. "Marriages are not made in heaven; they come in a kit and you have to put them together yourselves." For my husband and I, the "putting together" process still goes on; we keep falling in love all over again and again.

It has taken years to understand the difference: healthy love means giving one's heart, and obsessive love means giving one's soul—or expecting it from one's mate. The healing process has not been easy. In surgery, and in relationships, cutting away the bad while leaving the good is not a simple matter. Too often, with the slap of realization, there's a jump from denial to destruction. I've watched this in myself and others. A once submissive soul turns assertive overnight and destroys the relationship that could possibly be saved with a gentler touch.

While healing my own relationship, and getting the dance right—or at least more right—I learned insights that helped me and I believe can help others overcome heater problems, *prevent* masquerades and *prepare* for healthy love relationships. Healing in these areas can make all the difference, and can enrich life—whether single or married. Some put their life in a holding pattern till they are "together" with a Beloved, but this attitude leads to unhealthy bonding because they become too wanting, too desperate—like Sadie. There are other joys of being together—here they are.

The Four Joys of Togetherness

One: The joy of being together with the Higher Power—or God.

Together with God we love ourselves and fellow human beings more—not too much, and not too little. Together with God, love flows through us like an electrical current, and creates a resistance to the emotional starvation called poor self-esteem—which can lead to the masquerades. Together with God, our souls fill with the spiritual strength of peace, love, confidence and goodwill that prevent the craving to be loved—on any basis, at any price. Together with God, and true to ourselves, we create a climate of self-trust, and other-trust, that frees friendliness and goodwill, but also warns against relationships that would prove harmful. Being true to oneself comes before knowing who is right and true for us. Together with God, we naturally lose the inclination to worship his children.

A scene from C.S. Lewis', Great Divorce, illustrates this insight. It is a fictional scene in the afterlife when two lovers meet again. The woman died first, so the scene takes place as her husband greets her following his death. Evidently their old love was a *need* love—now she has healed. She tells him that she has been very happy without him; he becomes angry, and asks, "Do you mean to say. . do you mean to say you've been happy? . .Love! Do you know the meaning of the word?"

She answers, "How should I not? I am in love. In love, do you understand? Yes, now I love truly."

"You mean, you mean you did not love me truly in the old days?" he asks.

"Only in a poor sort of way. . .What we called love down

there was mostly the *craving to be loved.* In the main I loved you for my own sake: because I needed you."

"And now!" he screams, "Now you need me no more?"

"But of course not. What needs could I have now that I have all? I am full now, not empty. . . Strong, not weak. You shall be the same. Come and see. We shall have no need for one another now: we can begin to love truly." (C.S. Lewis, The Great Divorce, p.113)

Notice the line, "What we called loved down there was mostly the *craving to be loved.*" Masquerades—unhealthy relationships masquerading as love—begin with unhealthy motives and unmet needs, and, once again, the "craving to be loved" is at the top of the unhealthy motives. Those starving for food are not very discriminatory in what they eat; those starving for love are also not very discriminatory. In their longing to be loved, indeed, craving to be loved, they accept scraps from the possible banquet of love.

It is well documented that children whose need for love is never satisfied have a longing that can lead to the masquerades. This is often the case when young women of tender post-puberty age, bond with older men. They want the masculine touch that they never knew as a little girl. This emptiness can be filled by Divine love.

It was never better said than by Shakespeare's Sonnet XXIX:

When in disgrace with fortune and men's eyes,
I all alone beweep my outcast state,
And trouble deaf Heaven with my bootless cries,

And look upon myself, and curse my fate,
Wishing me like to one more rich in hope,
Featur'd like him, like him with friends possess'd,
Desiring this man's art, and that man's scope,
With what I most enjoy contented least;
Yet in these thoughts myself almost despising,
Haply I think on thee,—and then my state
(Like to the lark at break of day arising
From sullen earth) sings hymns at heaven's gate;
For thy sweet love remember'd such wealth brings,
That then I scorn to change my state with kings.

I have experienced the clear difference—the craving to be loved—emotional poverty—and the emotional richness satisfied by Divine Love. Basking in the warmth of God's love, true love and marriages can better prosper.

Terry, a classic blond, was the mother of two children. She was busily making a home for her family, and her life was going well, when her husband of fourteen years decided he wanted a divorce. I met her shortly after she returned to her home town to be near her parents. She seemed strung out—nervous. I sensed the divorce had been extremely difficult for her. Months later, she said, "I had a dream in which I was getting married again—to a very dark man." Several months later she married an African American, a wonderful, kind man.

One day we had a few minutes to talk. She began talking of her new marriage. "It has been a real struggle," she said.

"We're so different. Our backgrounds are different, our race is different, so we've really had to struggle. But every day it's getting better and better. I don't think we create a marriage; God does. It's like this: there's me and Aron, and we're two separate persons, but when we invite the powers of God into our lives, He creates the marriage."

"You make it sound like the marriage is a third person," I said.

"In a way it is," she answered, "it's the relationship that is formed when a husband and wife unite with God. You can see this in chemicals. Oxygen is one chemical, and hydrogen is another, but when they combine in a molecule a new identity is created: water."

I think of this idea often. It reminds me that we're not alone in our marriage journey. Wrenching moments of disappointment and despair have been diluted by calling upon divine power. I have no doubt that just as there is a force that heals up wounds of marital discord, so there is a force that like a raging wind would rip and tear us apart. Recall the last time a simple, platonic disagreement flared into an out and out war of intense bitterness and resentment. Such destructive passion reveals this dark force. Prayer and meditation heals and strengthens the bonds of love.

Healing Idolatry

Being together with God is a protection from the motive of the idolatry—wanting to worship another human being. In his popular book, Seven Habits of Highly Effective People,

Stephen Covey explains the negative consequences that occur when loving becomes idolatry:

> "Over the years, I have been involved in working with many troubled marriages, and I have observed a certain thread weaving itself through . . .that thread is strong emotional dependence. If our sense of emotional worth comes primarily from our marriage (or mate) then we become highly dependent upon that relationship. We become vulnerable to the moods and the feelings, the behavior and treatment of our spouse, or to any external event that may impinge on the relationship." (He calls such unhealthy relationships "Spouse Centered.")
>
> (In his book, he points out the symptoms:) "Your feelings of security are based on the way your spouse treats you. You are highly vulnerable to the moods and feelings of your spouse. There is deep disappointment resulting in withdrawal or conflict when your spouse disagrees with you or does not meet your expectations. Your direction comes from your own needs and wants and from those of your spouse. Your decision-making criterion is limited to what you think is best for your marriage or your mate, or to the preferences and opinions of your spouse. Your life perspective surrounds things which may positively or negatively influence your spouse or your relationship. Your power to act is limited by weaknesses in your spouse and in yourself." (p. 111, 112 and 119)

Healing Spiritual Weakness

Spiritual strength gives the courage and the fortitude to overcome the masquerades. This idea is important; healing from unhealthy motives requires more than just knowing. Is there anyone out there who does not know in their minds that smoking is harmful to one's health? Yet, millions still smoke.

Healing requires knowing and the strength to put into practice the knowledge. Most of us know what is right—it's the doing it that's the problem. We can heal our minds by replacing false or destructive ideas with truth, but the behaviors remain until we muster the strength to live that truth.

We can know our motives are unhealthy and self-destructive, and still not change actions. This was an amazing reality I discovered while reading several books on abusive relationships: men and women can fully realize that they're caught in a masquerade and yet remain. Many men and women will stay in abusive relationships because they're convinced, "It's all I deserve." Some women will stay with men who physically or sexually abuse the children. Healing includes not only the strength to see things right, but *to correct things right.* One comes from the mind, the other comes from strength of the soul—or being together with God's power. Again, being together with God we love ourselves and fellow human beings more—not too much, and not too little.

Spiritual strength is an important key—I would say, the most important— in preventing the motives that lead to the masquerades. Divine love generates peace, confidence and the courage to wait; it lifts our souls to a whole new dimension of loving—one that is free, filled, complete. Divine love helps us to overcome the craving to take control and dominate.

Restoring Love

Divine love increases our ability to love, and can replenish the fountain of love in marriage. The God who created us to love can fill that love again and again—if we but ask. Successful marriages are directly related to attributes of spiritual strength: love, patience, goodwill, understanding, compassion and respect. On the other hand qualities of impatience, ill will, intolerance, coarseness, disrespect—all symptoms of one who is spiritually weak. They erode the tender bonds of marriage.

The love and attraction that bond lovers together cannot be mandated. Husbands need to feel needed, respected, and important. Wives must feel cherished, and loved. Husbands and wives may stay together because of the legal contract, or because of the children, or because they fear divorce, but staying together is not the purpose of marriage. The purpose of marriage is to grow together, to be alive together, to love together, to build together.

Two: The joy of being together with oneself

The next joy came when I realized the need to be together with oneself— true to conscience, destiny, uniqueness, personality, and pursuits. Individuality is enhanced in true love, and no one can make us happy if we are not first happy with ourselves.

Several years ago I read the book, Escape From Freedom, and was fascinated with Eric Fromm's idea that the reason people support dictators, or others who would rob them of their conscience and identity, is because they want their conscience and identity robbed. In their loneliness and fear of freedom they surrender it to someone else.

This insight has powerful meaning in all human bonding, and most pointedly in the area of romantic bonding. He writes: "There seems to be the need to. . . give up the independence of one's own individual self and to fuse one's self with somebody or something outside of oneself in order to acquire the strength which the individual self is lacking. Love is based on equality and freedom. If it is based on subordination and loss of integrity of one partner, it is masochistic dependence of one partner, regardless of how the relationship is rationalized." (pgs 141, l61)

Dostoevsky, in The Brothers Karamazov, wrote that some men (and women) have "no more pressing need than the one to find somebody to whom he can surrender, as quickly as possible, that gift of freedom which he, the unfortunate creature, was born with."

Love obviously was never meant to be an escape from oneself. There will never be a way to feel right with someone else until we're right with and for ourselves. "To be or not to be, that is the question," said Hamlet, in Shakespere's play. "The whole life of the individual." said Eric Fromm, "is nothing but the process of giving birth to himself."

If we stop the birth process we begin the stagnation process. There can be:

No satisfaction without exertion,

No peace without obedience,

No knowledge without learning,

No self-respect without self-sacrifice,

No victory without teeth-gritting perseverance,

No winning without trying,

No mountaintop vistas without enduring the mundane of the valley floor. (Richard L. Evans, An Open Road, p. 169)

Healthy love is two whole and alive persons bonding together in one purpose, combining knowledge, gifts, talents, love and ambition—an important insight to remember before marriage as well as after marriage. Drop-outs make dull traveling companions. The way to healthy, growing relationships is to be healthy and growing. Health is always attracted to health—the intellectually alive are naturally attracted to others intellectually alive. The emotionally alive are attracted to the emotionally alive. Growing is attracted to growing, as if to say, "Hey, I can see we're on the same journey; let's journey together."

Healthy love is bonding with a soul-mate who is about the business of life—of becoming. Healthy love happens when two travelers—who are alive in heart, mind, spirit and body—discover they're on the same road. Unhealthy bonding occurs when two going nowhere decide to go together. It's as if to say, "I don't want to get out of bed. I want to stay under these warm covers and just sleep my life away. Isn't there someone out there who will join me, so I'm not alone in my sleep?" What a contrast to the travelers who are striving, learning, moving forward—about the business of life, whether that's playing ping-pong, trying out a new recipe, reading to a hospital-bound friend, hiking in the mountains, taking a class in deep sea diving, volunteering at the hospital, or singing in the choir at church. They find joy in giving birth to themselves. Their union is based upon progression, not stagnation. They join forces because they know that they can grow faster together than they could apart—not to escape the challenge of growing.

There's something within each of us that becomes frustrated when we cease to grow. Climbing the soul's mountain of destiny leads to personal exhilaration, and marital exhilaration. There's excitement in the air when everyone's growing, becoming, learning, aspiring—and sharing that growth with other members of the family. In marriage, family and friends, lives are intertwined; the growth and success of one contributes to the growth and success of all.

The trust and freedom of honorable, virtuous love sets the stage for personal progress. It requires time and space alone—time to exercise, time to think, time to read, time to study, time to pray. The alone time then brings life to the together time. On the other hand, obsessive relationships can stifle personal growth because everything and everyone outside of the masquerade is threatening. Fear bonds them together and fear keeps them *too* together.

Aaron David, our fourth son, said, "I'm anxious to get married, but I want more than a mannequin. I want a woman I can talk to—someone who keeps learning and reading. A woman who likes to hike and be adventurous."

I said, "In other words, you want a woman who's alive?"

"Right!" he said. Aaron married his "Beloved" Kaia two years ago; they hike together, fish together, study together—they "live" together!

We must create our own personal circle of love and happiness before we can create circles of love with another, and *personal happiness is directly connected with personal growth.*

Letting Go for Growth's Sake

Healthy marriages let go for growth's sake. My husband has always been supportive of my efforts to continue my education. The summers spent away from home studying at the university have not been easy for either of us; the telephone bill cost almost as much as the tuition. During my first summer at the university we had four children ranging from eight months to seven years. They all accompanied me. The summer that *we* graduated nine children accompanied me and we were expecting our tenth baby.

That summer we rented two apartments with three bedrooms apiece—one for the boys, and one for the girls. The children still comment that those summers were filled with some of the happiest memories of their childhood. We actually learned together—gathering bugs for a biology class, hiking mountains for a geology paper, attending concerts for a music class, etc.

While I am away, my husband usually plans a welcome home surprise. One summer, he said he would be unable to drive the family to the university because he had too much work at the office. I was hurt, but realized that there really was no need for him to drive us, after all I was a big girl and could drive the seven hundred miles. He came to visit the family once but was so busy he wasn't able to drive out again.

When I returned home I found out why he was so busy; he had completely remodeled our master bedroom, changing the design of the room, the carpet, the drapes—everything! He had purchased new bedroom furniture, and a huge old oak desk which he refinished for my writing projects. Even pots of yellow daisies were placed around the room. I was in such shock that for days I kept running back to the bedroom just to make sure it wasn't a dream.

These homecoming surprises have been sacrifices and signs of his supportive love: a remodeled library, a new play-house for the little girls, complete with window boxes with cascades of pink impatiens, play equipment for the children, a redecorated kitchen, etc.

Sometimes, my husband says to me, "Do you know what my business is?"

"What?" I answer.

"Making my wife happy," he answers with a mischievous grin.

Three: The joy of being together with the family of God

The third joy is experienced when we are *together* with the family of God—not divided from them with envy, ill will, competition, exploitation, or a masquerade. Together with the family of God, we see ourselves not higher than or lower than—just one of them. There's a glorious social freedom, a spontaneity, a confidence, that comes in no other way. This is one of the spiritual gifts that naturally come through being connected with God.

Warm-hearted, personable human beings draw others who are also warm-hearted, personable human beings. All love surrounds the lovable—friendship love, family love, associate love, and romantic love. Those who are waiting only for romantic love miss out on life and the opportunity to be in love every day of their lives. The greatest treasures on this earth are not things, but people—people with unique personalities, treasure chests of stories and experiences.

There's a joy that comes only through being together with friends—male and female—who love what we love, who cherish what we cherish—be that music, or movies, or the arts, or gardening, or caring for children, or work with the homeless. This is a joy that is open to anyone seeking a friend, anyone who is about the business of life.

Four: The joy of being together with those who leave a legacy of love.

Everywhere we look, we see the legacies that others have left so that our lives can be easier, or more beautiful, or more free. Lives have been lost so that we can live in a free society. Time and energy have been spent so that we can enjoy inventions that were not a part of our grandparents' lives. We live, and because we live we owe something. Striving to be faithful to ourselves—to the best that is within ourselves—we enrich our own lives and complement the lives of our loved ones.

"We have a moral obligation to exercise our personal capabilities of mind, muscle, and spirit in a way that will return to the Lord, our families, and our society the fruits of our best efforts. To do less is to live our lives unfulfilled. It is to deny ourselves and those dependent upon us opportunity and advantage." J. Richard Clark

---

The business of life is to move forward—and to leave to the world a legacy of love. We owe it to all those who have lived and sacrificed before, and all those who will come after us to enhance the quality of their lives. Our contribution does not need to be great, but it needs to be. Each one of us owes the world and humanity the gift of our unique selves, our talents, our strength. Our individual lives can make a difference—and in rolling up our sleeves to help others we gain peace within our own hearts.

"It makes people smile; I like that."

Several years ago, an elderly man in a nearby rest home shuffled outside to the corner intersection, and for several hours a day, waved and smiled to the people in every passing car. Some thought he was crazy, but this simple act of kindness brought a smile and a feeling of warmth every time I encountered his greeting.

I was, at the time, a writer for the local elementary school newsletter and I thought his story would make an interesting addition. The rest home had obviously been a private residence once. It stood suspended in time near a busy intersection. I approached the huge wood door, rang the doorbell and a man peeked out a small window and asked what I wanted. I told him I wanted to meet the man who stands out waving every day. He then opened the door, and said matter-of factly, "Follow me. His name is Emery Butcher."

As I was guided through the large, dark living room and down a hall, I attempted to greet the elderly men and women who were sitting about. Most of them did not look up to see me, but just sat motionless not seeming to notice my passing. Showing no emotion whatsoever, they sat staring into space, like they were watching television, but there were no televisions. Some looked at me when I greeted them, but did not answer. I wondered what they were thinking, what memories of pain had them so suspended in such a transitory state between life and death.

I sensed that some—if they had the strength and the inclination—would answer my, "Good morning," with, "No, it's not good and it's not morning—it's night—always night." Their despair radiated about them and weighed them down.

When I reached Emery's room, he was sitting at a desk reading. He immediately jumped to his feet like a high school athlete and said, "Good morning; my name is Emery," and held out his hand. After I introduced myself and the purpose for my visit, he quickly snatched the clothes off the desk chair and invited me to sit down. He then sat on the edge of the bed, obviously happy to have a visitor. He was an old man—he later told me eighty-one—but had the spirit of a new groom. He smiled a lot and spoke fast.

"I've come to interview you, Emery," I said. "have you ever been interviewed before?"

"No," he said smiling.

"I write for the local elementary school's newsletter and I know the children would love to know why you stand out there for hours every day and wave to the people in the passing cars."

He grinned, looked down like a ten year-year-old boy that was just caught with his hand in the cookie jar and said, "People like it; I like it. It passes the day. It could get pretty boring around here; besides the old people here are not much to talk with. When I wave at the people it makes them smile. Well, some of them. The children always smile and return the wave, but some of their parents look at me like I'm crazy. Maybe I am. I just want to make a few people smile before I die. It feels good."

He continued, "When you get to be my age, you look back over your life and wonder if you did anything that made any difference to anyone. Your body gives out, but your mind just keeps going back over the memories. Some of them are good, but most of them are painful to remember. That's why you see most of the people here staring into space; they're dealing with the painful memories of their lives. I used to do that, too. I was married to the sweetest girl in the world, but she died when she was only thirty-nine. We were never able to have any children, and I never remarried. Oh, I've got a brother some-where, but I don't know what ever happened to him. I used to sit the day away and hurt, but then one day I realized there's still time. I'm not in a pine box yet. It's not a big thing—standing out there like a fool and waving to everyone, but it does put a smile on people's faces, and that makes me happy. Now, it's like my job. Like I go to work every day and wave to the people. I probably am just a crazy old fool, but it's made me want to get out of bed in the morning."

He looked amused, chuckled to himself, then said, "I get a kick out of the little kids waving to me. They look for me to be there; I don't like to disappoint them."

Emery became famous throughout Napa Valley for his smile and wave. His mission lasted about three years, then one day he was gone. Emery was a modern day Don Quixote who grieved over life's sufferings and determined to "add a measure of grace to the world" with his simple gesture of goodwill. Like Quixote, Emery was considered an eccentric, a fanatic who had lost his marbles. But who were really the fools—those in the dark house sinking into death with despair or Emery, outside in the sun attempting to make a difference with a wave?

An Egyptian myth says that we will be asked two simple questions when our souls enter the afterlife, "Did you find joy?" and "Did you share joy?" And that all judgments will be based on the answer. Emery found a way to add joy to the lives of others. His contribution will never be mentioned in history books, but it will live in the hearts of those whose lives were brightened—by a wave.

"To surrender dreams—this may be madness."

In the popular play, Man of La Mancha, based on the book, "Don Quixote" by Miguel de Cervantes y Saavedra, we see a dramatic scene that could have taken place over and over in the life of Emery—different words, but the same idea.

Remember that Cervantes—main character of the play—

despairs over "life as it is" and resolves to begin a quest to right wrongs. He puts on the attire of a knight and sallies forth to help those in need. He is accused of being a madman, a lunatic. He is told that he "turns his back on life" and that he must "come to terms with life as it is!"

He answers, "I have lived nearly fifty years, and I have seen life as it is. Pain, misery, hunger. . .cruelty beyond belief. I have heard the singing from taverns and the moans from bundles of filth on the streets. I have been a soldier and seen my comrades fall in battle. . . or die more slowly under the lash in Africa. I have held them in my arms at the final moment. These were men who saw life as it is, yet they died despairing. No glory, no gallant last words. . .only their eyes filled with confusion, whimpering the question: "Why?" I do not think they asked why they were dying, but why they had lived. When life itself seems lunatic, who knows where madness lies? Perhaps to be too practical is madness. To surrender dreams—this may be madness. To seek treasure where there is only trash. Too much sanity may be madness. And maddest of all, to see life as it is and not as it should be."

Self-respect comes when we give respect to others, and when we assist in creating heaven here and now. The question is, "Did you find joy, and did you share it?" In choosing beauty, honorable love, goodwill, order, and virtue, our individual lives 'add a measure of grace to the world' and to our own lives.

Summary

Together with God, I have realized the difference between loving someone and worshiping them. Experiencing divine love has stopped the obsessive craving to be loved. Together with myself, I see my husband's image not reflected in mine, but separate—where I can see and admire him better. Together with myself, goals and aspirations, I have been awakened to a whole new realm of togetherness—my husband's talents complimenting mine—as we travel and build life as a couple. I now realize the difference between surrendering my individualism and enhancing that individualism in marriage. Together with the family of God, I have overcome the tendency to use marriage as an escape, a selfish turn-inward grooming like two monkeys at the zoo, primping one another as they look around in suspicion.

The final joy—purposeful living—has set my soul on fire and lifted my view beyond the clatter and confusion of the day. There's excitement in the air when there are plans, goals and aspirations—both personally and in marriage. Romantic love is more alive when the couple is seen as companions in a cause, rather than simply bed partners. My husband and I have raised eleven children together—his patience complimenting my impatience. We have directed Christmas productions together, his technical skills combined with my writing and directing skills. We have compiled books together (like this one), his story-telling ability combined with my idea-telling ability. We're happier together when we're working side by side. These insights have assisted in the healing process. Our masquerade-love is becoming a majestic-love—one day at a time. The hope is that these same insights will help you.

Notes on chapter thirteen:

1. Do not equate the birth process—caring for needs of oneself—with selfishness. Self-love and nurturing is not selfish; as it is said, "You cannot lift another person up unless you are standing on higher ground." Being true to oneself and the growth process, the emotional, intellectual and most of all the spiritual needs of oneself paves the way to truly love.

A great thought on this comes from the book, Escape From Freedom by Erich Fromm.

"Selfishness is not identical with self-love but with its very opposite. Selfishness is one kind of greediness. Like all greediness, it contains an insatiability, as a consequence of which there is never any real satisfaction. Greed is a bottomless pit which exhausts the person in an endless effort to satisfy the need without ever reaching satisfaction. Close observation shows that while the selfish person is always anxiously concerned with himself, he is never satisfied and is always restless, always driven by the fear of not getting enough, of missing something, of being deprived of something. He is filled with burning envy of anyone who might have more. If we observe still closer, especially the unconscious dynamics, we find that this type of person is basically not fond of himself, but deeply dislikes himself." (p. 115)

2. "When you set limits, you establish your boundaries. Your boundaries help to protect your integrity as an individual. They help to define you. . . Responding appropriately enforces your limits and reestablishes or confirms your boundaries. . .Awaken your mate to the fact that his behavior is inappropriate and is unacceptable to you. Some people change their behavior when they experience the impact of a strong response. Others are very resistant to change. . .Following are some questions which may help you to evaluate the quality of your relationship:

Does your mate enrich your life?

Does he bring you joy?

Do you feel a real connection to him?

Do you think in the same way and share the same dreams?

Does he show good will?

Good will in a relationship is a warmth and honesty which comes from one's deepest sense of truth. It is a concern for the other's well being as well as a strong desire to understand the other. . .if your mate shows good will and you can answer 'yes' to the above questions, there is a good chance he may give up (unhealthy behaviors) when you enforce your limits." (Patricia Evans, <u>The Verbally Abusive Relationship</u>, p.128,9)

3. "Studies show that more than half (60%) of the fathers of babies born to teenagers are over age 20. They are not boyfriends or peers. They are predators. They find young girls attractive because the girls are pliant, eager to please and probably free of sexually-transmitted diseases. . .If the girls are poor, and many are, older men can offer them material

rewards as simple as a trip to the beauty parlor." (Cynthia Tucker, S.F. Chronicle, Jan 27, 1996)

The Dark Side of Passion: The Mystique 14

*Especially for Men

"We use a most unfortunate idiom when we say of a lustful man prowling the streets that he 'wants a woman'. Strictly speaking, a woman is just what he does not want. He wants a pleasure for which a woman happens to be the necessary piece of apparatus. How much he cares about the woman as such may be gauged by his attitude to her five minutes after fruition—one does not keep the carton after one has smoked the cigarettes."

The Four Loves, C.S. Lewis

Insight #14

Men's strong physical side can lead into into the mystique: sex divorced from love and, honor.

Kerry captivated my heart instantly; he was fun-loving, adventurous, and admired by all, especially the youth of the church. One Saturday, he offered to take one of the boys, who was having struggles in his life, ocean fishing. Kerry had a small rowboat just right for the occasion. When they arrived at the coast, a warning sign greeted them on the beach: NO SWIMMING OR BOATING ALLOWED: TREACHEROUS UNDER CURRENTS.

Kerry chose to ignore the sign, after all, the sea was calm, the breeze was light, and there were just a few slight swells on the blue green water. He must have reasoned that there was really nothing to worry about; he was an experienced outdoorsman. He had been through plenty of close calls in his life, and there was never a situation thrust upon him that he couldn't handle.

Unfortunately his experience was, for the most part, in a totally different environment. He had been raised in the Rocky Mountains. And although he knew and understood the inherent dangers that exist on icy lakes and raging rivers, he had never experienced the undercurrents of the Pacific Ocean. This was the first of his two fatal mistakes.

As they loaded their little boat with fishing gear, sandwiches and snacks, he reminded the boy to wear a life jacket. He himself was an expert swimmer, and he definitely didn't want to be encumbered by a bulky life jacket. This was his second mistake.

They were on the water just over an hour when the wind kicked up and the waves began to crash with a frenzy of turmoil. It all happened so quickly. The little boat was no match for the sea. It finally gave way and capsized, throwing both of them into the foamy, icy waters of the Pacific.

The young man—with the help of his life jacket—was

finally able to reach the beach. Almost completely exhausted, he drug himself ashore and then turned, looking for his leader. Nothing. And then he saw him. About a hundred yards out, he was perilously clinging to the top of a rock. By now the sea was boiling. The young boy jumped up and down, waving frantically to his leader. Then he stopped and stared horrified as a giant wave came crashing down unmercifully over the rock, and his leader was gone.

The Undercurrents or Evil Force

Kerry was no match for the powerful undercurrents. Like a giant vacuum, they sucked him into the water, and to death. The powerful undercurrents of the ocean are like the powerful downpull of evil that pulls human sexuality away from love and into the dark side of passion: the mystique.

John Milton, in his classic epic poem "Paradise Lost" reveals the deep despair of the Evil One who will never know the joys of sweet, intimate marital love. The scene in the poem is vivid, looking upon Adam and Eve in loving embrace, ". . .with kisses pure. Aside the Devil turned for envy, yet with jealous leer malign eyed them askance and to himself thus pained:

"Sight hateful, sight tormenting! thus these two
Imparadised in one another's arms,
The happier Eden, shall enjoy their fill
Of bliss on bliss, while I to Hell am thrust,
Where neither joy nor love, but fierce desire,
Among our other torments not the least. . ." (p. 112)

Milton portrays the devil's horrible torment that He will never experience sweet marital love. Enraged by fierce jealousy, he attempts to corrupt and destroy it. Interesting idea. The emotions can lead women into dramatic, and often destructive relationships masquerading as love, while the adventurous physical side of men can lead into the mystique—seductive sex.

We need to just look around to see that there's a power intent on twisting human sexuality away from the Creator's intent. Everyone passing through puberty is endowed with this power, and must choose whether to use it for or against themselves and others. Sexual drive creates a need for others—either a need to love or the need to merely use another for sexual gratification.

What a prime target to corrupt! Think of the tragedy when the marvelous powers to bind men and women together is used as a game, a predatory sport, even a weapon of hate. Men viewing women as toys for sexual pleasure and women, fearful of exploitation, scorning all men, or looking upon men as toys for pleasure and men fearful of exploitation. Such fertile ground to seed contempt, greed, envy, lies, deceit, pretense, pride, vanity, between the sons and daughters of God!

Think of the pain and sorrow of unfaithfulness—when the circle of love is broken by infidelity. Disloyalty inflicts a wound on the soul that penetrates deeper and wider than any other kind of human suffering. Scarred-over hearts may never heal; the nausea of betrayal hangs on and on. Think of the tragedy when the powers of procreation become powers of prodestruction, as happens when they are used for exploitation, rape and child molestation.

In his fascinating book, The Screwtape Letters, C.S. Lewis adds to Milton's idea. It is written in the form of directives or memos from one devil to another. He writes,

"He [meaning God] has filled His world with pleasures. There are things for humans to do all day long without His minding in the least—sleeping, washing, eating, drinking, making love, playing, praying, working. Everything has to be *twisted* before it's any use to us. We fight under cruel disadvantages. Nothing is naturally on our side." (p. 102)

Sexual intimacy is naturally good, naturally uplifting, naturally the greatest force for happiness. It can create little heavens on this earth where husbands love their wives and wives love their husbands, and together they love their children. This wonderful power for happiness must be twisted away from its original intent in order to become bad, immoral, harmful to the human spirit. It must be twisted away from making love to making lust, then it can create literal hells of human suffering, because nothing penetrates and pains deeper than crimes against the heart. Those who seduce almost always feign love to get sex, and feigned love hurts deep. Wounds against the body can heal in a matter of days, but wounds against the heart sometimes never heal.

Twisted into an Act of Lust

How can human intimacy be "twisted" away from the original intent of the Creator? How can it be twisted away from its purpose? How can the Adversary, who will never experience intimacy, know how to twist it?

It must be twisted away from an act of love, and turned into an act of lust. Then instead of making love, it becomes an act of simply making fun, or making alienation, or making resentment, or making hate.

There are grey layers of the twist, and there ares black layers—when the power to love is twisted three hundred and sixty degrees away from the Garden of Eden version and cast into outerdarkness—when tenderness is twisted to callousness, when bonding sinks to alienation, when it is used as a game, a predatory sport, acting out under the cloak of love. There's a universe-wide difference between love and lust. Lust is best described as intense sexual cravings motivated by power rather than love. Dictionary terms: devoured by desire, mad with lust, frenzy of desire. These intense cravings have nothing to do with love, and everything to do with selfishness, pride, vanity, abuse, power. Lust drains spiritual strength, while love increases it. Lust drains feelings of the heart while love magnifies all good and tender feelings for everyone. Lust originates from sex organs; love originates from the heart. Lust is greedy while love is giving. Lust shuts down conscience while love enhances it. Lust confuses the mind and battles with reason, while love clears the mind and creates order. Lust doesn't care about the morning after, while love cares for eternity.

"Lust is a captivity of the reason," said Jeremy Taylor, 16th century clergyman, "and an enraging of the passions. It hinders business and distracts counsel. It sins against the body and weakens the soul."

Poet John Milton wrote, "When lust, by unchaste looks, loose gestures, and foul talk, but most by lewd and lavish acts of sin, lets in defilement to the inward parts, the soul grows clotted by contagion, embodies and imbrutes till she quite lose the divine property of her first being." In other words, lust cankers the soul and corrupts the very nature of a child of God into becoming animalistic. Those who prefer the barnyard romp, eventually belong in the barn.

There are more differences between love and lust. Love respects human life; lust disrespects all life. Love inspires honesty; lust inspires lies and deceit. Love sees hearts, minds, and feelings, while lust sees sexually, wants sexually. Love inspires one to bless the life of the beloved; lust inspires one to possess the life of another or merely to use that life for sexual gratification. Love inspires dignity in oneself; lust inspires depravity. Love inspires a deep adoration and admiration for the whole person—body, mind, spirit, personality, unique identity, while lust inspires only a deep craving for flesh-to-flesh intimacy. Love desires a soulmate while lust wants a playmate.

The Rape of Lucrece

William Shakespeare's "The Rape of Lucrece" gives a graphic picture of one who is enflamed with predatory lust. It reveals the internal conflict between conscience and fierce desire. Conscience pleads, but passions win.

It begins with a group of Roman soldiers discussing the virtues of their wives. Collatinus tells his friends that his wife Lucretia is most chaste and virtuous. They all agree to find out whose wife is most chaste by surprising them in the night suddenly and secretly. All the wives are "dancing and revelling" except Lucretia, who is spinning with her maids.

The king's son, Sextus Tarquinius, becomes inflamed by lust as he observes the beauty and purity of his friend's wife, Lucretia. That night, after Collatinus leaves again, "he treacherously stealeth into her chamber, violently ravished her, and early in the morning speedeth away."

Before surrendering to his lust, his conscience pleads:

"What win I if I gain the thing I seek?
A dream, a breath, a froth of fleeting joy:
Who buys a minute's mirth to wail a week?
Or sells eternity to get a toy?
For one sweet grape who will the vine destroy?
. . .I have debated, even in my soul,
What wrong, what shame, what sorrow I shall breed;
But nothing can Affection's course control,
Or stop the headlong fury of his speed.
I know repentant tears ensue the deed,

Reproach, disdain, and deadly enmity;
Yet strive I to embrace mine infamy."

The author continues,
"But she hath lost a dearer thing than life,
And he hath won what he would lose again.
This forced league doth force a further strife,
This momentary joy breeds months of pain,
This hot desire converts to cold disdain:
Pure chastity is rifled of her store,
And Lust, the thief, far poorer than before."

(p. 1170,1175, The Complete Works of William Shakespeare)

The Dark Side of Passion—The Mystique

The twist, or mystique, attempts to make lust appear more exciting, more sexually satisfying than love—as if fragmented sex could possibly be more satisfying than holistic intimacy of mind, heart, body and soul. The mystique would say, "Oh, of course there's sex in soul-bonding, and marriage, and all that family stuff, but the real thing, the real passion happens when you break out of all that and enter into a different dimension—a mirage only—that's beyond reality. Only in this way can you get the high that your sexuality deserves. Sure God knows about love, but I know about sex—raw, sweaty sex."

There are at least four layers to the mystique: **masturbative sex**, using a man or woman as an apparatus for sexual pleasure, **consentual and collusive sex**, pausing conscience to have a dead-end masquerade, **predatory sex**, satisfying the craving for sex and pride with the thrill of the hunt, and **criminal sex**, acting out the rage inside through sexual satisfaction that comes only with another's suffering and pain. (This last, darker form of the mystique is discussed later.)

Predatory Sex

Chris was waiting to take our daughter Anna out on a date. I had often heard her comment on his respect for women, and so I said, "I hear good things about you. My daughter tells me that you won't play the games with women, as many of the guys do. She admires the respect you have for women."

"I don't know how they can do it," he said. "Most of my friends see it like it's all a game. They'll go for the best-looking woman around like they're going for a trophy or something. Then if someone better looking comes along, they'll break off with the first and go for that woman. They don't seem to even care whether these women are getting hurt or not. I know that you might admire me for not playing the game, but sometimes I find myself wondering what's wrong with me."

"Wrong with you?" I asked.

"Well, everyone I know seems to be into the trophy

game, and I just can't do it, so I wonder what's wrong with me—like I'm not a real man or something like that. I guess I've been around too many women to just use them. I was raised with my Mom, my Gramma and my sister. I just can't look at women like they're toys when I've been so close to them all my life. But I know that some of the guys look at me and wonder if I'm just a wimp."

"You're not a wimp," I said, "You're a gentleman. You have respect for women; you have a good heart. You obviously still care."

Chris's friends might be adventurous, or mischievous, or maybe showing off to impress someone, but if they continue to fake love to get sex they may find they can't love at all. Chris noticed this when he observed, "They don't care whether the women get hurt or not." The disrespect for these women eventually extends to all human life—even one's own. We have the choice, to love with honor, or to dishonor and lose the ability to love at all.

Chris's friends have entered into the mystique—sex twisted away from creating circles of love—and turned to a predatory game.They began playing the game after they were seduced themselves by the lies: that a *real man* becomes more manly with each seduction; that a real man plays the game: sex for entertainment, sex for vanity, sex for pride, and that real men stay distant—cool and casual, even cold. They probably don't stop to think about the suffering they are inflicing upon women. If they did, perhaps they would reconsider what it means to be a real man. By some standards,

Chris isn't a *real* man—by the world's definition—but by my standards, he's a true man—true to himself and true to women. I was very impressed.

In the real world, men are never less like men and more like beasts than when they are trampling upon tender hearts to play the jungle game—seducing various and assorted women in various and assorted ways. On the other hand, nothing is more of a disgrace to womanhood than when women cunningly capture a heart that they do not even want in order to satisfy their craving for attention, vanity, or pride.

Behind the mask of the masquerades are bad ideas and bad motives, and behind the mask of the masturbation and predatory mystique there's a different set of bad ideas and bad motives that appeal to masculine pride and twist the longing to love and bond into a desire to use and abuse. Some of these bad ideas are:

Men who score with many women are more manly.

Some women or men exist, like toys, for sexual gratification and that it's okay to use them because they expect to be used.

Sex is simply a biological need.

Real men don't cry, feel or fall in love.

Sex is more exciting when it's immoral, or worse, when pleasure comes with another's pain.

It's okay to say, 'I love you,' even when it's a bold-faced lie to get sex.

Spending money gives you a right to her body.

Women secretly like being seduced into sex—even forced.

Sexual passions cannot be controlled.

Extra-marital affairs can actually help a marriage.

The lies go on and on; these are just the beginning, but they all lead to the same ending: creating circles of indifference and dishonor. In this section we will explore both the *power* and the *plan* behind the mask of the mystique.

"Sexual attraction creates, for the moment, the illusion of union, yet without love , this 'union' leaves strangers as far apart as they were before—sometimes it makes them ashamed of each other, or even makes them hate each other, because when the illusion has gone they feel their estrangement even more markedly than before." The Art of Loving, Erich Fromm, p. 54

The Web of the Mystique

The mystique is sex robbed of dignity. It is stripped down to the bare-bones of the physical act itself. It's seeing it all as a joke, a sport, a game, a hunt, a selfish pursuit. Recently, I read an article in which a group of young men in high school set themselves a challenge to see how many of their women school mates they could seduce by graduation—this is the predatory mystique. A middle-age man pursues a beautiful married woman for the challenge of it all—this is the predatory mystique. A woman plots to win her employer's heart and separate him from his wife—this is the predatory mystique.

In a very real sense, we could call the mystique a web, it ensnares, entraps and drains spirituality. It includes the five L's:

One: Lowering the value and dignity of human life

For clarity let's pretend that the mystique has a voice, and if it did it would say things like, "We are all just animals, so we have to get all the gusto while we can. . . Forget all that mushy stuff like love and marriage, and get right down to sex.. . .She does it all the time, what difference will this one time make? . .He's a love-machine; good till the right one comes along. . .What a woman; look at her body. . .Hey, you make me look good now, but if someone better looking comes along, I just may. . ."

Just as the case for moral virtue is founded upon a clear window perspective of the dignity of human life, the mystique is founded upon a distorted view—disrespect for human life and sexuality. It reduces human beings to sexual beings only. It's the attitude that there are some human beings—women and men—whose destiny is to sexually satisfy. They are not sons or brothers or daughters or sisters; they are warm mannequins without hearts and feelings, thoughts, or aspirations. What man ever thought the prostitute a sister, a daughter or a mother?

Recently, our family visited a video-rental store. As I walked up and down the isles, I noticed video after video exposing women's bodies, buttocks and breasts, but faces were hidden from view.

A World War II Japanese soldier was being interviewed. Now an old man, he related his experiences during the war. He told of young women, who were captured and kept as hostages for sexual exploitation by the soldiers. At the time, he said, he didn't realize how horrible this treatment was for the women. Then, with tears in his eyes, he said, "I only began to feel for these women after the war, when my wife gave birth to our own little daughter. I still wake with the nightmares of it all; that someone could do this to our daughter. I wonder if one day I will come face to face with the fathers and mothers of those women—women we somehow believed were just there for us to use. I still can't figure it all out; how could we be so callous?"

What a paradigm shift! Becoming a father, he realized he had been duped into believing a lie—that some women, and men, exist only as sexual beings for exploitation.

Two: Implanting the lie: secret and shameful

The mystique might say, "This is the secret of great sex: it has to be bad to be really good. You have got to go outside what's moral and all that rot in order to experience the thrill of the forbidden. Let me show you how much more exciting it is when it's in secret and shameful."

The mystique promotes the idea that the best sexual high can only happen outside God's wholesome boundaries of a loving, loyal and legal relationship.There's electricity to the lie, powerfully deadening, which can lead from one perversion to another, because once a "boundary" has been broken the thrill is gone. Just as a drug addict craves riskier and more dangerous drugs to get the same high, those caught into the web of this dark version of the mystique crave new flesh, variety, the bizarre, the vulgar, the perverted to get the same kick—to just feel again. This spiral-down cycle leads to the living dead—humans that walk and talk but exist without hearts, consciences, feelings of compassion. Take Gary Bishop—child molester and killer—for example. Before they executed him he said, "I continued to digress further and further into my perverted behavior (because) more stimulation was necessary to maintain the same level of excitement."

Three: Inflaming the lust

The mystique would say, "Let me take control of your sexual desire; let me show you how it can be powerfully satisfying without love. Let me inflame the craving to have, to hold, to use and then discard."

The mystique strips the desire for human love and tenderness down to lust—a game that always leaves the victim feeling less loved and more used. It's "*the felt evil. . .it is that 'tang' in the flavor which [the lustful] are after.* " (C.S. Lewis, The Screwtape Letters , p. 93)

Four: Spicing up the language

The mystique would say, "Let's talk sexy—you know those terms that make you melt with desire. Forget the real words—the words in the anatomy textbooks—they're so academic. I have created other words, words that entice and seduce your thoughts into the web."

Terms for body parts and passions must be twisted from the platonic to those with the "tang" in them—electrically charged. The inflection—how it is said—can be as seductive as what is said. I recall the junior high days when it seemed that everything said could be slanted towards the sexual—even the most innocent of conversations. For instance, a young girl says to a classmate, "How are you today, Bob?"

Her greeting is simply an expression of human warmth, but he answers, "And how are you, Babe? Is there anything I can do to make you feel better?"

"I just meant. . ."

"Hey, I know what you meant; you don't have to explain things to me. I know you are one fine chick. And I would love to get to know you better."

The inflection is as important as the language itself.

Five: Creating the look

The spider says, "Let me show you by the way I look, the way I walk, the way I dress, the way I smile, the way I sit, that I want you sexually. That's why my eyes are half-closed, my smile is seductive, and my body is twisted to look eager for you. It's what I call—the look."

Women and men models for pornography are taught to look a certain way—never like the girl-next-door with eyes open and mouth in a friendly smile. They have that look that says, "Hey, Babe, do you want me or what?" You can see this same look, though not so exaggerated, in some clothing catalogues. The models have their eyes half closed, heads thrown back, mouths open and hips thrust forward. Hardly ever do they they have a warm, friendly smile. Bodies are contorted into sexually arousing positions. Blouses are half-buttoned—jeans, too. It all looks so silly! When we have our heads on straight, we feel like saying, "Ah, come on. Get real."

You might get that same feeling when you're walking through the mall and a teenager walks by dressed with baggy pants sliding off his buttocks, high-top tennis shoes with laces dragging behind, hair dyed four variations of purple and shaved down the center. Next year the whole thing may flip flop, but right now it is called being *cool.* Who of us wasn't inclined—the first time we saw the new look in fashion—to say, "What are you trying to put over?" You just have to play dumb to enter the game.

The "knock, knock" jokes show how one must play dumb to

enter into the fun. If someone says, "Knock, knock." The response is, "Who's there?" If you say, "What do you mean knock, knock? You're not at a door." The joke is gone.

You just have to give in to the game, and forget all seriousness. It works exactly the same way when you enter into the mirage of the mystique. You must surrender logical thinking and sympathetic emotions. The rule of joke listening is to never think deeply. Same with the mystique— never think too deeply or the mirage disappears. Never feel too deeply, either, or your heart won't let you proceed! But if you continue to shut down your mind and heart, eventually they do just that: shut down.

Self-Evaluation

You know you're entangled in the dark side of passion when you think that men who score with many women are more manly; when you think that some women or men exist simply for sexual pleasures; when you are convinced that sex is just basic instinct; when you believe that real men don't cry or feel, or fall in love; when you have bought into the lie that sex is more exciting when it's outside the boundaries of honesty and honor. You know you're in the darkest depth of the mystique when you think that sex is better when it's illegal and immoral, when it's all right to fake love to get sex, when spending money on someone gives you a right to their body, when you actually believe that women really secretly like being seduced into sex, even raped, and when sexual gain comes only after someone else's pain—emotional pain, spiritual pain or physical pain.

"This was a game, like bridge. . ."

You know you're caught into the predatory mystique when you can see yourself in this scene from the book by Ernest Hemingway's, Farewell to Arms: "We were off the driveway, walking under the trees. I took her hands, then stopped and kissed her.

'Isn't there somewhere we can go?' I asked.

She looked at me, 'And you do love me?'

'Yes.'

'You did say you loved me, didn't you?'

'Yes,' I lied. 'I love you.' (I had not said it before.)

After she declares her love for him, she asks, "You won't go away?"

He answers, "No. I'll always come back." He then rationalizes his lie away, "I turned her so I could see her face when I kissed her and I saw that her eyes were shut. I kissed both her shut eyes. I thought she was probably a little crazy. It was all right if she was. I did not care what I was getting into. This was better than going every evening to the house for officers where the girls climbed all over you and put your cap on backward as a sign of affection between their trips upstairs with brother officers. I knew I did not love Catherine Barkley nor had any idea of loving her. This was a game, like bridge, in which you said things instead of playing cards. Like bridge you had to pretend you were playing for money or playing for some stakes. Nobody had mentioned what the stakes were. It was all right with me."

A few minutes later, however, Catherine calls the game for what it is. She says, "This is a rotten game we play, isn't it?"

"What game?"

"Don't be dull."

"I'm not, on purpose."

"You're a nice boy," she said, "And you play it as well as you know how. But it's a rotten game."

"Do you always know what people think?" He asks.

"Not always. But I do with you. You don't have to pretend you love me. That's over for the evening. Is there anything you'd like to talk about?"

In this story we see clearly the motives of the Predator. He wanted more than a warm body (masturbation sex); he mentions that there were women who "climbed all over you" st the officer's club. He wanted a challenging warm body. Catherine stops him short and calls it for what it is: a "rotten game" but leaves the opportunity for friendly conversation open.

The Longing to Share a Gift—the Gift of Love and Intimacy

Here's a little analogy that may help men see the dangers of exploitive sex, and the wholesome destination of human bonding. You're driving down the road, hoping to make your destination before night fall. You have a beautifully wrapped gift to give to someone, but you don't know who and you don't know where that person is. Something inside is leading you, but you're not even quite sure what that is—a strange longing.

You see a sporting event alongside the road, a soccer game. You've always loved soccer but you decide to continue on in the hopes that you'll get where you're going before nightfall. Besides, something within urges you on and tells not to get sidetracked.

A few hours later, you notice an amusement park. You stop your car, and wonder if you should spend the day on the rides—just for the thrill of it. You could open the gift and take it to a hock shop to get money to go on the rides, but the longing within urges you to continue on so you keep driving.

Evening has come. In the darkness it's getting harder and harder to see, especially since you don't know where you're going. Just as you're beginning to fall asleep you notice bright fluorescent lights against the black sky. The closer you get, the brighter and more bizarre the town seems. At first it looks offensive and gaudy. There's a dank and dark feeling, but as you drive through the town a errie kind of excitement takes over, and you long to be a part of whatever's happening. You park the car, and a young woman approaches you. She's dressed in a low-cut top, and a short short skirt. Her makeup is plastered on, and you wonder why, since without it she would be fairly attractive. She moves close to you, and says,

"Hi, Babe. I've been waiting all my life for you. Only fifty-dollars."

You realize it's all a joke—played on you, but for a moment your mind becomes confused; it all seems so fascinating, so intriguing, so flattering. You feel so manly, so powerful, so cool and casual. After all, you think, maybe this is different. Maybe she really does think I am more handsome, more manly, more wonderful than any other man that's she's ever been with before. In the darkness, she looks so enchanting, so appealing. You begin to think her not as a woman, but some goddess with mystic powers.

While all of this is racing through your mind, she urges, "Come on, let me make your dreams come true."

"I don't have any money, but. . .I do have whatever's in this package."

"Hey, I'm game," she says with a seductive smile. "Besides that, I'm bored."

As you get out of the car and begin to follow her, an inside alarm starts going off. It shouts, "Can't you see through this hoax? She's selling you something, like the barkers at the carnivals. Her flattery is all a scam; if you give away the gift you'll throw in a piece of your soul. She's confused, sure. Maybe someone molested her as a little girl so that she believes that this is all she's good for. If you go with her, you'll confirm that image that she has of herself. You'll be just another guy to cause her to think less of herself. Run, now!"

You attempt to shut the alarm down. "I know what I'm doing here. I'm an adult; I can do what I want with whom I want. Leave me alone. Besides, she'll think I'm a baby if I back out now. She'll think I'm a wimp. I'll think I'm a wimp myself. . .Wait, giving in is the wimp; I'm not giving in to this."

Suddenly, you turn away and run. Like a bad nightmare you search for your keys, but you cannot find them. You search for your car, but you can't find it. Finally, you see your car, and find your keys in your pocket. You jump into the car, breathing heavily. You're terrified—not of what someone could do to you, but what *you could do to yourself.*

As you proceed down the road, you cannot get the whole thing out of your mind. The smokescreen clears and now you can see it all for what it was. You sigh a breath of relief—grateful that you had the courage to get away. You remember that idea that when you have sex with someone, you also have sex with everyone they've already had sex with, and feeling of ominous fear comes over you. You realize what tripped you up: pride, vanity, fear of humilation. You wonder how you could have been taken in at all by such an obvious scam, and you realize the baggage you would have walked away with had you surrendered to the moment. The baggage of bad feelings, the baggage of possible diseases, the baggage of bad memories, the baggage of being a part of those who have made her feel so desperate for love that she accepts anything—even if it's opposite the real thing.

After several hours, the morning rays of sunshine cast soft light on the landscape. Everything looks fresh and beautiful and clean. The giant oak trees are radiant with their new spring leaves. The lake on the right is blue and clear, with misty vapors rising. You see a campsite near the lake. There's a sign that says, "Welcome".

As you approach the parking lot, you notice a family nearby on a picnic table. They're laughing and talking together. You notice that there's a young woman throwing a ball to a group of children—an older daughter maybe. She's beautiful, radiant, athletic looking. As soon as you are out of the car, the father of the family comes over to you, and invites you to their picnic. Reluctant, but hungry, you join them. You feel awkward at first, but within a few minutes it seems like you've always known them. You join in the conversation; they actually listen. They even invite you to be a part of the cleanup after dinner.

Later, as everyone gathers around the campfire, you sit next to the young woman, who you've learned is the eldest daughter in the family. You're stunned by her beauty. Her light-brown hair seems to dance about her face; her warm smile is inviting. Within a few minutes you realize that somewhere, somehow you've always known her. You find yourself telling her things you've never told anyone. You discover yourself in her presence. After awhile, you start thinking: I never knew I could be this way; I love the way she makes me feel. I'm falling in love with her—and myself at the same time. I love the me I am with her.

The warmth of the fire blends with the warmth of the conversation, and for a moment you realize that this is one of the happiest moments of your life. Then, with horror you remember the night before. You realize that if you had succumbed then, you wouldn't feel comfortable with her now.

You begin thinking, what a contrast in these women: one made me feel excitement, the other makes me feel alive: one made me feel bold and powerful, this one makes me feel warm and wonderful. I would have been ashamed if anyone saw me with that woman, but I would be proud for anyone to see me with this woman. The one made me feel like a macho man, this one makes me feel protective—like a big brother over a little sister. The one made me think of nothing but sex, and this one makes me think of nothing but love—not just love for her—love for everything and everyone, including myself. The other woman would look dark even in daylight; this woman looks light and sunny even at night.

As the family members start going to their tents for the night, you realize it's time to part. After saying, "Good-night" you return to your car, place the key in the ignition, and begin to drive off. Then a flash of awareness: this *is* the destination..

The gift he was carrying was the gift of loving, the gift of honoring, the gift of cherishing, and the gift of intimacy. The point: there's a longing within—to give the gift of love—that leads us, in time and maturity, to create a circle of wholesome and honorable love, but there is also a force that attempts to detour away from that destination and to squander the gift frivolously. The soccer game, and the amusement park represents the detour courses of using the gift for sport, entertainment or the thrill of the hunt.

The prostitute woman in the story represents the darker side of passion, the one that's shrouded with the "tang" of evil. Those who become detoured into dark sex, can miss out on ever discovering the real thing, and can become sucked into the powerful undercurrents that deaden the soul. Sex cannot be divorced from sincere love without severe consequences.

Studies have shown that most men and women—even the promiscuous—want eventually to have a one-and-only Beloved, but promiscuous sex can endanger the possibility of ever finding and recognizing the real thing.

Sex for masturbation, or sport, or thrills may seem like an innocent form of entertainment on the surface, but it's an act of self-betrayal and other-betrayal. It betrays the longing that guides to the real thing, it betrays oneself, it betrays conscience, it betrays sincere feelings of love, and betrays those who are used and abused in the process.

Hocking the gift, or giving it away piece by piece, naturally reduces the joy of gift opening together with one's Beloved. There's something disappointing when someone offers a gift that has already been opened and used. (I realize that this statement may make some readers uncomfortable, but it also may give those who want reasons to stay virgin until marriage incentive to do so. However, the commitment to virtue—and the inner joy of being virtuous—can take place at any time in our lives. Like the expression, "Today is the first day of the rest of your life." Never, never, never think that because you have made mistakes in the past that you need to make the same mistakes in the future. After interviewing young men and women, I realized that most became involved in unhealthy "love" relationships, because they did not know or did not understand how to recognize unhealthy love or the value of waiting until a loving, loyal and legal relationship. One young woman said, "If I had read one page of this book when I was a teenager, I would have remained a virgin.")

Summary

There is a Higher Power that lifts us, and strengthens us to become all that we were created to become as children of God, and there is a Lower Power that's like a dangerous undercurrent, pulling us away from our divine selves. Again, one energizes our natural capacity to love, to be sensitive, to be compassionate, to appreciate and value all human life, and the other pulls us down into complacency or worse—contempt for ourselves and others.

We're not created to do bad and feel good. Betrayal leads to a loss of emotional feelings and spiritual strength, and this loss creates a frenzy of desire to feel again. If we choose not to feel compassion and sympathy for our fellow human beings, we will end up not feeling at all. Some people are looking for partners in love, others are looking for playmates in sex —who pretend to be in love. Playmates miss out on sexual fulfillment in its highest and most satisfying level. The human soul longs to have it all—sexual fulfillment, emotional fulfillment, intellectual fulfillment and spiritual fulfillment. Getting sidetracked has a high price.

I have no doubt that there's a power working to destroy the sweetness and glory of sexual intimacy. Isn't it interesting that sexual intimacy—most holy and sacred act of all—is the butt of a million vulgar and disgusting jokes? Isn't it interesting when what is most light is made to appear dark? When what is a pure fountain for inspiration, progress, ambition, sweet friendship, angelic babies, happy homes is robbed of its dignity and honor. What a mighty target for the powers of darkness.

Healthy sexuality is founded upon loving, honoring and cherishing; the mystique is founded upon dishonoring and despising. It begins with the selfish, self-centered desire to use a warm body for masturbation, but can descend to the challenging warm body—the exploitive hunt—and then on down to the desire to use and abuse. Next we will explore the connection between pornography and the desire to use and abuse.

Notes on chapter fourteen:

1. The mystique—loveless sex—has had devastating effects upon young men's chances for fatherhood. By the

turn of the century 50% of American children will not be living with their dads. Sex without real love may bring babies into the world, but it seldom produces a father. "Men are not biologically attuned to being committed fathers. Left culturally unregulated, men's sexual behavior can be promiscuous, their paternity casual, their commitment to families weak." This article points out that men who are married are much more likely to take an active role in the raising of their children. Also, children raised without fathers are more likely to have emotional and social problems. They are more likely to engage in crime, less able to succeed in school, more vulnerable to sexual abuse, child neglect, etc. They are more likely to drop out of school. This list goes on, and on. (David Popenoe, "Life Without Father", Reader's Digest, Feb. 1997)

2. "Female juvenile prostitutes, most of whom are runaways, have extensive histories of child sexual abuse. Such studies report that between 30 and 90 percent . . .experienced some form of sexual abuse as children or adolescents." U.S. Department of Justice, The Sexual Exploitation of Missing Children: A Research Review, October 1988.)

The Deadly Hazards of Pornography 15

"Today no one in the world shall suffer because I live. I will be kind, considerate, careful in thought and speech and act. I will seek to discover the element that weakens me as a power in the world, and that keeps me from living up to the fullness of my possibility. That weakness I will master today. I will conquer it, at any cost."

William George Jordan

Insight # 15

Pornography is like a training manual for the mystique; it dulls the conscience, corrupts the mind, cankers the heart, deadens the soul, and stimulates natural passions until they become unnatural.

Therapy goes with the territory of mothering. Young children have only one real mother, but teenagers seem to need a few more—just to work things through—to clear out the cobwebs of confused thinking. I've enjoyed these conversations with my children's friends. Curt was one of these, but not in the beginning.

Curt was a friend of one of our sons. He seemed extremely shy; my natural friendliness seemed to irritate his right to privacy. He kept his face covered with a baseball cap that was tipped downwards, and he shadowed our son in silence whenever they passed through our home. Often I attempted to bring him out of his shell, but conversation seemed painful. Their friendship gradually faded away, but years later he came to visit—alone.

I was watering flowers when he drove up. I didn't recognize him; he no longer wore the baseball cap. This time, he started the conversation,"Hi, Mrs. Sorensen; it's been a long time."

"Well, Curt," I responded, "it has been a long time. How are you doing?"

"Better, thank you," he said.

"Better?" I asked.

"Definitely better," he responded.

We sat down on the lawn and began catching up. I learned why he was doing better when he learned about this writing project. He said, "That's great. I'm so glad that you're writing on the dangers of pornography. I wish that someone would have warned me years ago when I got hooked on the stuff. It's bad—really bad."

"Tell me about it," I said.

"Well, it all started when I went over to a friend's house to play. His older brother had a collection of porno magazines. The three of us climbed into a closet and started looking at them. Wow, I had never seen anything like that before, but once I got started I couldn't stop. There seemed to be a magic to it all—I loved and hated the way they made me feel."

"What do you mean?" I asked.

"Well, they're exciting to a guy. They make you feel powerful, excited on the outside, but terrible on the inside. The guys think there's nothing wrong with the stuff, but all I know is how I felt at the time, and I felt bad. I couldn't be around Mom or my sisters without feeling bad. I couldn't be around you, or Micah's sisters without feeling bad. I wanted to hide from everyone—except my friends. You're always scared that someone is going to find your stash.

"I started out having sexual fantasies; I could sensationalize anyone. They would be just sitting there, but I would sensationalize them."

"What do you mean by sensationalize?" I asked.

"I could, just by thinking, make any woman look sexy, inviting," he said. "She could be just sitting there, or jogging down the street, or working alongside me at the restaurant, it didn't matter; I was convinced that she wanted me sexually like I wanted her. I know it's bizarre, but I was controlled by sexual fantasies."

"How did you get out?" I asked.

"I don't know, well, yes, I do. I met someone—a girl—that I really cared about. I never thought she would ever even look at a guy like me, but one day I got up the courage to ask her out. She just looked at me; she stood there looking at me. I turned around, walked away and went home and hid out with my stash of magazines. I kept thinking to myself, Who does she think she is? Who does she think she is? My love turned to hate in just a few minutes, then I realized I didn't hate her—I hated myself, or what I was doing to myself. I realized that I would never be able to date a girl like that unless I cleaned up my act. I threw all the magazines in a paper bag, and went out in the backyard, dug a hole and buried them."

"That's fantastic," I said, "Did you ever dig them up again?"

He smiled, looked down, then said, "Hey, to be honest, I wanted to. Whenever I got depressed, I really wanted to, but I never did. Oh, there's times when I walk pass the magazine rack at the grocery store and glance over at them, but I don't open'm. I know what they do to you, and I don't want it anymore. By the way, I'm with the greatest girlfriend now. She has helped me to get back on track—I mean with school and goals. I met her in a class at the college. We're probably going to get married in a couple of years."

"How did you get up the courage to ask her out?" I asked playfully.

"I didn't actually, she asked me out," he said. "Hey, really that's one of the things that happened after I got away from the stuff. Women started noticing me. I think what happened there is that before I scared them; they didn't know, but I think they sensed it—that I didn't respect women, or myself for that matter. That's a laugh; you think that it's all in secret—that nobody knows what you're doing, but you just can't hide the bad feelings."

"Can I use your story in my book?" I asked.

"Are you kidding? If it helps some kid, I'm happy for you to use it."

Curt walked away, then as he got into his car, he smiled and waved.

"Hey, say hi to Micah," he said, "and thanks for listening."

"Thanks for telling," I said. As he drove away, I sat thinking about the difference in him. The Curt that used to hide his face, and cower in my presence was gone; the new Curt was open, alive and free.

The Pollution of Pornography

Remember the sign that was posted on the beach in the story about Kerry? It read: NO SWIMMING OR BOATING ALLOWED: TREACHEROUS UNDERCURRENTS. Pornography should have a warning sign that says: Beware, Dangerous Substance that Dulls the Conscience, Corrupts the Mind, Cankers the Heart, Deadens the Soul, and Stimulates Natural Passions until They become Unnatural.

Let's set the record straight: we're not talking about censorship of classic novels and beautiful art portraying undressed men and women. I walked through the Louvre in Paris, France and saw more naked men and women than I have ever seen in my life, but their nakedness increased—not decreased—my reverence for human life! The paintings portrayed human dignity, poise and grace. As I walked away I realized for the first time, how society has fallen from such a view. We live in an age of technological advancement but spiritual darkness.

Nakedness is not the issue; neither is the discussion of sexuality, even the scriptures are open and candid about sex. It's the "tang" or "brutal force" in pornography that makes it so destructive. The art at the Louve, France inspires an awakened sense of wonderment for human life and form; pornography breeds contempt for human life and form. We know it by it's rank smell—the smell of lust, the smell of vulgarity, the smell of mocking, the smell of ridicule.

Our inner guide tells us that it is not good for the human soul by the dark, depressing bitter aftertaste. Women are quick to call it for what it is, but men can get addicted to the "tang" of it—the passions roused, the pride, the fascination with power. The addiction is not only to the pornography, but to the dark power that inspires it. Pornography has two parts— what we *see* and what we *feel*, and it's that feeling that's the brutal force.

The Brutal Force Behind Pornography

We can better understand the brutal force behind pornography by contrast. My husband and I love to listen to classical music; there's a energizing, uplifting, ennobling force to it. (Perhaps such compositions are immortal because they have been inspired by the Immortal, Eternal God.)

Good books such as scriptures and other inspired writings can have the same edifying effect. They enlighten our minds, and generate tender feelings of our hearts. The after effect is that we feel more alive, more peace, more direction.

Pornography is pornography because of the power it generates towards the dark side of human life and the dark side of sex.

Pornography rips the mask off of the mystique; it openly exposes all the five parts of the mystique: it **lowers** the vision of human life, instills the **lie** that sex is better when it involves only body parts; inflames the **lust** that reduces the act to a graduated form of masturbation, uses charged **language**, and has the seductive **look**.

Now let's take a closer look at the dangers mentioned: It dulls the conscience, corrupts the mind, cankers the heart, and deadens the soul, and stimulates natural passions until they become unnatural.

1. Dulls the conscience

"Pornography," said Susan Brownmiller, "(is) designed to dehumanize women, to reduce the female to an object of sexual access. Bodies are stripped, exposed and contorted for the purpose of ridicule, to bolster that 'masculine esteem' which gets its kicks and sense of power from viewing females as anonymous, panting playthings, adult toys, dehumanized objects to be used, abused, broken and discarded." (Against Our Will, p. 975)

Pornography opens the door to exploitation—using and abusing others for sexual gratification—by dulling the conscience and dehumanizing women—and in some cases, men and children. The Nazi's of Germany first launched a campaign to dehumanize the Jews, and then they exterminated them. The dehumanization process dulled the consciences of the people into believing that the Jews were less than human. Throughout history, this simple plan has been used: dehumanize through ridicule and humiliation—justify the conscience that this abuse is an exception—then carry out acts of abuse, or even murder. Christians were mocked and killed by the Romans—because they were considered less than human. In our American history, Indians were killed for sport—because they were considered less than human. The ridicule comes first, then the act of violence.

In this same way, pornography seduces the conscience into thinking that it's okay to take advantage of women because they are less than human. They're not human beings, they're just "chicks" or "babes". Pornography ridicules all human life, but especially the women who are portrayed as "anonymous, panting playthings, adult toys, dehumanized objects to be used, abused, broken and discarded."

Our collective conscience is wide-eyed and alert when it comes to any mistreatment of blacks or Jews, but dull and into denial when it comes to women being held up for ridicule in pornography—reduced down to toys to satisfy men's desire for power and play. If the photos in the magazines were only of Jewish women, we would see them for what they are, but the photos are simply of *women* so we excuse them by saying, "It's freedom of speech. This is what these women want to do with their lives. These women choose to become sex toys; We can't help that. Besides—everyone knows—censorship is bad."

Such expressions confirm exactly the message: that it's perfectly acceptable to hold women up for ridicule. However, to portray any woman (or man for that matter) as a toy for sexual exploitation is to dehumanize all women—and men—even ourselves.

2. Corrupts the mind

Pornography is like a training manual for the mystique—sex divorced from love. It programs the mind with ideas and attitudes that lead to sexual exploitation, just like seeds planted eventually produce a harvest of food.

Men who have a steady diet of these ideas form a distorted perspective of women, seeing them as "sex toys".

3. Cankers the heart

Pornography increases the power for lust, while decreasing the power to love. Normal intimacy is empowered by feelings of love and the desire to make life together. Lust is empowered with intense sexual desire to have sex for masturbation, sex for pride, sex for power. When a man makes sexual-lust the master control center of his identity, he becomes the "upside-down" man ruled by passion rather than compassion, rashness rather than rationality.

4. Deadens the soul

There are natural laws that govern the universe, there are

natural laws that govern the soul. We can choose to love, honor and cherish the family of God, or we can choose to hate, dishonor and despise, but in doing so we cannot escape the natural consequence—the deadening of the soul. (This extremely important idea is explored next.) That which is no longer used, needed, or wanted becomes extinct. It's called natural selection. It works in nature and in humans. Souls that are dying seek sensual stimulation and shock to feel alive again. Sexual illnesses are the result of spiritual starvation and the craving to feel alive again.

5. Stimulates natural sexual feelings to make them unnatural, twisting love into lust.

Pornography creates the upside down man—ruled and controlled by sexual passions—void of heart and mind. Remember, the nourish and neglect principle: we are endowed with powers of mind, heart, spirit, and sexuality, but we choose which to nourish and which to neglect, which will be the masters and which will be the servants. Those who concentrate time and energy consuming pornography deliberately make lust their master. We see the same effect when time and energy is concentrated into one area at the exclusion of others. The jock who puts all efforts towards the game of football, but neglects studies and mind development, or the computer nerd who sits in front of the monitor hour after hour and forgets how to communicate with humans. Pornography stimulates the sexual, exaggerates the sexual, gives more power to the sexual, and ultimately enthrones the sexual to become the master of all control centers.

Psychologist Patrick Carnes, currently the leading United States researcher on sexual addictions, found that among 932 sex addicts studied, 90% of the men reported that pornography was significant to their addictions. (Don't Call It Love, p. 67) A sexual addiction occurs when deviant sexual behaviors get out of control, regardless of how severe the consequences. It occurs when "inordinate amounts of time are spent in obtaining sex, being sexual, or recovering from sexual experience(s). . .[to the] neglect of important social, occupational, or recreational activities" (Ibid. p.12). The thrust of his message is that with regular use of pornography, there is a loss of personal power to resist self-destructive and other-destructive behaviors.

The Five Effects of Pornography

Victor Cline, PhD., a clinical psychologist, has treated over three hundred persons suffering from deviant sexual behaviors; 96% of his clients are male. Among them are child molesters and rapists. In an article titled, "Pornography Effects: Empirical and Clinical Evidence," he noted, "with only a few exceptions" pornography was a major "contributor or facilitator" in the acquisition of sexual illness. He found that pornography affected men in five ways. (Notice how Dr. Cline's findings agree with the five that have already been mentioned.)

First, there is an addictive effect.

"They got hooked. . .they could not throw off their

dependence on the material by themselves despite many negative consequences such as divorce, loss of family, or problems with the law as with sexual assault."

While normal sexual desires can be contained and controlled, pornography stimulates or inflames passions until they become like a massive case of poison oak—the more you scratch, the more you itch. The sexual desire is a stimulus/response control center—the more stimulation—either in thought or touch—the more control it takes. The social scientists call this a stimulus/response attribute of our natures. Seeing food causes our mouths to salivate in preparation for the meal. Seeing seductive looking women hardly dressed creates a stimulus for men to respond sexually.

Second, there was an escalation effect.

"With the passage of time they (those addicted to pornography) required more explicit, rougher, more deviant and kinky kinds of sexual material to get the highs and sexual turn ons.. . ."

Gary Bishop, a molester and murderer, said before he was executed, "Pornography was a determining factor in my downfall. . .I spent hundreds of dollars on magazines and films. . .Some of the material was shocking and disgusting at first, but it shortly became commonplace and acceptable.

"As I continued to digress further into my perverted behavior, more stimulation was necessary to maintain the same level of excitement. Finding and procuring sexually arousing materials became an obsession. For me seeing pornography was like lighting a fuse on a stick of dynamite. I became stimulated and had to gratify my urges or explode—[those portrayed in the pictures] became mere sexual objects. My conscience was desensitized and my sexual appetite entirely controlled my actions."(Ibid. p. 17,18)

Third, there is a desensitization effect.

Dr. Cline points out that pornography which depicts violence and aggression against women, causes men to "take lightly" such acts of abuse. What had been shocking and repulsive became acceptable and commonplace. Another word for desensitization would be unfeeling, unsympathetic. In other words, *those who become addicted to pornography increase sexual lust while they decrease emotional love.* They do not stop to remember that the women are not sex toys, but daughters, sisters, maybe even mothers—many of whom have been trained to please sexually when they were little girls—by grown-ups who should have protected them.

Fourth, there is disruption of intimate relationships.

Along with the desensitization effect, there is a disruption in marital bonding. Dr. Cline said, "The major consequence of being addicted to pornography is . . .it diminished their capacity to love and express affection to their partner in their intimate relations. The fantasy was all-powerful, much to the chagrin and disappointment of their partner. Their sex drive had been diverted to a degree away from their spouse. This disturbance of the fragile bonds of intimate family and marital relationships. . . is where the most grievous pain, damage, and sorrow occurs." In other words, the more they gave into the pornography, the less they were able to express marital intimacy. The mystique can become so compelling that reality is discarded for a mirage—not unlike the fantasy masquerade which longs for the love that's "hidden in the mist".

Fantasy masquerades can prevent women from experiencing real love, and fantasy sex can prevent men from experiencing real marital sex. Remember the story of Bob, whose wife was addicted to romantic novels, or the fantasy masquerade? Here's a story that shows how a man can become addicted to the fantasy side of pornography.

I attended a seminar on sexual addictions with speaker Patrick Carnes, author of Don't Call It Love. During the break, a young wife and mother confided, "I never understood it before—why my husband would rather make love to a magazine than me. We haven't made love in over a year. After listening to the discussion on pornography I realize that a man can actually prefer the fantasy over the real thing. It really doesn't make sense."

We cannot look through two windows at once if we look at human sexuality through the mystique, we miss out on the magnificence of soul-bonding intimacy. In wholesome bonding, the man and woman are magnetized to each other, the sexual attraction reinforcing their love and commitment.

The apostle Paul taught, "The wife hath not power of her own body, but the husband; and likewise also the husband hath not power of his own body, but the wife." (1 Corinthians 7:4-5) Some have suggested that Paul meant sexual "power" or the right to ignite sexual powers. In other words, the wife gives to the husband the power and right to ignite her sexual passions, and the husband, in turn, reserves that right for his wife. Pornography is voluntarily giving that right to a stranger's image on paper or film.

Fifth, there is the acting-out effect.

There is an increasing tendency to sexually act out the behaviors viewed in pornography. One time I interviewed several inmates at the Vacaville Medical Facility, a local prison. One of the questions I asked was, "Do you believe that pornography leads to sex crimes?"

Everyone of them answered, "Absolutely!"

A young man who was serving time for rape said, "I know that's what led to my crime. I had been sitting in my room for several hours just looking at the stuff. The pornography created a sexual frenzy that I just couldn't control. When I left my apartment, I started stalking the first good looking woman I saw. I waited until it was dark and went into her apartment through a back window. I know when I get out, I won't ever look at that stuff again. Men just don't realize what it does to them. They think it's just innocent entertainment; it's not. It makes you think that women want to raped—that they prefer it, that it's more exciting."

A three-year-old girl in Oakland, California, was kidnapped, her head shaved so that no one would recognize her, then locked in a filthy van, and abused for four years before someone tipped off the police. When the police found her, they also discovered the van was full of pornographic material. Another molester who abused little boys said, "I became so stimulated (by pornography) that I had to gratify my urges or explode. All boys became mere sexual objects. My conscience was desensitized and my sexual appetite entirely controlled my actions."

Summary

Pornography dissects everything away from the sex act except the sex act itself. It disregards romance, feelings, kindness, tenderness, courtship, friendship, honesty, honor, respect, and a protective spirit. It presents a picture of human sexuality that's a fake and a lie, just as the masquerade presents a picture of love that's a lie. It distorts the view of human life to a sexual slant. It bypasses the intellect, the feelings, the uniqueness, the personality. It twists and spoils natural feelings of love, sympathy and compassion into indifference, disgust, and callousness. It strips sex away from love, honor and cherish, and turns it towards hate, dishonor and despise. It promotes out-of-control sexuality while at the same time it drains moral strength and spirituality.

Each one of are needed to battle the pornography in our society; one voice can make a difference. As I say over and over to our children, "We need to let people know what we stand for, and what we won't stand for." As Edmund Burke said, "All that is necessary for the triumph of evil is for good men to do nothing."

Notes to chapter fifteen:

1. The American Medical Association recently released a report stating that sexual assaults are the most rapidly growing violent crime in America. Over 700,000 women are sexually assaulted each year. More than one in four college-age women surveyed had been the victim of rape or attempted rape. 57% of the assaults occurred on dates. 73% of the assailants and 55% of the victims had used alcohol or drugs prior to the assault. 76% of the boys surveyed believed that forced sex was acceptable under some circumstances. *This was absolutely shocking,* 51% of boys and girls surveyed (between the ages of 11 to 14 years-of-age) said that forced sex was acceptable if the boy "spent a lot of money" on the girl. 75% of the boys, and 47% of the girls said it was acceptable for a boy to rape a girl if they had been dating for more than six months. In a survey of male college students, 35% admitted that they would rape a girl if they thought they could get away with it, 43% admitted that they had used coercive behavior to have sex, including ignoring a woman's protest and using physical aggression to force intercourse. (quoted by Ann Landers, Feb. 28, 1997)

2. "In academic studies, males exposed to even 'soft' pornography take a more lenient view of rape and empathize less with rape victims. Writing in the Duke Law journal, Professor Cass Sunstein concludes that 'the liberalization of pornography laws in the United States. . .has been accompanied by a rise in reported rape rates' almost fourfold

between 1960-88 in the United States—while 'in countries where restrictions have been adopted, reported rapes have decreased.'

"The correlation is even more stark regarding child molestation. John Rabun Jr., ex-deputy director of the Justice Department's National Center for Missing and Exploited Children, says that in 40 prosecutions, 'All adult predators were found with adult pornography and in most cases child nudes and/or pornography.'

"But forget rapists and pedophiles. The invisible victims in this sex-saturated society—where every new telecom technology opens orchards of forbidden fruit—are countless families where loving male-female relationships die the slow death of porn-poisoning. 'Normal' men who use pornography which portrays women as one-dimensional sexual objects, often come to view their wives similarly, importing porn-fueled fantasies into the marital bed. . .with love and tenderness drained from marital sex, wives become mere means of enhanced masturbation. They sense it. They resent it. And discord follows. Perhaps, not accidentally, the Divorce Age and the Porn Age almost perfectly overlap. (Paul Akers, Scripps Howards News Service, S.F. Examiner, January 19, 1997)

4. "More than a decade ago, Attorney Beneral Edwin Meese III's commission on pornography issued its controversial report asserting that sexually explicit materials were harmful and called for strict enforcement of the federal obscenity laws. The report prompted President Ronald

Reagan to launch one of the most far-reaching assaults on porn in the nation's history, a campaign that continued under President George Bush. Hundreds of producers, distributors, and retailers in the sex industry were indicted and convicted. Many were driven from the business and imprisoned. The Reagan-Bush war on pornography coincided, however, with a dramatic increase in America's consumption of sexually explicit materials. . .According to Adult Video News. . .the number of hardcore-video rentals rose from 75 million in 1985 to 490 million in 1992. The total climbed to 665 million, an all-time high, in 1996. Last year Americans spent more than $8 billion on (pornography). . . (Twenty-five years ago it was estimated that Americans spent between 5 to 10 million on pornographic materials.) Despite having some of the toughest restrictions on sexually explicit materials of any Western industrialized nation, the United States is now by far the world's leading producer of porn. . ." (U.S. News & World Report, "The Business of Porn", Eric Schlosser, February 10, 1997)

16

The Black Side of Passion: Monsters

"It seems to me quite extraordinary that anyone should have failed to notice, especially during the last half century, a diabolic presence in the world, pulling downwards as gravity does instead of pressing upwards as trees and plants do when they grow and reach so resolutely and beautifully after the light. A counter-force to creativity; destructive in its nature and purpose. . ."

Malcolm Muggeridge, Jesus, The Man Who Lives

Insight #16

Mortals can become supermen or superwomen in their ability to love and bless through connecting with the powers of God—and they can become supermen and superwomen in their ability to hate and hurt by choice and connecting with the powers of evil.

When I was a little girl, I was terrified of the closet at the foot of my bed. I would lie awake expecting something or somebody—a monster—to jump out and get me. When I could stand the fear no longer I would call to my Mother, "Momma, Momma. Help! Wake up. I'm scared!"

Eventually she would wake up and call out, "What's the matter?"

"I'm scared," I would whimper, "I'm scared of monsters."

"There are no monsters." She would call out. "Go back to sleep." Her soft voice and presence in the night comforted me, so I went back to sleep, but I still wondered if there were monsters in the closet.

As a mother myself, I say the same thing when one of my little ones call out in the middle of the night, "Go back to sleep; there are no monsters." But it's a lie and I know it. There *are* monsters, I read about them almost every day in the newspapers, or see them on television. They do not look like the ones that I created in my imagination as a child, with huge, hairy heads and red flaming eyes. They look like ordinary people—like those who fix the telephone, or those who bag our groceries. It is not what is on the outside that makes them monsters, but what's missing on the inside—their hearts; they no longer feel sympathy or empathy. They go about life with a brutal, cold callousness that sets them apart from normal people.

Monsters are those whose sexual passions are twisted completely opposite the Creator's design—to create circles of love. Their sexual cravings have nothing whatsoever to do with love, honor and cherish, and everything to do with hate, dishonor and despise. They are recreated to become a weapon to kidnap, rape, molest—even murder. Their pleasure comes only after another's suffering and pain. Their crimes—when committed without feeling—show the absence of love and the *presence of an evil, destructive force.*

The Brutal Force

Tolstoy, the Russian novelist, refers to this the force of evil when he wrote: "besides the blessed spiritual force controlling (our) souls, there (is) another, a brutal force. . . (which will) not allow. . . humble peace. . ." To ignore this power is like ignoring the existence of electricity.

This force that battles against virtue is like a constant undercurrent pulling us down and away from our divine selves. The youth—and we ourselves—need to clearly understand that entering into the mystique can lead to darker and darker forms of sexual exploitation. Masturbation sex—using someone's body as an apparatus for sexual gratification, can lead to collusive sex—pausing conscience for a mutual masquerade, then to predatory sex—satisfying the craving for sex and pride with the thrill of the hunt, and then to criminal sex—acting out the rage inside through sexual satisfication that comes only with another's suffering and pain.

Feeding on a steady diet of the dark attitudes towards sexuality (usually involving pornography) they eventually develop a disease that modern medicines can't touch. Again, a disease that dulls the conscience, corrupts the mind, cankers the heart, and deadens the soul, and stimulates natural passions until they become unnatural—and destructive. This is one of the most important factors in the journey of understanding. When sexual satisfaction only comes with the high price of another's suffering and pain, a monster is created. Monsters no longer feel; they no longer care, they are children of the darkness—by their own choice.

The research into the black side of the mystique—criminal sex—was not easy; I read book after book on pornography, perversion, and prostitution. I interviewed police officers and attended seminars on sexual addictions. I listened to personal stories. I prayed for divine guidance to understand—and find answers. I learned everything I didn't want to know about sexual deviancy. Through it all, I recognized the "brutal force."

Super Powers to Hate and Hurt

We are recognizing the monsters and the powers of evil when sexual crimes are committed that go beyond our comprehension and beyond normal human capacity to hurt. We are recognizing a monster when the act is cold-hearted and callous. We are recognizing a monster when we find our minds spinning with thoughts such as: I understand sexual desires, but to go that overboard?. . Why?. . Why would anyone do such a thing?. .It's absolutely senseless. . .It's sick, bizarre. . I just don't get it. . .It's beyond me. . .I can't understand it; what gets into these people? "

We can maybe understand this better by contrast. Those who are true to themselves, and together with God, have Divine spiritual strength to live and love more abundantly. They may even experience miracles in their lives. Moses' power to love and bless the Israelites was magnified by the Lord when he parted the Red Sea. Deborah loved and blessed her people by leading the armies of Israel to victory. When the lame man asked Peter for alms, he answered, "Silver and gold have I none; but such as I have give I thee: In the name of Jesus Christ of Nazareth rise up and walk." (Acts 3:6) Peter lifts the man up, and he walks. *Mortals can become supermen or superwomen in their ability to love and bless through connecting with the powers of God—and they can become supermen and superwomen in their ability to hate and hurt by connecting with the powers of evil.*

We will never begin to understand man's inhumanity to man, or the dangers of exploitive sex until we recognize the undercurrents or the "brutal force" as Tolstoy calls it. Our spirits *feel it,* and naturally fear it—at least in the beginning—especially as children. Little children are extremely sensitive to these feelings—like I was when I called to Mother in the middle of the night. But if we gradually accept this force into our lives, it can become addictive. Then in a spiritually deadened condition, there's a craving for it—even a temporary rejuvenation in it all—for the energy, the excitement, the thrills.

This power is addictive and spiritually deadening. It drains the human soul of the ability to control thoughts and actions. If we plug a lamp into the electrical socket, it connects with a power source to light the room. When we stay connected to God—the Creator—we maintain feelings of love and the power to manifest that love, but if we choose to disconnect from that source, we lose feelings of love and the spiritual stamina to keep from sliding into the dark side of passion.

Again, there are natural laws that govern the universe, there are natural laws that govern the soul. We can choose to love, honor and cherish the family of God, or we can choose to hate, dishonor and despise them, but in doing so we cannot escape the natural consequence—the deadening of the soul. That which is no longer used, needed, or wanted becomes extinct. It's called natural selection. It works in nature and in humans. Souls that are dying seek sensual stimulation and shock to feel alive again.

In a Moment of Panic, She Ran

Several years ago, we owned and loved a gray, appaloosa horse named Wednesday. One morning I went out to her corral and discovered a huge pool of blood where she usually stood; she was gone. I knew that with the loss of so much blood, her life was at stake and every second counted. In a panic, I grabbed her halter and began running, frantically searching and praying to find her. I ran through the bushes that lined the creek thinking that she might seek refuge in the brush, but she was not there. Over and over I prayed for help, but the impression kept coming that I should stop looking and call the Humane Society. I wouldn't listen; I had to find her—*now*! I didn't have time to call anyone.

I kept running through the creek bed, thinking she had to be hidden in the bushes. Finally, not finding her, I ran into the house and called the Humane Society, wondering at the time how this call could possibly make any difference. How could they know where she was? I told the man who answered the phone what had happened and asked if anyone had seen an appaloosa. "There's been a horse found just off Monticello road," he said, "she collapsed and died on the side of the road; maybe that's your horse."

The place he described was just a few blocks away from our house. I jumped into the car and drove to it. A crowd had gathered around her; she was lying in a pool of blood stone dead. It took time, but eventually I pieced together what had happened. She evidently punctured herself on the rusted handle of an old plow that had been overlooked in the brush, bled through the night, then in a moment of panic, began running until she collapsed from the loss of blood.

I think this story has great meaning because when we are disconnected and drained from life, we too can panic and run aimlessly, searching for anything to feel alive again, especially sexual stimulation. We cannot understand the dangers of the the black side of passion without understanding the reality of the undercurrents or evil. Journalist Malcolm Muggeridge, a great British writer, describes his belief in the Adversary:

"Even those who are prepared in a vague way to acknowledge the existence of a deity draw the line at the Devil," said Malcolm Muggeridge, British journalist. "a Devil representing the contrary principle, destructive rather than creative, malevolent rather than beneficent, is another matter, and quite out of the question. Personally, I have found the Devil easier to believe in than God; for one thing; alas, I have had more to do with him. It seems to me quite extraordinary that anyone should have failed to notice, especially during the last half century, a diabolic presence in the world, pulling downwards as gravity does instead of pressing upwards as trees and plants do when they grow and reach so resolutely and beautifully after the light. A counter-force to creativity; destructive in its nature and purpose, raging far and wide like a forest fire, and burning in the heart's core—pinpointed there, a fiery tongue of fierce desire. Have we not seen this Devil's destructiveness making a bonfire of past, present and future in one mighty conflagration? Smelt him, rancid-sweet? Touched him, slippery-soft? Glimpsed him, sometimes in a mirror, with drooling, greedy mouth, misty ravening eyes and flushed flesh? Who can miss him in those blackest of all moments, when God seems to have disappeared, leaving the Devil to occupy an empty universe?" (Jesus, The Man Who Lives, p.51)

Monsters are those who, like the appaloosa, are so spiritually weak that they lose the strength to resist the forces of the undercurrents. Westley Dodd, a monster who collected pornography and stalked children while they played in parks, said, “I liked molesting and did what I had to do to avoid jail so I could continue molesting . . My behavior became predatory and uncontrollable.” (Time Magazine, The Devil's Disciple January 11, 1993, article, by Nancy Gibbs.) Note: The title of this article, “Devil's Disciple” says it all. Having given into the undercurrents, Dodd lost all control of himself and his sexual cravings, and followed like a zombie the biddings of the black side.

Gary Bishop, a molester and murderer, said before he was executed,

“Pornography was a determining factor in my downfall. . .I spent hundreds of dollars on these magazines and films. . .Some of the material was shocking and disgusting at first, but it shortly became commonplace and acceptable.

“As I continued to digress further into my perverted behavior, more stimulation was necessary to maintain the same level of excitement. Finding and procuring sexually arousing materials became an obsession. For me seeing pornography was like lighting a fuse on a stick of dynamite. I became stimulated and had to gratify my urges or explode. . .My conscience was desensitized and my sexual appetite entirely controlled my actions.”(Victor Cline, Ph.D., Pornography Effects: Empirical and Clinical Evidence.)

Taking a Life or Using a Life

Sexual crimes have been equated with the horrible crime of murder and some have thought this to be too harsh. But is it? Is there much difference between taking a life and using a life? The rapist who finds pleasure only with another's pain—is this not close to the cold-blooded heart of a murderer? The child molester who steals innocence and childhood is kindred spirit to one who steals life. Life once taken, cannot be restored; the peace of mind of the rape victim cannot be restored, and the bloom of childhood cannot be restored. Such twisted abuse of the powers of sexuality reek of a dark force. Those who find sexual satisfaction only when they destroy innocence are monsters.

There are actually few who will become monsters, but continuing to exploit others for sexual advantage can eventually create a monster—without conscience, without sympathy and raging with uncontrolled lust. This is the greatest danger of sexual exploitation—hardly ever mentioned, but vital in understanding the dangers.

Summary

Just as there is a Higher Power that lifts and energizes our natural capacity to love and value human life, so there is also a lower power that drains and deadens our capacity to love. Under its influence, we find ourselves less and less in control of our thoughts and actions. We slip into complacency or worse—contempt for ourselves and others. We have the choice to either reach up for the light or allow ourselves to be pulled down to the darkness—both powers are real.

Each of us has the potential to become either beauty or beast, to become more like the beautiful child we were, or to become less—less alive, less loving, less free. We are born loving, open and explicitly honest, but we can choose to be insensitive, closed and cunning. Born to be alive, but we can choose to sink into stagnation. Born to be free, but we can choose the bondage of drugs, or worse—the bondage of out-of-control sexual passions. Born to bond together in loving relationships, but we can choose to twist this power away from love. Monsters do not turn wax cold overnight; it's a process, a process that goes in fast forward with pornography, sexual exploitation and the forces of the undercurrent. Then decision by decision the capacity to love is weakened while the capacity for indifference, apathy, even despising is strengthened. Twisting the powers to love into powers to use and abuse opens us to the brutal forces of the undercurrents. We are not created to breed without also bonding in love; even the most cunning of predators know that almost always they must use the magic word "love" to open the way for sex. Those who degrade it all to a barnyard romp can eventually expect to become animalistic.

I still don't like to believe in monsters. I would love to believe that there are no monsters—no one who would come in the middle of the night, jump out of closets and hurt me or my children. I would love to see the world like it is at Disneyland—beautiful, no litter, freshly painted, smiling kind faces and happy sounds, but *my denial will only increase their power.* Monsters are out there, but none were born that way. There are no babies who come to us without hearts vibrant and overflowing with love; something happens along the way. Monsters are not born; they are a recreation. Created by giving away their light, and taking in the darkness.

The next section will explore how we seduce ourselves in the process of seducing others.

17

Betrayal Against Oneself

"Fear not them which kill the body, but are not able to kill the soul, but rather fear him which is able to destroy both soul and body in hell."

Matthew 10:28

Insight #17

Twisting the powers to love and bond into powers that hate and alienate inflicts a soul-deadening disease, a disease that shuts down the guidance of conscience, the clear thinking of reason, and the compassion of the heart.

The universe is abundant with signs of divine direction, order, uniformity, growing, blooming, bearing fruit, building nests, spinning webs, spawning, teaching, protecting, exploring, conquering. Each particle of life, from the microscopic to the macroscopic, has plan and purpose. Each has a career—a profession—and pursues it with unwavering dedication. Just as there is plan and purpose for every creature on earth, so there is a plan for the children of God. Obviously, God's plan for us is that we continue as we were created: children of light and children of love, but we have the choice to follow conscience or to reject it and recreate ourselves. However, once we choose, we cannot escape the natural consequences of our choices—to flourish living within the natural laws of happiness, or to fight against those laws and find ourselves dying from the inside out. Simply put, we cannot choose to harm others without first harming ourselves; seducing others begins with ourselves. We can capture this understanding by looking back—to the way we were as children. Of course, seeing the end of the road is helpful, too—the monsters, but for most of us, the point is to become aware of the deadening process itself.

The Way We Were

Children are the peak performers of life—open, loving, free, spontaneous, candid, real, sincere, curious—in short, ALIVE. Their minds are bright and searching; they want to know how this works, and why that doesn't. They want to know who put the moon in the sky and why water freezes. They delight to discover butterflies, ants, bugs, rocks, rainbows!

Their consciences are extremely sensitive. One time I left our three-year-old Micah in the main house on our property while I went over to the other house to organize some papers I had stored there. I gave him instructions, "Micah, don't eat the chocolate chip cookies; they are for after dinner."

After awhile he walked over to where I was working, stood silent for a few minutes, then asked, "Do you smell cookies?"

"Did you eat the cookies that I told you not to eat?" I asked.

He answered, "How did you know?"

Once in awhile our family plays hide and seek through the house. The youngest of our children may go along with the game and hide, but it never lasts for long. Pretty soon, we hear, "I'm here, hiding in the closet."

Little children are brimming with the capacity to love; they are so tenderhearted and sensitive that they cry over a cartoon character's pain. Chubby little bodies, spilling over with rolls and rolls of fat, match their *hearts*, spilling over with waves and waves of love. Time after time, my husband and I have returned from a date night to find love-notes pinned to our pillow, taped to our bedroom door, or even stuck on the computer monitor. Our children have given us every token of love conceivable: mustard flowers, love notes left on our pillows, hearts scrawled on our bathroom mirror and candies. Micah—at the tender age of eight—did not have a gift for my birthday so he found a scrap piece of wood, water colored a landscape scene and then wrote "I Love You" in bold print across it. Years later I lacquered it to preserve it.

Just recently, eleven-year-old Jessica put love notes on everyone's bedroom doors—even our guests whom she barely knew. (What an honor parenthood is! Kings and queens have imprinted their images upon coins, but with time such images are worn away. Through the powers of procreation we stamp our image upon our child, and all the children that come after—what an honor!)

The Way We Choose To Become

We were all once children with active hearts, minds, spirits and consciences, but we can choose for ourselves whether to keep those control centers alive or to allow them to go dormant. We were created to be loving, but we can choose to be unloving and cold. We were created to be guided by conscience, but we can refuse to listen. We were created to reason logically and clearly, but we can choose to live in denial. We were created to unite together in intimacy of mind, heart, spirit and body, but we can redesign the powers of love into powers to hurt and to harm. But when we insist upon shutting down the guidance of the conscience, the arguments of the mind, and the sympathies of the heart that attempt to stop us from exploiting and using others, *a soul-deadening disease begins that rots from the inside out.*

Mush Oaks

After our eighth child, Jennifer, was born, my husband and I decided that it was time to buy a home with property. After searching all over Napa Valley, we bought a farm just across the street. We had admired the property studded with giant oak trees for years, and we were awe struck by the way the trees arched like a canopy over the charming farmhouse.

The trees were magnificent; they had stood in the valley over two hundred years. They stood over seventy feet tall; their gnarled branches spread Cathedral-like over an area the size of a football field. Their trunks were over five feet in diameter at the base.

After living under the trees for over twenty years, we have learned to both love and fear them. When a windstorm races through the valley, one or two of the giant limbs, weighing a ton or more, breaks and falls to the ground. Such a crushing blow would be lethal to anyone in their path.

The oak trees that stand like gods across the Napa Valley are prone to a disease that rots them from the inside out—giving them the nickname "mush" oak. When the wind blows, the children come inside and we watch in fear. We love our oak trees. They shade us from the hot sun in the summer, delight us with snow-like leaf flurries in the autumn, surprise us with the explosion of baby green leaves in the spring, but most of all, they warn us to beware of the disease that rots the soul from the inside out.

Betrayal Against Oneself

The idea that we can inflict a disease upon ourselves came to me as I researched for this writing project. It was fascinating and answered many questions that were puzzling to me. I wondered how women and men could not see through the masquerades. I wondered how little boys, who were once tender-hearted towards their girl friends, could grow up and think nothing of saying "I love you" to get sex. I wondered where men could get the idea that they are more manly with each sexual conquest?

Most of all, I was haunted by the monsters—those whose

sexual gain always involves another's pain. I found my head spinning with questions, "How do monsters become monsters? What happens to their feelings of sympathy for their victims? How do they become so hardened? What happens to their consciences? What happened to these babies—how could some turn from chubby, soft and lovable beings to cold-hearted monsters?

There are no simple answers, and definitely family and societal conditioning plays a part, but it makes sense that with the right to life comes the right to choose, whether to become more the child of God we were created to be, or less, even less than the animals. Less than the animals, because animals do not have the ability to choose; they follow instinct. We of all the creations of God have with the gift of life as well as the ability to direct that life.

The idea that we can recreate ourselves, and inflict a soul-destroying disease upon ourselves became intriguing. I kept coming across this idea in my research.

Destroyeth His Own Soul

David, an Old Testament king who knew by hard experience, said, "Whoso committeth adultery with a woman lacketh understanding; he that doeth it destroyeth his own soul."

The first part of this sentence, that we err because of ignorance or "lack understanding," supported my cause to write this rationale, but I had copied this quote over and over before I noticed—really noticed—the ending, "he that doeth it destroyeth his own soul."

With the first realization, it seemed so strict, so extreme; it no longer does. David uses the term "soul destruction", and C.S. Lewis spoke of "soul-destroying surrender to the senses."

Rob You of Your Very Self

The psychologist Viktor Frankl, said that while he was imprisoned in a German Concentration Camp:

> "Every day, every hour, offered the opportunity to make a decision, a decision which determined whether you would or would not submit to those powers which threatened to rob you of your very self, your inner freedom; which determined whether or not you would become the plaything of circumstances, renouncing freedom and dignity to become molded into the form of the typical inmate." (Man's Search For Freedom, pgs. 86-87)

There are natural laws that govern the universe; there are natural laws that govern the soul. We can choose to love, honor and cherish the family of God, or we can choose to hate, dishonor and despise, but in doing so we cannot escape the natural consequences. Like the process of adaptation, that which is no longer used, needed, or wanted becomes extinct. It's called natural selection. It works in nature and in humans.

Turn-of-the-century Christian philosopher Henry Drummond wrote,

> "This destroying process, goes on quite independently of God's judgment on sin. . .The soul that is left to itself unwatched, uncultivated, unredeemed, must fall away into death by its own nature. . .It shall die, not necessarily because God passes sentence of death upon it, but because it cannot help dying. It has neglected the functions which resist death. The punishment is in its very nature, and the sentence is being gradually carried out all along the path of life by ordinary processes which enforce the verdict with the same faithfulness as natural law." Natural Law In the Spiritual World, p. 104

The greatest danger of twisting sex into a tool for exploiting others is not the physical consequences, but the emotional and spiritual consequences. We cannot seduce others without first seducing ourselves and inflicting a disease of the soul; a disease that shuts down the guidance of conscience, the clear thinking of reason, and the compassion of the heart.

The Guidance of the Conscience

Conscience guides us towards happiness and protects us from unhappiness, but if we intentionally shut it down, we inflict a disease that destroys from the inside out. Realizing that the hot stove will cause pain, we avoid touching it, but if we shut away the knowledge that it is hot and touch it anyway, we are flirting with disaster and pain. Remember, conscience is a protection to the soul just as pain is a protection to the body. Previously, it was called the peace/sorrow mechanism. Thomas Jefferson believed, "that the moral sense is as much a part of our constitution as that of feeling, seeing or hearing." "A good conscience," said Joseph Addison, "is to the soul what health is to the body."

The guide within says no when we attempt to entice another into bed by empty promises of love; it says no when we use another's body for an apparatus or tool for sexual pleasures, but if we refuse to listen, it eventually goes silent. In other words, when we deliberately feed lies to ourselves in order to silence the conscience, we set ourselves up as an enemy to ourselves. Like a car without a steering wheel, the engine keeps going while the mechanism to guide it becomes defective—and made defective by the driver's own tampering—a self-inflicted craziness! Those who will not listen to their built-in alarm systems—the protective device for spiritual safety and mental sanity— eventually shut it down.

When we deliberately feed lies to ourselves in order to silence the conscience, we set ourselves up as an enemy to ourselves; fooling ourselves, we eventually create a fool. Like a car without a steering wheel, the engine keeps going while the mechanism to guide it becomes defective—and made defective by the driver's own tampering—a self-inflicted craziness! Those who will not listen to their built-in alarm systems—the protective device for spiritual safety and mental sanity— eventually shut it down.

"You have to convince your conscience. . ."

A young man who was caught into the web of the mystique, explained the process of shutting down the conscience, "When you make the decision to take advantage of others for sexual gratification, you suffer from horrendous guilt. Then you have to create a whole bunch of lies to convince your conscience that it's okay to proceed. Otherwise, it keeps bugging you and messing up the whole thing."

We can imagine the conversation. The young man, burning and churning with desire, says, "It's all right; I love you. I will always love you."

"But I don't know that," she sobs. "I'm afraid that you will leave me."

"I'll never leave you," he says, not even believing himself. "We'll be married as soon as we're out of high school, and then. . . "

His conscience attempts to reason with him,"You know you don't love her. Don't say that. Don't take advantage of her; she loves you," but it is silenced with the commands, "I want her now. Leave me alone. Back off."

See the process? He commands the conscience to leave him alone, and in time the conscience does just that—leaves him alone, without protection, without guidance.

Popular psychologist and author, M. Scott Peck has observed that,

> "All mentally healthy people submit themselves to the demands of their own conscience. In evil people however, in the conflict between their guilt and their will, it is the guilt that must go and the will that must win"(People of the Lie).

This danger to exploitive sex is one of the hidden hazards—it needs more explaining. A thief who steals a car may silence his conscience with the excuse, "I need that car more than they do." An employee who takes money from the boss might say, "He's rich; he'll never miss the money." The husband who berates and belittles his wife may rationalize to himself, "It's the only way to get things done around here." Those involved in an extra-marital affair might excuse their dishonorable behavior by saying, "My husband is not meeting my needs. . . She doesn't love him like I love him. . .That's not what I call a marriage. . .No one will ever know. . .Just this once. . .This is an exception to the rule. . .This is different. . .We love each other. . .I couldn't help myself. . . We're adults, we have a right to. . ."

Notice the deliberate effort to cloud clear and rational thinking: "If you really loved me, you would. . .It's the only way to tell if we're compatible. . .When you're really in love, you can't help yourselves. . .You don't understand men and their needs. . .This is prom night—a special occasion, just this once. . .This is our last date before summer break. . .This is our last date before the end of the summer. . .This is our last date before the Macy's Flower Day sale. . .Don't deny yourself such pleasure. . .We're adults, we can't help it if we married the wrong people; it's the only way. . . No one will ever find out. . . I don't know what's right and wrong, but I know that we're right for each other, so just forget that I'm married."

Such arguments against the conscience eventually silence it and leave a form of insanity in the wake. Again, fooling ourselves eventually creates a fool.

No One Will Ever Know

We see the betrayal of conscience in the story of King David of the Old Testament. He had many wives and concubines, but the woman bathing on the rooftop—Bathsheba—offered the challenge, the fascination. While her husband was off to war, he enticed her to lay with him. When she later announced that she was pregnant, he devised a plan so that her husband Uriah would think that the child was his.

David ordered him to come home. After pretending to be interested in the happenings on the battle front, David suggested that Uriah go to his home and he even sent dinner with him. But Uriah refused to go home, and slept with the servants at the king's door. When David found this out, he was shocked and asked Uriah why he did not go to his house.

Uriah answered, "The ark, and Israel, and Judah, abide in tents; and my Lord Joab, and the servants of my lord, are encamped in the open fields; shall I then go into mine house, to eat and to drink, and to lie with my wife? As thou livest, and as thy soul liveth, I will not do this thing."

I have always been touched by this! Uriah reminds us of the untouched Sir Lancelot of Camelot—so dedicated to the cause! He refused to enjoy the pleasures of food, drink or the marital bed so long as his buddies were roughing it out in the fields.

David tries one more time to get Uriah to go sleep with his wife; he gets him drunk and sends him home the next night, but still Uriah sleeps with the servants on the doorstep. Now David orders him to be sent to the front lines of battle where he is sure to be killed—and he is. After a decent period of mourning, David marries Bathsheba and thinks the whole thing is over. No one will ever know. Then God sends Nathan the prophet to confront David with his great sins. (2 Samuel Chap. 12)

David's descent may have begun with pride. I can imagine that he may have attempted to shut down the whisperings of conscience by saying to himself, "I am the king. Should not the king have the most beautiful woman in his kingdom? If I keep it a secret, no one ever needs to know. Her husband will believe the child is his. So what if he dies in battle? This could have happened anyway, had I not intervened."

While nothing is as painful to the human soul as an uneasy conscience, nothing is worse than the silence of it.

David may have shut down his conscience, but afterwards the guilt was crippling. John Calvin said, "The torture of a bad conscience is the hell of a living soul." We can feel the "hell of a living soul" in David's own words, "Have mercy upon me, O God, according to thy loving kindness: according unto the multitude of thy tender mercies blot out my transgressions.

"Wash me thoroughly from mine iniquity, and cleanse me from my sin. For I acknowledge my transgressions: and my sin is ever before me.

Hide thy face from my sins, and blot out all mine iniquities.

"Create in me a clean heart, O, God; and renew a right spirit within me.

"Cast me not away from thy presence; and take not thy holy spirit from me." (Psalm 5l: 1-3, and 9-11.)

David not only suffered from pangs of guilt, he feared the loss of the spirit, when he cried, "and take not thy holy spirit from me." Losing the spirit—the energizing force of the Higher Power—means losing life, feeling drained, weakened, and to a man who had known the glory of God's presence in his life, feeling terribly alone. This is important. Disconnecting with conscience is also disconnecting with

God and that life force that rejuvenates, and restores spiritual strength, enhances love, peace and joy; this factor alone makes all virtue tremendously worthwhile and rewarding.

Just as David attempted to cover for his wrongdoing, we do the same thing when we make war with ourselves to feel good about doing bad.

Deliberately altering the clear thinking of our minds in order to proceed with an act of self-betrayal or other betrayal sets a course to shut down the conscience and rational thinking. We cannot become an enemy to others without first becoming an enemy to ourselves.

"I still possessed my soul."

In a scene from the novel, Jane Eyre, we see one woman's battle to hold onto virtue, conscience and powers of reason to protect her soul. As a young woman, Jane goes to work for a wealthy man, Rochester. They fall in love, he proposes marriage. She accepts, but then discovers that he has a mentally ill wife hidden in the attic. When she tells him that she will not be a part of the masquerade, he pleads for her to become his mistress. Using the rationale of the current "situation ethics," he tells her he isn't really married. Besides, "you have neither relatives nor acquaintances whom you need fear to offend by living with me."

She battles within herself, "Oh, comply! Think of his misery...soothe him; save him, love him; tell him you love him and will be his. Who in the world cares for you? or who will be injured by what you do?"

She gives her answer to herself and him with these words: "I care for myself. The more solitary, the more friendless, the more unsustained I am, the more I will respect myself. I will keep the law given by God and sanctioned by man. I will hold to the principles received by me when I was sane, and not mad—as I am now.

"Law and principles are not for the times when there is no temptation; they are for such moments as this, when body and soul rise in mutiny against their rigour; stringent are they; inviolate they shall be. If at my individual convenience I might break them, what would be their worth? They have a worth—so I have always believed; and if I cannot believe it now, it is because I am insane—quite insane: with my veins running fire, and my heart beating faster than I count its throbs. Preconceived opinions, foregone determinations, are all I have at this hour to stand by: there I plant my foot." Then she says to herself: "I still possessed my soul, and with it the certainty of ultimate safety."

I loved the expression that with her soul, she was "certain of ultimate safety." Jane Eyre knew what so many do not know today—that happiness comes mainly from ourselves, and being true to ourselves. We cannot be happy with someone else, unless we are first happy and at peace with ourselves. Being true to herself—and her conscience—she was assured of the "safety of her soul" and an inner happiness.

Summary

We are free to be conscious or to force unconsciousness upon ourselves. We are free to follow the gentle voice of conscience within or to ignore it, but we are not free of the consequences of ignoring it. Piecemeal dismantling of our vital and God-given control centers—mind, heart, conscience— eventually destroys not just one's positive self-image, but any image at all.

The expression "abuse it and lose it" applies to both the conscience and the heart. Next we explore the damage to the heart, when it is used as a pawn for exploiting others—sexually or otherwise.

Betrayal Against The Heart 18

A young man is leaving to go off to war. With his last kiss to his wife and love she asked, "But why must you do this?" He explains, "I could not love thee, dear, as much if loved I not honor more."

Insight #18

If we choose to turn away from the Creator—and away from the gift of love—we decrease our capacity to love, and increase the power to hate. What we use is added upon, but what we abuse is taken away—by our own choice.

There are lessons of life to be learned from chickens. Several years ago, our Rhode Island Red hen laid eggs in the ivy, and sat on them faithfully for weeks. Then one day we noticed she was out and about again, with a dozen or so yellow baby chicks following her around.

Our family loved watching the mother hen with her brood following close behind, but if we approached them to get a better view of the baby chicks, the feisty mother hen would stop, look sternly as if to say, "Stay away!" Then she would fluff up her feathers into an umbrella-like fan, and all the baby chicks would immediately run and hide under her protective wings. When all of them were nestled safely beneath her wings and completely hidden from view, she looked like a huge, fat chicken.

In time, the baby chicks grew to become as large as their mother—some even larger, but they still followed her around the yard, brushing aside leaves and pecking for bits of this and bites of that.

One early evening, I watched the mother hen and her brood as they prepared themselves for the night. You've probably heard the expression, "going to bed with the chickens". Chickens retire for the night with the first shadows of the evening—sometimes as early as three or four in the afternoon. They like to roost high in a tree or atop a structure to feel safe and protected. The mother hen and her brood climbed to the top of a peaked roof out building to roost for the night.

Once she settled into a spot, she spread her wings out to snuggle her chicks, but since they were now grown, and since they were on top of a roof, there were only two spots next to mother—one on the right and one on the left. I stood watching them for several minutes as the almost fully grown chickens challenged each other for the two prized spots next to mother. Two would settle next to her, then others would push them aside and take their places. The chickens would tumble down the roof, and then climb back up again. This happened over and over. When I was wondering if they would spend the whole night in this tussle—fighting and struggling for position—it was over. Two, probably the strongest and most determined, secured themselves next to mother, and the others surrendered to being in second, or third, or fourth spot. The mother hen tried to compensate by reaching out her wings to touch them all.

Why Casual and Exploitive Sex Damages the Heart

Love and a protective spirit are an endowment from the Creator—to animals and humans alike, but only humans have the agency to reject these gifts. We can choose whether to reach out in love and protection to the family of God, or we can choose not to love, and not to protect, and eventually feel nothing at all.

The heart is damaged in several ways when it's used to play love games or as a pawn for exploitation (for actual sexual conquest or for a vanity conquest): by turning off feelings of love and sympathy that would hinder the conquest, by faking feelings of love to gain conquest, and by surrendering to the forces of the undercurrent—consequently, increasing the ability to hate. (Actually, there is one other way that the heart is affected: those who have been victimized become resistant to love, naturally suspicious and cynical of anyone who says, "I love you.")

This is the most damaging consequence to twisting the

powers to love and bond into powers for pleasure and sport—or worse for the hunt. *When the natural functions of the heart are shut down in order to take advantage of another, caring turns to indifference, compassion turns to callousness, goodwill turns to ill will.*

The Intent of the Heart

The motives of the heart determines whether an act is merely mischievous or malicious. It is possible to do harm to another unintentionally. As we mentioned before, our justice system is set up to determine the crime itself and the premeditation—or intent of the heart—that went before the crime. To forget to return a borrowed book is a case of neglect, or irresponsibility, but not a hateful act. But when the passion to love and bond together is recreated for the game—sex for sport, sex to exploit, sex for pride, sex for vanity, sex for sex—the heart becomes damaged. Such intentional harm to oneself and others inflicts a disease upon the heart.

The damaged heart—one that no longer feels love or sympathy—then proceeds with malicious acts with a "so what and who cares" attitude. The heart that no longer cares and longer loves is the *cause* of hurting others, and the *result* of hurting others.

We call those who commit crime without remorse "hardened criminals". In other words, their hearts have become so hardened—without softness, without compassion—that they no longer care. We read their comments in the newspaper, "Do it to them before they do it to you. . .He deserved what he got. . .Why should I care?. . She was just an ol' lady. . .You either take or be taken. . .She was askin' for it."

"The longer we continue to make the wrong decisions," Eric Fromm said, "the more our heart hardens; the more often we make the right decisions, the more our heart softens—or better perhaps, comes alive. . . each act of surrender and cowardice weakens me, opens the path for more acts of surrender, and eventually freedom is lost. Most people fail in the art of living not because they are inherently bad or so without will that they cannot lead a better life; they fail because they do not wake up and see when they stand at a fork in the road and have to decide." (The Heart of Man: Its Genius for Good and Evil, pp. 173-178)

Behind the Mask of Love

Sexual seduction is particularly harmful to the heart because it must begin with the mask of love and involves the most deceptive and cunning of strategy. Even those who have reduced sex to a graduated form of masturbation are aware that *love cannot be dismissed.* For example, a man is obsessed with lust for a woman at the office. If he says bluntly, "I think you're beautiful and I would like to use your body," he is likely to get a slap in the face and a lawsuit for sexual harassment. But if the man fakes "love," it may open the emotional doors to her heart, and thus to her bed. Women were not created to surrender sexually without believing that they are loved and cherished. Men are not created to comfortably launch into the sex act without feelings of love. So whether the motive is sex, vanity, power, or pain, the empty word of love is still used—*making the abuse all the more abusive.*

Someone may steal your car, and the motive is clear—greed and ill will. They want what you have. Someone may slander your name and the motive is clear—ill will. They want to put you down. In exploiting another sexually however, the real motives are disguised. We have all seen the woman who flatters in order to flatter herself, the smile that entices only to win another heart. We have also seen the man who gives thoughtful gifts—of flowers, of cards—in order take sexual advantage. The flattery, love words and love acts mask the real motives of the heart. Stealing doesn't require the fake—the malice begins and ends the act. At least there's an honesty about the motives, but almost always sexual seduction begins with a false front—dishonesty, deception and a mask of love.

The mask says, "I love you." Behind the mask, "I want to use you."

The mask says, "I think you are the most beautiful women or handsome man I have ever met." Behind the mask, "I think you would make a great challenge to add to my trophy case of beautiful women that I have seduced. The guys will be impressed when they see me with you." The mask says, "I'll always be faithful to you," but behind the mask, "Hey, right now it sounds good, but who can tell what will happen tomorrow? Actually, I plan to move on as soon as it gets old, which is usually about two weeks." The mask says, "You're the only one who has ever made me feel this way." Behind the mask, "At least this week. Actually I said the same thing to someone else last week."

Turning Off Feelings of Sympathy and Compassion

A thief doesn't feel for his victims—otherwise he likely would not steal at all. If he thought, "Oh, gosh, what will he think when he wakes up in the morning to find that I have stolen his car? He probably won't be able to go to work. Maybe he doesn't have the money to buy another one. I just hate to think of how he's going to feel!" Such feelings of sympathy would likely eliminate the desire to steal. In this same way those who are stalking for sex, or to win a heart for vanity, must turn off feelings of sympathy in order to proceed. Turning feelings off to take advantage eventually shuts down any feelings at all.

If the predator—either to win heart or body—were to think, "She is such a sweet girl; and she's so happily married. How can I do this to her? She is such a good friend to me, and I would ruin that friendship if I took advantage of her," such thoughts would hinder the act—so they are intentionally dismissed. And when the heart is being instructed—even commanded—to turn off, it eventually does just that.

Each act of surrender and cowardice weakens me, opens the path for more acts of surrender, and eventually freedom is lost.

The Heart, Center of Happiness

Damaging the feelings of the heart is to the soul, like a heart attack is to the physical body. It affects everything. We can damage a leg, even have it amputated, and still be who we are. We can become completely paralyzed and still be ourselves, but when we damage the heart's ability to love, the entire identity is altered: feelings, ambitions, motives, personality, character, sense of humor, conversation, everything!

Just as the heart is the key vital organ of the body, so the feelings of the heart are the key vital part of our soul. All that makes us warm human beings comes from feelings of love, sympathy, empathy, compassion, kindess, thoughtfulness, etc. The heart—love—is the source of all virtue, of all internal peace, of all true happiness.

Jesus Christ taught a simple formula for happiness here and hereafter when the lawyer asked him, "Master, which is the great commandment in the law?" He answered simply, "Thou shalt love the Lord thy God with all thy heart, and with all thy soul, and with all thy mind, this is the first and great commandment. The second is like unto it, Thou shalt love they neighbor as thyself. On these two commandments hang all the law and the prophets." (St. Matthew 22: 36-40) So simple, but so all-encompassing.

Those who love will not have the *heart* to harm others. In other words a person with a healthy heart—healthy emotionally—will naturally do those things that are kind and virtuous.

A Diseased Heart

I have found it fascinating that Jesus Christ pointed out the symptoms of a spiritually diseased heart the way a medical physician would point out the symptoms of a diseased body—symptoms that if untreated can be fatal. He said, "Ye have heard that it was said of them of old time, Thou shalt not commit adultery: but I say unto you, that whosoever looketh on a woman to lust after her hath committed adultery with her already in his heart." (Matt. 5:28)

When I first read this I thought: "Wait a minute! That doesn't seem fair. Is he saying that just by looking at a woman a man has already committed adultery? Are we to be held accountable for our thoughts as well as our actions?" Then I started noticing that Jesus did not say that the man had committed adultery, but that he had committed adultery "in his heart." Also, the problem is not that the man looked upon the woman to admire her, to converse with her, or to befriend her, but that he looked "to lust after her." Now lusting is a whole different matter. To lust after someone means to have an intense sexual desire—to want them—to have an intense craving to use them for gratification.

It is as if to say, "This man's heart is diseased; it's in danger. He has already begun the dying process—from the inside out." In other words, sick actions that hurt self or others always begin with a sick heart or motives. This same idea shows up in the counsel, "Ye have heard that it was said by them of old time, Thou shalt not kill; and whosoever shall kill shall be in danger of the judgment: but I say unto you, that whosoever is angry with his brother without a cause shall be in danger of the judgment." (Matt. 5:22)

Some have interpreted this to mean that we are never to be angry—but Jesus displayed anger when he cleansed the temple. Anger isn't the problem; it's being angry "without a cause." In other words, when your heart is so sour that you go around getting angry with people for no reason, you've got a diseased heart—maybe even a heart that has become hardened by the brutal force.

The spiritually diseased heart has symptoms just like a physically diseased body: pride, vanity, jealousy, hatred, bitterness, lust, callousness, anger, malice, apathy, hostility. Eventually, as the feelings of the heart shut down, a numbness takes over and the soul yearns to feel alive again—to feel anything again. This is when the comatose descend to a lower level of sexual exploitation in order to experience the excitement again—more explicit, more immoral, more shocking. They are crying out, "Oh, do something! Anything! But make me feel again. Am I alive?"

There's a path that leads into this darkness of life; it happens gradually: taking one step out of the light and another step into the darkness. We have the choice whether to love and protect or to recreate ourselves to neither love or protect.

I recently overheard one man say to another—with great pride,

"Women are so easy. They want so desperately to believe that they are loved that when you tell them those magic words 'I love you' they believe it. It doesn't really matter how you treat them. Even if you treat them like dogs, they still believe they're loved if you say it. They're so easy. It's like putting crumbs on the ground to capture a bird. You just keep putting the crumbs down—the compliments—and they walk right into your lap."

He was showing symptoms of a spiritually diseased heart—even dead.

"That's what every woman says."

The predator's inability to feel for his victim, and the victim's resistance to feeling again are depicted beautifully in a scene from the novel, Tess of the d'Urbervilles by Thomas Hardy.

Tess, a young, innocent woman, leaves her home and goes to work for a neighbor, Alec. He seduces her against her will. She eventually yields to an affair—a masquerade of love— then comes to her senses and returns to her family—pregnant. The following scene takes place as he is driving her home—horse and carriage—and notices that she has begun to cry:

"What are you crying for?" he coldly asked.

"I was only thinking that I was born over there," murmured Tess.

"Well—we must all be born somewhere."

"I wish I had never been born—there or anywhere else!"

"Pooh! Well, if you didn't wish to come to Trantridge why did you come?"

She did not reply.

"You didn't come for love of me, that I'll swear," he says.

"Tis quite true. If I had gone for love o'you, if I had ever sincerely loved you, if I loved you still, I should not so loathe and hate myself for my weakness as I do now!. . .My eyes were dazed by you for a little, and that was all."

He shrugged his shoulders. She resumed—

"I didn't understand your message till it was too late."

"That's what every woman says."

"How can you dare to use such words!" she cried, turning impetuously upon him, her eyes flashing as the latent spirit (of which he was to see more some day) awoke in her. "My God! I could knock you out of the gig! Did it never strike your mind that what every woman says some women feel?" (pg. 94)

Later, Tess tells her mother that she is pregnant by Alec. Her mother, poor in money and integrity, scorns Tess—not for becoming pregnant—but for not getting Alec to marry her.

Tess is repulsed by the idea: [She]. . . "had never wholly cared for him, she did not at all care for him now. She had dreaded him, winced before him, succumbed to adroit advantages he took of her helplessness; then, temporarily blinded by his ardent manners, had been stirred to confused surrender awhile: had suddenly despised and disliked him, and had run away. That was all. Hate him she did not quite; but he was dust and ashes to her, and even for her name's sake she scarcely wished to marry him."

"Oh, Mother, my mother!" cried the agonized girl, turning passionately upon her parent as if her poor heart would break. "How could I be expected to know? I was a child when I left this house four months ago. Why didn't you tell me there was danger in men-folk? Why didn't you warn me?" (pp. 94, 100)

Summary

All life forms bloom and grow by turning to the light, not away from it. If we choose to turn away from the Creator and conscience and become spiritually weak, we eventually decrease our power to love, and increase the power to hate. What we use is added upon, but what we abuse is taken away—by our own choice.

If you're sensing a desire for change in your life, the next chapter is for you. These writings may have awakened within you an uncomfortable awareness. The ideas inspire change; that's exactly what they're intended to do. They changed my life, and my hope is that they change yours.

19

One Warm Sunny Afternoon

"Souls are made sweet not by taking the acid fluids out, but by putting something in—a great Love, a new Spirit. . ."

Henry Drummond

Insight # 19

The Creator who gave you life can give you a new life—a new heart, a new chance.

One man said, after reading this book, "It reminds me of the man I was, the man I am now, and the man I hope to become." This chapter is personally directed to those who "hope to become" more loving and more honorable. It's the conversation that maybe you and I would have together—one, warm, sunny afternoon.

Stephen came to me one summer afternoon. I had known him before—when life was still with him. His mother and I had been friends; she died in childbirth several years before. His appearance was eerie, but there was an earnestness about him. The kids would say he looked wasted and old for his twenty years of age. His hair had been dyed so many times that now it resembled the lifeless straw of a cheap doll—the synthetic look. His complexion was ghostly white; his eyes had a lost look. I see that same look on many of the youth who hang around town dressed all in black.

After some initial small talk, he told me that he had come to see me because he thought I might be able to help him. He had heard that I was writing a book on chasity, and he remembered that I had been friends with his mother. We went out to the front porch where we could be alone. The warm summer sun seemed to lighten the mood.

"I don't know if I can help," I said, "but let's talk about it. What's happened to you? "

"Since you were a friend to my mom, I thought maybe I could tell you a few things," he said. "I really need help."

Two hours later, while the sun sank behind the trees, his horror story was over. He had gone from addiction to pornography to being addicted to sexual exploitation and adventurism. For several minutes we sat in silence. My heart was heavy; his heart was breaking.

"What do I do now?" he asked.

"Go back," I said.

"Go back to what?"

"Go back to the way you were; go back to being alive again."

"I've gone too far," he said with despair.

"If you really had gone too far you wouldn't be here today," I assured him.

"How do you know that?" he asked.

"You're here because you're looking for help; that means

your conscience is still working. You haven't shut it down all together. You're in pain. That's good, too. It's telling you to stop doing what you're doing. You seem to still care; that means your heart is still alive. You haven't gone too far, but you're dying, and your soul knows it."

"Dying? You mean suicide?" he asked.

"A piecemeal kind of suicide that's already begun—I suspect that's why you're feeling the way you are now. It's uglier than death—it's dying while you're still alive. You know what I mean; you maybe see it more clearly in some of your friends. They don't care. They don't feel. Nothing matters anymore."

He was listening. His heart was still feeling! His conscience was hurting. Oh, blessed guilt that nags to let us know when we're off course! His mind was still functioning and searching for answers. His soul was dying of spiritual starvation, but he knew it! He was listening. The sun hid behind a gray cloud. There was a chill in the air.

Go Back To Being Alive

A scene popped into my memory of the first time I ever noticed Stephen. He was a young boy. I went to his house to visit with his mother. As we sat in the kitchen talking over lemonade, the children peered at me from behind doors. They seemed excited that someone different was there.

As I was leaving, Stephen came up to me holding a huge pumpkin he had grown all by himself. He said, "Mrs.

Sorensen, would you like to have one of my pumpkins?"

I looked over to the garden spot. "Are you sure you want to give me this one?" I asked. "It's the biggest you have."

"Yes," he said, "I want you to have this one."

I took the pumpkin, amazed by the giving heart of this young boy.

"Stephen," I said, "do you remember when you were just a little boy and you gave me the largest pumpkin that you had grown?"

"I did? No, I don't remember that," he said.

"It was the first time that I really noticed you. You had a heart that was so sensitive and caring. It's still there! Reach back to the Stephen that was full of life and love."

"Go back to being a kid? Are you serious?" he asked.

"Go back to being alive," I said once again.

"You're right; I actually feel like I'm dying inside; I don't feel anything anymore. I've gone from one sexual experience to another just for the high. Now I don't get a high on anything. But I don't know how to change. I don't know how to get back."

"Remember the Stephen that was, and at least you have some idea of what you're shooting for. You walked away from him, but you can go back if you really want to. You can turn it around."

"I don't know. I'd like to think that. I don't have sex anymore; it has me. Every minute—it has me. Everywhere I look I see sex. I can't even see a jogger on the street without thinking of him or her sexually, and I imagine in my mind that everyone wants to have sex with me. I know it sounds bizarre, but it's the way things are with me all the time. I've created a monster and now I can't control it."

While I listened I was reminded of the upside-down man—led around by twisted sexual passions. He had become a slave to himself.

"How can I stop doing something when it's always on my mind? Worse, how can I stop doing something that I want to do? I can't stop thinking about it; I can't stop the thoughts that keep haunting me. I want to change; I want to be like other people. I want to get on with my life, but I'm caught in one sexual relationship after another. Some of them last for just a night; others last for a few weeks, but I'm a slave to it all. Life's hell."

"You've created your own hell," I urged. "We're not created to do bad and feel good. Something inside is trying to tell you that you're off course. Think about it, Stephen. There is no other more disgraceful abuse of our brothers and sisters than in reducing human intimacy to a meat market. If one lies, the truth can be told; if one steals from another, the stolen property can be returned. But the deliberate plotting to use someone's body to gratify sexual cravings or pride is like the cravings of an evil spirit to possess the body of the living. It's to say, 'I care not for your soul, I merely want to use your body.' Nothing takes the life or the love from the human heart like sexual exploitation. But you can change."

"Right now, the only way I think I can handle it is to shut it off completely."

"I recently read the book, Don't Call It Love, by Patrick Carnes. He deals with people who are in one way or another addicted to sex—either pornography, destructive affairs, or prostitution. In the book he tells the value of the celibacy treatment—no sex at all—even in marriage. It makes sense—allowing time for the mind, heart and conscience to regain control of the flesh.

"I recall reading that one of his patients said it was like returning to childhood and starting all over again. It really helped his patients."

"I know that I need to stop the acts, but how do I stop the thoughts that are continually haunting me?"

Clean The House, Junk the Lies

"I think the first step would be to clean house."

"Clean house?"

"Your house—your spirit. Well, actually, you could begin with your actual house—clean out all the junk. Stop allowing yourself to be seduced by propaganda. Get rid of the pornography—magazines, movies, books.

"You'll feel fantastic with this first step, but the next step won't be as easy. It takes minutes to clean out a house, but it takes months, even years to clean out your mind—your thoughts that led to the sexual addiction. You've allowed your mind to be programmed by pornography to believe lies about human life, love and sex. Now, you've got to junk the lies—or do a housecleaning on your mind."

"Lies?"

"You've bought into lies about human life and human sexuality. You see yourself first as a sexual being—wrong. First you're a spiritual being. You said that you're always thinking that the person you're looking at wants to have a sexual experience with you. That's another lie.

"You can only see people from your own perspective. Because you're a sex addict, you think that everyone else is, too. You're like the thief who thinks that everyone's going to steal from him, or the gossip who thinks that everyone's talking behind her back. How can it be any other way? We see others through ourselves, and by what we are. That's one reason why we can't hurt others without first hurting ourselves. You've given your life over to lies that have corrupted the way you think, how you feel and how you act. To get back, you need to exchange the lies for truth."

Not only does pornography misrepresent the whole issue of human sexuality, there's an evil power in it, a power that drains your strength to love. That's the reason why you feel so weak, so helpless. You've invited this power into your life, and now it has taken control. That's why you feel so out-of-control. You've allowed another power to take control of your life."

"So you believe in evil? Are you serious?"

"Absolutely. You would have to have your head in the sand not to believe in evil powers. Every day we hear about gross, bizarre things. They are inspired by something. Besides, I have felt this power in my life. I know both the powers that strengthen and the powers that weaken. Both are very real."

He shook his head. "I guess the whole idea of a Devil seems like something out of Halloween; I don't know if I buy into that. I do know, though, that I feel helpless. I don't know what's a lie and what's not. I don't know what reality is. I don't even know what normal is."

"Normal? Um. Maybe that's the wrong word. What's normal is not necessarily right and wholesome. It gives the idea that we ought to determine what's right by what's popular.

"Probably a better word would be 'natural.' It's natural to have sexual feelings, but it's not natural to want to use those feelings as an excuse to take advantage of someone. It may be natural to get angry, but it would be wrong to allow feelings of anger to lead you to clobber someone over the head. We were given the sexual power, but we can use this power to love, or to use and abuse. You've used this power against yourself and others. It will take time to change, but you can do it with divine help."

"What do you mean?" he said. "Are you talking about God? I hear that all the time from my Dad and I get tired of listening to him."

"Then stop listening to him and start listening to yourself; it's there deep inside."

Stephen was sitting with his head bowed; hands covering his face. The sun was fading behind the rows of trees on the other side of the lawn. It was almost time to begin dinner, but

I hoped that the family would fend for themselves. Our time together was precious; healing was taking place.

Without looking up, Stephen said, "I know I want to change, or at least I think I want to change. The truth is, I don't know what I want. Life without sex seems so boring; I don't know what would get me up in the morning. It's been my reason to live."

Dying From the Inside Out

"Now it's become your reason to die. You're dying and you know it. You have to do something. Before you started the sex thing, why did you get up in the morning? What was your motivation then?"

"I don't know if I can remember back that far. I got excited about the things that kids do—you know, going for a bike ride, playing a game of basketball with the guys—things like that."

"Just being alive? That's what you're talking about—just being alive! Have you ever thought that the sex addiction might be a way of trying to feel alive again? Like pouring hot salsa on food to give it some taste, pretty soon you can't taste anything at all. Food can taste pretty bland after you've been pouring on the hot salsa. But eventually the taste buds come alive again, and everything tastes better than ever. Since you can't see the future and how life will be better once you're healthy again, it might be a good idea to think of your past. Keep remembering what life was like as a child."

Stephen looked across the lawn where a group of neighborhood children and our two youngest were jumping on the trampoline, talking, laughing, sometimes colliding into one another.

With a sigh, he said, "It seems so long ago. No, more than that, it seems like a former life. But I remember feeling like that—so happy, so strong, so excited about doing anything—even jumping on a trampoline. I remember being with girls and not even thinking about them sexually. Now I feel so weak, so lost. I don't think I can change, but I know I can't go back to that."

"I bet if you ran across the lawn right now and started jumping along with the children, you would recapture it—at least a little. I've been thinking about that lately. As we grow up we hate being called a child or a baby or immature, and yet look who's happiest—the children!"

Reach for Divine Strength for a New Life

We sat in silence, watching the children. My mind wandered to a simple event that day. Jessica (9) and I had gone to visit the ducks after she came home from school; we have a whole family of ducks—a mom named Mollie with eleven babies. Jessica named each baby after her brothers and sisters. We gave them some grain, filled their pond with water, and just sat watching them. They chased one another through the pond and explored every nook and cranny seaching for a bug or worm. We've had the ducks for several weeks now, but I still can't tell the babies apart. They all look alike to me—with their grey streaked bodies and black-green wings. One of the ducks approached us, cocking her head to the left, then to the right.

I asked Jess, "Who is this one?"

"That's Signe," she said. "She's the prettiest one because her head is thinner than the others and the white lines around her eyes are just perfect. She's my favorite."

"Do you know each one?" I asked her.

"Well, sometimes I get them mixed up," she said, " but I can usually tell them apart. The one in the pond is the one who teases everyone all the time. The one over by the water is always getting in fights with the one over in the mud. That one playing with the bag is the curious one who is always checking everything out. I kinda know them."

She knew each of them; I was amazed. That's the way children are. They see what we don't see. They love with such tender hearts. We go around half alive, while the children are totally alive. No wonder Jesus said that the way to enter into the "kingdom of Heaven" is to become as a little child. His advice to those who have become lost is to look to the children.

Stephen was still staring at the children; his spirit seemed in despair.

I broke the silence, "Look at them, Stephen, Look at them. That's the way you used to be. Go back. You've chosen to go to the dark side of life, but now you can choose to go into the light just as well. You can choose to go back to the wonderful child you were when life was sweet. The Creator who gave you life can give you a new life—a new heart."

"A new life? A new heart? Is that possible?"

"That's what it's all about. The scriptures call it being born again, or having a change of heart. Promiscuous sex uses and abuses others and is a problem of the heart. The man who hits someone with his fist doesn't have a problem with his hand, but his heart. I used to have a passion problem, too—a horrible temper that caused a hell for me and everyone else in our family. In fact one time, I was "going off" as the kids say, and one of our sons who was about sixteen at the time said, 'You're the problem in this family, Mom—you and your temper.'

"I hated to hear that, but I knew that he was right: I was the problem—or my temper was. I knew I had to change, but I didn't know how to do it. My temper would just flash before I was even aware of it happening. I kept asking myself, 'How can I control my temper when it just happens? By the time I realize what I'm doing, I've already done it.'

"Over and over I would make a resolve that it would never happen again. Then it would. One time I got so mad at one of the children that I slapped him across the face—something I absolutely abhorred. I think children might need a spanking once in awhile, but never a slap in the face. I hiked up a mountain, determined to ask God for help—to know that it would never happen again. I pleaded with God all day and into the evening. I had to know that I would never lose my temper to violence again.

"Finally the impression came into my mind that it was not within the powers of God to grant my wish, but that it *would* never happen again if I stayed spiritually strong and connected to divine power. Upon returning home, my son was happily playing with friends. I asked for his forgiveness; he hugged me and said, 'It's all right, Mom. I pushed you, too far. I'm sorry, too.'

"I realized the temper was a symptom of being spiritually weak, so I tried to stay spiritually strong. I read scriptures daily and prayed a lot; once in awhile I fasted. I also kept track of the circumstances that led up to losing my temper. I found that when the house was a mess, I was a mess. The false idea that I had to be a Supermom and have an immaculate house at all times didn't help.

"Eventually I experienced a total change of heart and disposition. I haven't lost my temper for some time, and when I do get angry I'm not destructive like I was in those dark days. I used to think that there were some people who were just good, and others who were naturally bad—and that I was one of the bad guys. Now I see it in a different perspective. When we aren't spiritually healthy, we're prone to all sorts of diseases of the soul. Mine was the passion of anger; yours is passion of the flesh. Both need Higher Power to overcome. And by the way, ask explicitly for what you need and don't think that God will be shocked; He already knows."

"If He already knows, why doesn't He just help me—without my asking for it?" Stephen asked.

"Because He waits to be invited. Evil power just barges in uninvited, but God waits to be invited. "

"Yeah, well, I don't think I can go to God. I used to pray, but I would feel like a hypocrite praying now—after making so many mistakes."

"Do you ever have dinner at your Dad's house?" I asked.

"What are you trying to say?"

"Do you feel like a hypocrite going for dinner?"

"I don't know what you're getting at. Of course I don't feel like a hypocrite going to my Dad's house for dinner."

"Well, look at it this way—when you're hungry you might go to your Dad's for dinner. He's happy because you've come over and he gets to see you, and you walk away happy because you get to see him and your tummy's full. In this same way, our Heavenly Father is happy to feed us when we're spiritually hungry. We make Him happy and ourselves happy at the same time. I don't think that either one is going to say, 'Hey, Stephen you're a hypocrite coming to me for food when you've made some mistakes in your life.' "

"I always thought that you first have to get your life together before you start praying or going to church," he said.

"By praying and going to church we connect with the power to get our lives together."

"You're saying I shouldn't wait."

"You're starving spiritually; you need the help now. Go for it."

"You make it sound simple," he said.

"The concept is pretty simple," I answered, "and I know that it works. But you're right. Doing it is not easy, especially if you have walked so far and so deep into the darkness. You have given yourself to the dark side of passion—as I call it. You've surrendered to a power force that drains your spiritual strength. That's why you feel so out-of-control—so weak. It takes time to build strength again. If you really want to change, the Higher Power is there to help you."

"You think so?"

"Think of it this way—you were given the gift of life and the right to direct that life by making choices. You have chosen to make choices that don't work. You know they don't work because after doing them you feel like you're dying. You're like someone starving, but it's not your body that's starving, it's your soul. So go to the source of life and get the strength to live again. Plugged into the power source, the human heart becomes energized to a newness of life like putting a charger on a battery. Paul taught that when we've got the battery charger on our hearts they will become filled with ". . . love, joy, peace, longsuffering, gentleness, goodness, faith." (Gal 5:22)

"Many of us have the idea that God is critical, judgmental, harsh, impatient, unkind, aloof, cynical, preachy. I think He would say simply and with love, 'You have chosen to disconnect from the powers of life and love. This has resulted in your weakness and pain. Reconnect with the life force and your heart will be healed.' "

"I'll try," he said, and left.

Summary

It has been several years since this conversation with Stephen. I see him every once in awhile, and when I do I'm amazed. He's Stephen again—happy, whole, alive and loving. Through sincere effort and divine help, he has healed. Once again, he looks like the bright, smiling young man who long ago held a huge pumpkin out to me in love. His experience with the dark side of passion, comments and suggestions have made a tremendous contribution in the research for this book. Thank you, Stephen.

The Freedom of Chastity 20

"I will pass through this world but once. Any good thing therefore that I can do, or any kindness that I can show to any human beings, let me do it now. Let me not defer it or neglect it, for I shall not pass this way again."

Henry Drummond

Insight #20

Honorable men and women—without hidden motives—are free to be spontaneous, warm and friendly; the mutual trust and respect releases and increases the freedom to love.

You never forget where you are and what you're doing when a great idea strikes you. It was a very hot, summer afternoon. While the children were cooling off, and happily playing in a small plastic pool, I sat reading The Great Divorce by my favorite author, C.S. Lewis. Then it happened. I read a few paragraphs that changed my life. They captured the vision of the wealth of chastity, and the love it can create. I remember feeling as if I had just uncovered one of the most precious and valuable jewels of a lifetime.

The book is a fictional story of a man who is allowed to leave hell and explore heaven for a day—accompanied by an angel who acts as a tour guide.The man sees a procession of people coming toward him. There is a radiance of light surrounding them, but particularly around one woman. There are young boys and girls on either side of her, throwing petals of flowers at her feet.

He asks the guide, "Is it. . .is it?"

"Not at all," said the guide, "It's someone ye'll never have heard of. Her name on earth was Sarah Smith and she lived at Golders Green."

The man asks, "She seems to be. . .well, a person of particular importance?"

"Aye. She is one of the great ones. Ye have heard that fame in this country and fame on Earth are two quite different things."

He asks the guide, "And who are all these young men and women on each side?"

"They are her sons and daughters," the angel answers.

"She must have had a large family, Sir," the man responds.

"Every young man or boy that met her became her son—even if it was only the boy that brought her meat to her door. Every girl that met her was her daughter."

"Isn't that a bit hard on their own parents?" he asked.

"No, there are those that steal other people's children. But her motherhood was a different kind. Those on whom it fell went back to their natural parents loving them more. Few men looked on her without becoming, in a certain fashion, her lovers. But it was the kind of love that made them not less true, but truer to their own wives. Every beast and bird that came near her had its place in her love. In her they became themselves. And now the abundance of life she has in Christ from the Father flows over into them. . .It is like when you throw a stone into a pool, and the concentric waves spread out further and further. Who knows where it will end? Redeemed humanity is still young, it has hardly come to its full strength. But already there is joy enough in the little finger of a great saint as yonder lady to waken all the dead things of the universe into life." (107-108)

Over and over I thought about the line: "Few men looked on her without becoming, in a certain fashion, her lovers, but it was the kind of love that made them not less true, but truer to their own wives." This simple story gave me the vision of the wealth of chastity. Before discovering this passage, almost everything I had read on chastity was from the slant of fear, duty or law. This captured the joy that comes from openly and honestly loving others. It was as if I could see the very woman herself planting in others seeds of patience, love, tolerance, faith, hope, and confidence. Filled with the qualities of life, love and joy, she stands out as a beacon of light in this world of despair, indifference and depression. I was filled with the desire to become this kind of woman. A woman that every wife would want for their husband's secretary—friendly, loving but in a warm, sisterly way—a woman who compliments all women.

We, too can awaken the life within ourselves and then awaken the lives around us by being true to ourselves, virtuous and connected to the Creator. How this dark world would come to light with such individuals!

Freedom in Men/Women Friendships

Moral virtue does not decrease our ability to show love to the human family; it releases and increases it! It sets us free to love, to be open and friendly. Women who are true to their husbands are able to be true to their men friends and associates—to compliment, encourage, and have a sisterly concern for them. Men who are true to their wives are able to be a true friend to their women friends, to compliment, encourage, and to have a brotherly concern for them. Everyone wins there's mutual integrity; everyone loses when there's dishonesty.

Henry Drummond captured the freedom of such a society when he said, "In an atmosphere of suspicion men (and women) shrivel up; but in an atmosphere (of love and trust) they expand and find encouragement and educative fellowship. . .What a delightful state of mind to live in! What a stimulus and benediction even to meet with it for a day!" (The Greatest Thing In the World, p. 38)

Free from the entanglements of hidden motives, men and women are free to love and share with a warmth and intimacy of feelings that could never take place in a predatory society.

The freedom comes from sincerely loving others, trusting motives, and wanting to "add a measure of grace to the world," as Don Quixote called it. Imagine a society in which everyone felt comfortable to be open, spontaneous and friendly.

My husband is a musician; I am an author. He has many women friends who enjoy the love of music with him. I have men friends who complement my writing abilities. We are both comfortable with these relationships because we trust ourselves and these friends. I often think of the extraordinary men friends in my life. Michael, scholar and author, who edited my first book and gave me the encouragement to have it published. Cliff, who is thirty years older than I am. We delight to discuss politics and gardening together. Ed, an inventor who thinks deeply, and cares passionately for the welfare of his two small children. There's a love and respect between us that would be impossible if one wants friendship and the other wants a secret affair, or if one wants to sincerely talk politics, but the other wants a masquerade.

Every so often someone mentions that it is impossible for a man and a woman to have a friendship without it becoming sexual. Loving with honor naturally inspires friendships, even Jesus Christ did not limit his ministry to men; He was sensitive and loving to brothers and sisters. He had men and women friends.

The Universal Attraction

Let's step back and take a wide-angled perspective on the male/female attraction. There's the desire to be bonded together in total intimacy, to create a circle of love, but outside that center circle, there's a another circle, the universal attraction between men and women. Within this outside circle there's still an attraction, a brotherly/sisterly attraction that's a part of being in the family of God. Honorable romantic love creates ambition, this outside circle of love creates ambition as well—the desire to do better and be better to win respect and attention. This creates a tremendous force for good.

Erich Fromm explained it this way,

> "(There is) the psycho-biological aspect of sexuality, the masculine-feminine polarity, and the desire to bridge this polarity by union. There is masculinity and femininity in character as well as in sexual function. Sexual attraction between the sexes is only partly motivated by the need for (sexual release); it is mainly the need for union with the other sexual pole. . ." (The Art of Loving, p. 37)

There is a natural and wholesome desire for nonsexual "union" between men and women, to be associated with one another in a friendly/family manner. Such association is possible only with trust, honesty, fidelity in marriage, and chastity before marriage.

In the book, Illusions and Realities, Dr. Brown, a family

therapist, explains,

> "A man glimpsing a neighbor woman might be aroused by her body and try to seduce her. Encountering an icy refusal, the shock of her children, or the anger of her husband would teach him that his fantasies were an illusion. On the other hand, if he were to share gardening tips, social activities, and mutual love for summer sunsets with this woman, he might well develop a real, though nonsexual, intimacy with a whole person—a neighbor, a talented human being, a wife, a mother, and a daughter." (p 5)

Think of a community where such wholesome interaction could flourish. The freedom of friendly non-sexual interaction among the sexes would decrease temptation towards infidelity, because women would receive not only the attention of their husbands, but also of their brothers in the human family. Men would not only have the attention of their wives, but of their sisters. Men and women often slide into an affair to reassure themselves that they still "have what it takes" to impress someone of the opposite sex. If friendly, innocent interaction were a part of daily life this need would be filled. Marriages would be stronger in a community of trust, chastity, and mutual respect.

I could see the single, unmarried woman saying, "Though I am not 'in love' with that special someone, I'll be in love with everyone. I will reach out to fall in love with a new friend every day! I will share a smile, my personality, my hopes. The love I give freely will come back to me freely.

Maybe I will never meet the magic man—but I'll make every day a magic day through the power of my love."

The wife who feels unappreciated in her marriage might say, "I realize that my marriage needs an overhaul, and it's slowly happening. But right now, here, today, I can surround myself with the love of friends and family." Each of us can live with a wealth of love if we're willing to reach out to others.

Note of warning: Beware thinking that it's all right to have a romantic encounter if it doesn't include sex, or if your spouse had one, or if this person is meeting your needs in a way no one else can. These are excuses to shut the conscience down. Signs of married individuals going over the boundaries: investing too much time, too much energy in another relationship, pretending it's only a friendship when the conversation includes sensual comments, discussing sexuality, and disclosing private aspects of one's marriage, entering into a romantic fantasy, using the relationship to create jealousy and mistrust for husband or wife, assuming that this relationship is so special that it deserves an exemption to the rule of fidelity in marriage.

Free of Hidden Motives

We naturally find ourselves on guard whenever someone is trying to get something from us—when there's hidden motives. This same resistance occurs when we suspect the motives of men and women who use their friendliness and charm to gain a new heart, boost vanity, pride, or the worst, merely a warm body for the night. We find ourselves thinking, “Just what are you going to want from me? Is this just a friendly guy, or is he trying to get something?”

For instance, about once a year a bright, energetic young man comes to our door to sell us a miracle cleaner. “Ma’am,” he says, “This is your lucky day! I’m here to introduce you to the most fantastic cleaner the world has ever known! It makes carpets look and smell like new. It can....” While giving the sales pitch, he begins spraying the door frame and wiping off dirt smudges. I am usually impressed by the cleaning job, but unimpressed by the cost—thirty-five dollars a pint.

As I begin my “thank-you but no-thank you” speech, he makes a last-ditch effort for a sale, telling me that almost all of our neighbors have purchased it. Then while pulling out the sales tags to prove it, he says, “Nobody else thought it was too expensive.”

The more passion he piles on, the more irritated I become. When he realizes that I am not going to purchase his cleaner, he turns and stomps off. I know he feels he wasted time with me, and I feel I wasted time with him. No matter how pleasantly I say “no,” the young man walks off feeling rejected.

Now whenever I see a young man walking down the driveway with a spray bottle in his hand and a rag hanging from his pocket, I want to run and hide. He is going to resent me when I won’t buy his product, and I’ll resent myself if I do. It’s a no-win situation.

Salespeople may be friendly, but we find ourselves always suspecting their motives; there's the money factor. When we suspect motives, social interaction is shut down. A predatory society—men conning women for a warm body for the night, or women cunningly trying to win another heart—causes suspicion and resistance to open, friendly conversation. When the predatory spirit prevails, everyone begins to question even innocent acts of kindness:

The boss wonders why the new secretary is so friendly.

The secretary is suspicious of the surprise raise.

The mailman suspects the woman who leaves cookies in the mailbox.

The grocery clerk fears the "look" in the eyes of a customer.

The teacher sneaks out the back door before a certain student needs help again.

A male doctor is afraid to call a woman patient at home to see how she's doing.

Parents wonder about the motives of a teacher who takes special attention with their daughter.

An attractive woman is afraid to accept a date out of fear that he'll expect sexual favors.

What a nightmare of distrust! Warmth, personality, smiles, friendliness, and touch cannot flourish in a society of hidden motives.

You're not the fortress; you're the assault.

One man I interviewed for this book had an interesting perspective on the idea that a predatory society attacks mutual trust. He was in his late thirties, husband, father, and an African-American who had grown up in an area of a large city known for racial tension and crime.

"I was taught to be a predator from before I can remember," he said. "I thought that was just the way it was. Men are supposed to stalk and prey upon women. Women expect it. Men fall into it because they want to be normal. They're trained for the game—to capture as many women as they can. The hunt is thrilling."

We discussed the effects of the "hunt" upon women. He said, "Women become uneasy in their wait to be attacked. What a dreary outlook on life! They're afraid to be feminine or to look feminine. Some become masculine and harsh to protect themselves. Then some women have resorted to becoming hunters themselves. The only way to escape being hunted is to hope for the first strike advantage."

We discussed the harm to social interaction when humans prey upon one another. His insights were powerful! "The sexual game puts everything in question. This predator syndrome creates a harshness in men—they're not allowed to be sensitive. Sometimes men want to nestle into the bosom of someone who can comfort them; they want sometimes to be childlike. They want someone who can give strength, but that's all lost in the game. You're not the fortress; you're the assault. You're always on the prowl. Your whole nature begins to go for the target. Not only your actions but your words and thoughts are geared to the conquest.

"In a relationship without trust, you can't really communicate. It's just business at hand. Human interaction is based upon trust and fair play. In the sex game, there is no way to really tell what another is thinking; it attacks the whole system of trust and liability.

"I saw the effects of adultery in a military service camp in Texas. The day after a woman's husband left to go out to duty, another man moved in. There was no trust. And when there's no trust, everyone begins to suspect everyone else. People are on the verge of killing because of the distrust. No word—no bond. Everything is up for grabs. Everything's at risk! When we lose the ability to make clear choices, we become like safari hunters. We get a thrill just with the hunt. We become prideful of our displayed trophies or conquests, but even if you've just captured someone, you're still anxious for the next hunt. The hunger continues because there's no satisfaction. You're always jealous because someone has a bigger and better trophy than you. So you push for newer and better trophies.

"When you become a hunter you're willing to do whatever it takes to get what you want. You lie, deceive—anything. The issue comes up, whether to lie and say you love the gal. You do it just to get what you want. At the end of the game, you have to admit that it was a lie all along. You've presented a picture of a Shangri-la relationship. Eventually you have to admit that it was all a lie. You come to the realization that it's podunk (nothing)."

The idea came up in our conversation that moral virtue is a dividing line between people. Husbands who are loyal to their wives are not comfortable with women who do not respect their position of loyalty. Women who are faithful to their husbands are uncomfortable with men who pose a threat to their marriage. The freedom of interaction can happen only when everyone shares the same values.

For instance, while I was taking an evening music appreciation class at the local college, I often enjoyed after-class discussions with the teacher. I appreciated his vast knowledge of classical music, especially since my husband was a master pianist. After awhile I began to realize that while our friendship was totally platonic for me, he had a different perspective. One night he said, "We've got to stop meeting like this. Why don't you come over to my apartment. We can talk there, and be alone."

It was not so much what he said but the way he said it that set off the alarm. That was the last night that I stayed after class to talk. *The freedom of friendship shuts down when one sees it as friendship, but the other sees it as romance.*

Since most human interactions are based upon trust and truth, a predatory society attacks everyone. In a relationship without trust, you can't really communicate—it's just business at hand.

If only women knew the wondrous power of influence they have when they simply love their brothers with warmth and friendship! If only they knew that when they dress to attract the "upside down" man, they will do just that and suffer the consequences. If only they knew that layer upon layer of makeup says, "I need a mask." If only they knew that honest men will always be attracted to honest women—women who are first a sister, then a friend, and then, if right, a lover.

If only men realized how foolish they look when they repeat the same same old lines, "Where have you been all my life? . .You're the most beautiful woman. . .I've been waiting for you . . .You and I, babe, that's how it's going to. . ." If only they knew that honest, sincere women are attracted to honest, sincere men. If only they knew that woman of class are only attracted to men of class, and that the most manly attributes are not muscles or charm, but sincerity and integrity.

"I love you for yourself."

A beautiful story that illustrates the wealth of chastity was written by Kahlil Gibran in his book Jesus, Son of Man. Gibran created fictitional stories from actual New Testament persons to give glimpses into the character of The Son Of Man. The woman in this particular story, Miriam, has, like Aldonza, known few men who loved with honor; she herself is without honor. She views from the upside-down sexual slant, and attempts a relationship the only way she knows how—sensuously. He, on the other hand, relates to her as brother and friend, with respect, warmth, and friendliness.

She tells the story: "It was in the month of June when I saw Him for the first time. He was walking in the wheat field. . .The rhythm of His step was different from other men's, and the movement of his body was like naught I had seen before. . .and I gazed at Him, and my soul quivered within me, for He was beautiful. His body was single and each part seemed to love every other part. Then I clothed myself with the raiment of Damascus. I walked to Him with my scented garments and my golden sandals, the sandals the Roman captain had given me, even these sandals. And when I reached him, I said, "Good-morrow to you."

And He said, "Good-morrow to you, Miriam."

And He looked at me, and His night-eyes saw me as no man had seen me. And suddenly I was as if naked, and I was shy.

Yet, He had only said, "Good-morrow to you."

And then I said to Him, "Will you not come to my house?"

And he said, "Am I not already in your house?"

I did not know what He meant then, but I know now. . when (he spoke to me) life spoke to death. . .for mind you, my friend, I was dead. I was a woman who had divorced her soul. I was living apart from this self which you now see. I belonged to all men, and to none. They called me harlot, and a woman possessed of seven devils. . .but when His dawn-eyes looked into my eyes all the stars of my night faded away, and I became Miriam, only Miriam, a woman lost to the earth she had known, and finding herself in new places.

And now again I said to Him, "Come into my house and share bread and wine with me."

And He said, "Why do you bid me to be your guest?"

And I said, "I beg you to come into my house." And it was all that was sod in me, and all that was sky in me calling unto Him.

Then He looked at me, and the noontide of His eyes was upon me, and he said, "You have many lovers, and yet I alone love you. Other men love themselves in your nearness. I love you in your self. Other men see a beauty in you that shall fade away sooner than their own years. But I see in you a beauty that shall not fade away, and in the autumn of your days that beauty shall not be afraid to gaze at itself in the mirror, and it shall not be offended. I alone love the unseen in you."

As He walks away, she cries to him again, "Master, come to my house. I have incense to burn for you, and a silver basin for your feet. You are a stranger and yet not a stranger. I entreat you, come to my house."

He turns, smiles, and says again, "All men love you for themselves. I love you for yourself."

This is the end of the story, but the beginning of her new life. She says, "On that day the sunset of His eyes slew the dragon in me, and I became a woman, I became Miriam, Miriam of Mijdel." (Jesus, The Son of Man, Kahil Gibran, p. 14,15)

There is so much to be learned from this story. Notice how Miriam views Jesus. She only observes his form and feature as a man—not a person. Notice how she views herself! She sees only the sensual, and accents the sensual to entice—the perfume, the soft clothing, the scented sandals. Notice that as she comes to experience the true warmth of friendship, she realizes that she is "divorced from her soul." She longs for him to come into her house because while they can carry on a friendly conversation outside, she wants to move quickly towards the arena in which she feels most comfortable—physical intimacy.

He, on the other hand—man of honor and virtue—views from an abundance of love, respect, and friendliness. He is already in her house, because he is already in her heart. He sees her first as Miriam, sister, and friend. As a kind friend, he exposes the hidden lie. Men may say that they love you, but they "only love themselves in your nearness." It is a powerful statement, and shows the masquerade—that such an act is an act of vanity and pride. Instead of an act of love, it is an act of selfishness. The focus is still on oneself—not giving but getting, not loving but using.

We see the vivid contrast between one who loves with honor and one who does not, and how true love can transform lives. The love of the Savior changed her life—just as it can for us.

Summary

Forgetting—even discarding—the virtue of chastity has produced a poverty of social interaction, love and goodwill. A predatory society keeps everyone running scared and suspicious. On the other hand, chastity releases and magnifies the freedom to love, to be spontaneous and open, to have warm and loving friendships. This freedom is a natural outcome when men and women of virtue sincerely love others, trust their own motives, and want to "add a measure of grace to the world". The virtue of chastity could create a huge nest of love, where the lonely and unloved are pulled in and cared for.

"The greatest thing," wrote Henry Drummond, "a man can do for his Heavenly Father is to be kind to some of His other children. I wonder why it is that we are not all kinder than we are. How much the world needs it. How easily it is done. How instantaneously it acts. How infallibly it is remembered. How superabundantly it pays itself back—for there is no debtor in the world so honourable, so superbly honourable, as Love. 'Love never faileth.' Love is success, Love is happiness, Love is life. . . Lavish it upon the poor, where it is very easy; especially upon the rich, who often need it the most; most of all upon your equals, where it is very difficult, and for whom we each do least of all. . .Lose no chance of giving pleasure. For that is the ceaseless and anonymous triumph of a truly loving spirit. I will pass through this world but once. Any good thing therefore that

I can do, or any kindness that I can show to any human being, let me do it now. Let me not defer it or neglect it, for I shall not pass this way again." (The Greatest Thing In The World, pages 28-29)

Envision such a community where men and women are free to interact with one another without fear. Think of the good will, the innocent acts of mischievousness. Think of the jesting that could brighten life! Think of the self-esteem and respect that would flourish because everyone would be free to give and receive friendly interaction. It would be the beginning of heaven on earth!

I love to experience this freedom to love. My children tease me from time to time saying, "There she goes again. She's talking to a woman in the store. I'm sure the woman is telling Mother her life story; they all do." This *complaint* has been the greatest *compliment* .

"The real treasures of this life aren't the cars or houses," I explain to them, " they are the people. There is no human being that does not have a unique personality and captivating story. There are no ordinary people. Each one has so much to share; most people are waiting for someone to care enough to listen."

There's a man who works at the local post office. His name is Howard, and he seems to be very shy and insecure. Whenever I see him, I ask, "How are you doing, Howard?" He is almost always amazed that someone is calling him by name. He responds quietly. Then I ask, "How are your two baby girls doing?" Or, "How's the garden coming this year;

are you raising those giant pumpkins again?"

He is usually in such a state of shock that he hesitates to answer. Recently he asked, "How can you remember my name? How do you remember that we had another baby girl last year? How many people do you do this to?"

"Not enough," I answered. "I hope to do better."

Virtue in Marriage 21

"When two people loved each other they worked together always, two against the world, a little company. Joy was shared; trouble was split. You had an ally, somewhere, who was helping."

Paul Gallico

Insight #21
Men and women of virtue, by their very nature of integrity and respect prepare for successful, marriages; virtue after marriage keeps love and intimacy fresh and evergreen.

On one speaking engagement, I was worried because my assigned hour to speak was right after the lunch break—on the last day of a four-day university conference. Usually the youth stay up all night talking at such conferences and the worst time to attempt to teach them anything is after the lunch break. As they entered the lecture hall, my fears were confirmed. Some sat down and stared blankly ahead—without showing any vitals signs of life. Others didn't even try to stay awake; they simply laid their heads on the desk in front of them and fell promptly asleep.

With enthusiasm, I launched into my topic of chastity, but they were just too exhausted to listen. Then it occurred to me that their weariness might be linked to discouragement—discouragement with the possibility that they would ever really have a lasting love, and the belief that romantic love happens only in fairy tales.

I stopped teaching and began telling a simple story, "In order to continue my education, I have spent fourteen summers at a private university away from home. The children usually accompany me, but my husband is unable to leave his business, so he stays home. After one of these summers spent in separation, the children and I were walking through the airport to pick up Daddy. Six weeks had passed since we last saw him, and we were all excited to be together again. As we were rushing to get to the gate where the plane would arrive, I noticed a man to my left walking towards us who was the kind of guy you want to look at twice, or maybe three times. I forced myself to look away—after all, I was a married woman. The attraction was electrifying; in a flash of surrender, I turned to look just once more. What a hunk—blond, tanned, and handsome! A wave of guilt came over me, then the realization: this handsome man was my husband! How convenient!" The youth broke into a frenzy of applause; I continued.

"I sense that some of you are discouraged; you're skeptical of waiting till marriage when maybe that marriage won't last anyway. You're also wondering if there's a chance that the excitement of sexual intimacy can last and survive the day-today hassles of life. I want you to know that I know love can last, and that sexual feelings can continue to bloom in an honorable marriage.

"Have you ever stopped to think that chastity before marriage is like a training period to prepare you for the glorious powers of love and intimacy after marriage? We have the wrong idea about chastity; we think it's like a grueling test before marriage, and that after marriage the test is over and the virtue of chastity is not needed. But that's not true. True chastity isn't just what we *do* with our actions, it's what we *are* in our attitudes. Someone could have the actions and practice abstinence—but not have the attitude. A guy that tells off-color jokes and makes fun of women and sexuality is not chaste in attitude—even if he is chaste in body. Marriage contracts don't change attitudes, they merely change marital status; coarse, vulgar men or women leave their mates feeling cold and unloved—even in marriage. The promiscuous, loose, undisciplined or sexually flirtatious do not change their attitudes or nature with marriage. Sowing wild oats before marriage contributes to the same craving for oats after marriage.

"The whole point of chastity isn't just to *not* have sex, but to *have* love and respect. The love and respect before marriage keeps the love alive, and marital intimacy fresh and evergreen after marriage. Those with a disrespectful attitude towards sex before marriage will have that same attitude after marriage. The promiscuous before marriage are more likely to be promiscuous after marriage as well. It takes self-discipline not to have sex before marriage, and it take self-discipline not to have extra-marital sex after marriage.

"But let's look at the action part of chastity—the self-discipline part. It, too, is needed after marriage. While it might be always *legal* in marriage to engage in sexual intimacy, it's not always *loving*. Nothing shuts these tender, fragile feelings down in a woman more than the attitude of her husband, 'You owe me—because you're my wife.' There are natural seasons of desire for intimacy. Sometimes we just need and want to be alone—to think, to pray, to meditate-but these times alone, if respected, make the times together all the more wonderful.

"There's a time 'for embracing and a time to refrain from embracing.' There's a time for romantic passion, and a time for emotional, even intellectual passion. There's a time for intimacy of spirits, and a time for intimacy of bodies. There's a time for building a patio together, or caring for elderly parents together. There's a time for caring for the baby together. There are also times for a healthy constructive disagreement that clears misunderstanding. It's all a part of the love making.

"A loving husband doesn't simply want sex, he wants his Beloved to experience the joy of intimacy together. He realizes that will never happen if he tramples over feelings, and disrespects the natural seasons of desire. This requires self-control and patience. He is willing to protect the glorious—and I do mean glorious—honor of sexual intimacy from the world's vulgar perspective, from infidelity, and even from himself. Again, true chastity—the attitude of love, respect and self-control is the very key to keeping love and intimacy fresh and evergreen after marriage.

"Now let's turn to marital intimacy itself. The deepest sexual feelings and sexual joy come from the feelings of the heart, not simply sensations of the body. The attitude of respect for sexuality—lifts it all to heights that those who make a joke of it will never know. Cherishing the life of their Beloved makes it an honor to even hold hands; consequently sexual intimacy is a banquet of delight. True lovers have the greatest sexual stimulator of all: they treasure the whole life of their loved one—not simply the body, or the face, or the muscles, but the wholeness of life. Because of this, love-making becomes a multi-colored tapestry as rich as life itself. Sometimes the body leads the way. Sometimes the emotions lead the way. Other times the depth of the soul leads to rebonding. Wholesome sexual intimacy inspires ambition, purpose, direction, security, comfort, safety, compassion, goodwill. Those who only experience physical or fragmented sex will never know such glory of intimacy.

"C.S. Lewis, Christian philosopher, was a bachelor and professor until he met and married a woman named Joy—a woman who brought him complete joy. After a few brief years together, she died of cancer. He tells of the banquet of love-making that they had together, "For those few years (we) feasted on love; every mode of it—solemn and merry, romantic and realistic, sometimes as dramatic as a thunder-storm, sometimes as comfortable and unemphatic as putting on your soft slippers. No cranny of heart or body remained unsatisfied."

"Sometimes we get the idea that marital intimacy is not as exciting or as passionate as sex outside of marriage, but maybe that's because those who truly experience this magnificence of love making realize that it is so wonderful, so sacred, that it needs to be kept private and separate from the world.

"The world's perspective is totally different: the emphasis is upon the bodily senses, and satisfaction, but for those who truly love the emphasis is from the inside out—the emotions, the spiritual bonding, the depth of gratitude for the life of the Beloved. The world looks to physical stimulation and variety to bring back the feelings again, but it's like pouring hot salsa on everything to bring back the taste again. In time the taste buds become so seared they taste nothing at all. The better plan is to restore the ability to taste again, or the ability to love again, to value with intense appreciation the life of one's Beloved.

"This time of practicing self-control is preparing you for the most glorious opportunity of your life—the opportunity to fall in love and to keep that love alive, fresh and evergreen forever. It's the height of human happiness; nothing comes close to it. Don't do anything to jeopardize it."

Original Construction and Maintenance

Our journey of understanding together is almost over,

but I want to share a few personal scenes from my marriage for a couple of reasons—first of all, I want those who are single to realize that true romantic love is not luck, it's a process of building together on a foundation of loving, honoring and cherishing. And for those who are married, I hope to assist you to capture the glory of your sweet love together.

We have learned some valuable lessons about marriage from remodeling our almost century-old farmhouse. We've learned that there are two important factors that determine the success of houses—and love relationships—original construction and maintenance.The original construction is important, in houses and marriages. No doubt, relationships bonded together with healthy motives and maintained properly have the best foundation and the best chance for progressing ever after. Those with deception, betrayal, and collusion (loss of conscience together) start out on a shaky foundation.

There's a way to restore houses and relationships: junk what's bad, replace with good, and beautify. This process keeps houses new and love growing.

As I mentioned, our turn-of-the century house was built before building codes, accurate measuring, and uniform building materials. The wood had been obviously recycled, the plumbing and electrical was jimmied together with the attitude: whatever works. The remodeling process always has some unexpected surprises: termites, water damage, even frayed electrical wires. We've uncovered beams too small to support the weight, and weathered old lumber crumbling into a sponge-like texture. My husband says there's a rule to remodeling. You determine the cost and the time, then triple it. Remodeling houses takes time, money and energy, and maintaining love relationships does the same; it doesn't *just* happen.

We've learned that some things just don't work in love relationships; others work every time. Feeling honored, feeling loved, feeling respected, feeling cherished, feeling trusted works in any heart, any home, any friendship, or any marriage. On the other hand, some things we do to one another eat away the tender and fragile bonds of love like termites in the foundation of a home: disrespect, disloyalty and dishonor eventually destroy.

There are other poor maintenance practices: thinking that once love is won it will last without nourishment, demanding respect without earning it, flirting with other men or women to get even, staging a battle with one's mate, arguing to win rather than to understand, craving more love and attention than the other can freely and honestly give, thinking that sex is a marital right, using marriage to escape life rather than using it to enhance life, hiding away together rather than bringing others into the love circle, thinking that marriage means ownership.

Remodeling a house creates clutter, confusion and lots of dust storms—so does remodeling a marriage. Sometimes it's hard to keep the end in mind. One of our first projects in our home included remodeling the kitchen, living room, and bathrooms. The first few weeks were not difficult; I endured the mess with the vision of the completed project in mind, but after several months my patience wore thin. I kept saying to my husband, "I thought this was going to take just a couple of months; I wish we had never started."

In this same way, sometimes it's hard to keep the vision in mind when we're in the remodeling, refining process of marriage. A few years ago we struggled for months through the most extensive remodeling project of our marriage. We had accumulated the clutter that destroys marriages: resentment and misunderstanding. Besides, we were still dealing with defects of original construction and dysfunctional upbringing. (My husband's alcoholic heritage has been difficult; he still hides from the pain, embarrassment and guilt. Do all children of alcoholics inherit this guilt?) So much had to be put on the table, discussed, resolved and forgiven.

We talked, talked, and talked—sometimes through the night. Our daughter Jessica, then eight, started urging, "Please don't talk to each other anymore." Sometimes the talking seemed to be tearing away what was good, and sometimes it seemed to be building again. There were times in the dust storm that we lost vision. Prayer helped. Sometimes, we stopped talking and just started praying.

One night, our talking was digging a deeper and deeper hole. I was sitting on the floor, and wondering how we could ever climb out of all this. In my emotional turmoil, I began to pray. Even as I was praying, it all seemed hopeless; there were no words that would resolve the conflict. Then, for some reason, I reached out my hand to my husband. He was standing across the room, looking completely drained and depressed. Even as I reached out my hand, I wondered, "Why?" My stubborn pride wanted resolution of issues before affection. My husband walked over to me, put out his hand, lifted me into a hug, and for the moment the issues were resolved. Drawing upon divine power can make all the difference. It can refill an empty tank with faith, love and hope again.

During another difficult remodeling season of our marriage, my husband had to travel to Southern California to bid on a construction job. While he attended a business meeting, I sat in the car and waited. I prayed for the strength to see things clearly. I prayed for renewed faith. Then I opened my journal and wrote words that I hoped would recapture the vision of my love for him. I knew that without vision, I could not, I would not, go on.

Recapturing the Vision

"Is it time to leave, or time to begin again? Are all marriages like mine—a never ending, wrenching process of becoming one by being forged together in pain? My mind reasons that I am not loved, but my heart clings desperately to whatever there is, for it loves this man now more than ever. Why do I love you? I need to remember.

I love you because you give me that look of love—sweetest of all—the look that is my life's purpose.

I love you because you are tender-hearted, and cry through movies.

I love you because you have the most wonderful hands ever created, masculine, strong, yet, soft, creative, artistic.

I love you because you have a delightful, original sense of humor that always catches people off-guard.

I love you because you're ambitious; I love you because you're smart.

I love you because you're so stable, so constant.

I love you because you don't give up. In the blackest hour, you come home—you simply come home.

I love you because you're not like me, you think first and speak later; you are reserved, calm, predictable.

I love you because you have such class; you never need to be first, or outshine others or have the last word.

I love your willingness to do laundry, to get in to get the job done.

I love your hair—and your no hair.

I love the way you play the piano; I love sitting with you on the bench, watching your hands make love to music.

Because of this love that consumes me at times—consumes me with such longing, I so fear your silence! I fear pretense. I fear separation. Even more I fear feeling separate when we're together."

"How do I love thee?"

When my husband returned to the car, I read to him

these words of hope, and recaptured vision. A few days later, he wrote a similar letter.

"How do I love thee? Let me count the ways. . .

I love the way you look. . . I love your face, your hair, your figure.

I love the way you look in your clothes; you dress with class and at the same time you always look very gracious.

I love the style in which you present yourself—not gaudy with things hanging all over you and over-made up, but simple and gracious.

I love the way you carry yourself with poise and confidence.

I love to watch you walk—especially from behind.

I love your femininity which is not cute or mushy, but mysterious.

I love the look in your eyes and the small smile reserved only for me—it's the look that tells everyone else you and I share a secret that is so good, so unique that it's explainable only with the 'look and smile.'

I love the electricity that you generate in me when I see you.

I love your acceptance of me and your willingness to work with me.

I love you for your intimacy with me—body, mind, heart and spirit.

I love you for making an atmosphere that makes everyone feel welcome in our home.

I love you for making people more important than things.

I love the way you have developed your special gifts: writing, speaking, caring, sharing; I'm extremely proud of your accomplishments.

I love the way you teach without putting on any airs, and your willingness to expose yourself to the whole world if it will help someone with their life and problems.

I love you for your drive to learn, to grow, to progress, and I love the way you inspire these feelings within me.

I love you for making the best soup in the world."

We both read these letters over and over; gradually the vision returned. We were able to get through that remodel project with our love stronger. In this world of pragmatic pessimism, it is hard to hold onto the vision of love. Even those of us who have discovered the sweetest of soul-bonding are ever taunted by the voices that would say, "It's only chemistry. . .It can't last. . . Monogamy isn't natural. . .True love is a teenage fantasy. . .Soul-bonding is a myth."

Our environment, and the attitudes that surround us, are love-unfriendly; it takes remembering to hold the vision. We have come to believe that most marriages, and loves, are lost because the vision is lost. Emerson wrote, "One of the illusions of life is that the present hour is not the critical or the decisive hour. Write it on your heart that every day is (a decisive day). . ." A decisive day to fall in love again, to recapture the vision again, to be more loyal and true, and keep building.

Most of us will never realize how precious our loved ones are, or how glorious the present hour is, without a tragedy to awaken our senses. Young husbands are notorious for their complacency, and young wives destroy happiness over a lawn not mowed. My heart aches for human inclination to overlook the love that exists for the love that is "hidden in the mist". (Remember, Scarlett O'Hara in the novel, Gone With the Wind.) Those of us who are in an honorable marriage, have a portion of majestic love in our midst, but the smoke-screen of apathy prevents us from seeing and realizing. When will we learn to glory in the present hour? When will we learn to truly cherish the lives around us?

They Still Hold onto the Dream

As I was walking through the main living room of a convalescent home, I noticed that a group of elderly women were talking together. One was saying, "My husband will be here any minute to pick me up. We're going out for the evening." Another woman responded, "You too? Well my husband will be coming to take me home any moment now. I'll be so glad to be home."

I asked my friend, who was staying there to recuperate from a stroke, "Are their husbands really coming for them?"

"No," she said. "They say those things every day. Most of their husbands have died long ago, but they still hold onto the dream."

As I drove home, my heart ached for these women; I

wondered if they captured this appreciation for their husbands before or after their deaths. I believe that there's glory and romantic bliss in most marriages if complacency is overcome. Too many of us miss out on our only "glimpse of eternity" by trampling upon our happiness with petty arguments and put-downs. Worst—we bomb it with the tragedy of disloyalty.

Survived Everything That Life Could Throw at Them

Love is meant to be a refuge and a buffer—too many of us run during the remodeling and miss out on the newness and enhanced beauty that could follow. I found this sweet little story by Ernest Havemann. It captures the process of becoming one:

"You can see them alongside the shuffleboard courts in Florida or on the porches of the old folks' homes up north: an old man with snow-white hair, a little hard of hearing, reading the newspaper through a magnifying glass; an old woman in a shapeless dress, her knuckles gnarled by arthritis, wearing sandals to ease her aching arches. They are holding hands, and in a little while they will totter off to take a nap, and then she will cook supper, not a very good supper, and they will watch television, each knowing exactly what the other is thinking, until it is time for bed. They may even have a good, soul-stirring argument, just to prove that they still really care. And through the night they will snore unabashedly, each resting content because the other is there. They are in love, they have always been in love, although sometimes they would have denied it. And because they have been in love they have survived everything that life could throw at them, even their own failures."

One Self-Centered Passion or Another

Remember the play "Our Town"? Emily, who has died, is allowed to return to her mortal life for just one day. She picks her twelfth birthday. She is ecstatic to see everything and everyone again—as they were when she was a girl. She cries, "Oh, that's the town I knew as a little girl. And, look, there's the old white fence that used to be around our house. Oh, I'd forgotten that! Oh, I love it so!" Looking at her parents, she moans, "I can't bear it. They're so young and beautiful. Why did they ever have to get old? Mama, I'm here. I love you all, everything—I can't look at everything hard enough."

With intense appreciation, and sharpened awareness, she sees the contrast—how apathetic everyone appears. She cries to her mother, ". . .just for a moment now we're all together. Mama, just for a moment we're happy. *Let's look at one another.*"

As she returns to the hill and to her grave, she calls out, "Oh, earth, you're too wonderful for anybody to realize you." Then turning to the stage manager, she says, "Do any human beings ever realize life while they live it?—every, every minute?. . .that's all human beings are! Just blind people."

Then Simon Stimson, a man who warned her that her day in mortality would be discouraging, says, "Yes, now you know. Now you know! That's what it was to be alive. To move about in a cloud of ignorance; to go up and down trampling on the feelings of those about you. To spend and waste time as though you had a million years. To be always at the mercy of one self-centered passion, or another. Now you know—that's the happy existence you wanted to go back to. Ignorance and blindness."

If we could just capture the vision of how important our lives are—our loves are. If we could just really *look at each other*. If we could remember to love, fully love, each day. Why do we wait so long to realize?

If we could maintain such awe, reverence for human life there would be no wars, no mobs, no gangs, no poverty, no contention, no murders, no molesters, no pornography, no prostitution, and hardly a divorce.

In the novel Anna Karenina, Tolstoy writes of the love Levin had for Kitty, ' . . all the women in the world were practically of another planet to that on which Kitty had been born.' This has been the story of my life. For me there has only been one *real* man—Norm Sorensen. We still thrill to see each other across the room. We've discovered the tapestry of love-making: watching the baby together,putting gardens in together, putting on plays together, singing around the piano together, making dinner together, writing books together, cleaning windows together, raking the leaves together, riding the tractor together, making love together.

We share the same vision of "life as it should be". We certainly don't have a happily-ever-after relationship, but we do have a progressively-ever-after relationship—the type that's available to almost everyone who wants it bad enough. Our lasting love has not been a gift, but a day-to-day victory over the forces that would drive us apart. It's a victory after tremendous struggle, and lots of remodel projects.

A Last Word

As my husband and I were editing this part of the book, he began to chuckle. I sensed that he didn't really want me to ask why, but I did. "Oh," he said with a twinkle in his eye, "I was just thinking about that happily-ever-after idea, like the time you planted yourself on the hood of my car so that I couldn't get away from the argument. By the way, that really wasn't fair. And the time that I exploded and tore off across town on my bicycle to brood in my cave at the office. I know it seems kind of stupid riding a bike instead of taking the car, but there was no way you could sit on the hood of my bike. Besides, bike riding is a great way to work off frustration and anger. I'll have to say we've got the passion and excitement stuff down pat—but happily-ever-after? I'm not so sure what that means. This much I do know though; we love each other now more than ever, and I think it's because when the going gets rough, we ultimately pull together rather than pull apart."

22

Postscript: Take The High Road to Glory

"You are surprised that the world is losing its grip? That the world is grown old and full of pressing tribulations? Do not hold on to the old man, the world; do not refuse to regain your youth in Christ, who says to you, Do not fear, thy youth shall be renewed as an eagle."

St. Augustine

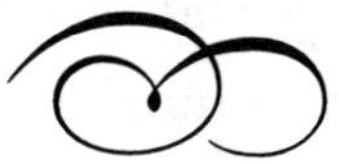

For the last few days I have been absolutely, out-of-my-mind silly. I have chased children around and around the house to tickle their knees. I have jumped from one silly accent to another in portraying the various and assorted kinds of "Mommies" that live at our house. My children say that I am "weird" but it's not true; I am a multiple personality. I say to them,

"Think of how boring it would be to only have one mommie—you have a dozen or so all rolled into one."

In truth, the reason that I am bouncing off the walls is because I am immensely happy. After years and years and years of reading and thinking, and writing and rewriting, and missing out on the abundance of life going on around me, I am gloriously happy to be finished with this writing project. Actually, I am not finished; I am spent. More could be said, and maybe one day. . .but not now.

Second to mothering, writing this book has been the most difficult task of my life, but for some reason—probably my German stubbornness—I have stuck it out. However, whenever we say "yes" to any task, we are also saying "no" to others. My whole soul seems now anxious to be released to do the "others."

A couple of days ago, while constructing a duck cage to keep the ducks off the patio and out of the garden, our daughter, Jessica said, "Isn't this fun, Mommie? If you weren't doing this you would probably just be working on your book or something boring like that."

While my heart is happy, my mothering instinct still worries: did I say enough? Will the reader understand? Have I stirred up more questions than I have answered? Will those caught in masquerades find their way out? Will those who have given in to the mystique of the dark side—like Stephen—find their way out? Did I make it clear that sexual intimacy is the most wonderful, glorious experience within the bonds of a loving marriage?

Like a mom worried over her babes, I worry for you. But it is time to part. What is unsaid must be left unsaid. I wish that there were time for you and I to sit on the porch in the warm sun and just talk things over. I'd like to leave just a few thoughts before we part.

To the unmarried:

Don't sit around and wait to be in love, create a circle of love for yourself and your loved one by staying spiritually strong. I have this idea that we need to create our own heavens before God will ever accept us into His. There is nothing sweeter, on earth or in eternity, than having "the force" with us.

Surround yourself with friends who are part of the "honor society" of virtue. Share in wholesome activities and adventures. There are so many who are lonely and unloved; reach out to them. Discover the exciting world of human treasures—people who are waiting for someone to come along and simply care to listen. Volunteer at the local hospital or elementary school. Share great movies together that portray love relationships of honor. You'll need all the help you can get to climb up and away from our sex-saturated society.

Invest in good, uplifting music, art, literature and movies. Reseed your mind with truth, wisdom, higher ideals, etc. Stay in school, and continue your education. Travel, if you possibly can, and discover God's wonderful children all over the world. Collect books that will become like friends, ever there to teach, to uplift, to guide. If you cannot afford to buy, then borrow from the local library. Be adventurous: hike the beautiful mountains, swim in cold lakes, learn country dancing, chess, anything! Have fun adventuring.

Usually, we get caught into the negative because there's not enough positives in our lives. Seize every day! Capture a mission that will lift your sights high, and that will "add a measure of grace to the world." We cannot change the world, but we can make a change in our own hearts, our own families, our own communities. Find a cause or launch your own.

Most of all, remember who you are; you are a child of God. What a tragedy to miss out on the soaring of the human soul because we have been convinced we're nothing more than "chickens" destined to spend our lives pecking out a living and "grabbing all the gusto we can." When we do not see the greater view, we settle for less. We are not simply animals with a more advanced computer. We are not slaves to appetites and passions unless we surrender to them. We have a divine purpose and destiny that extends beyond our mortal view.

When I began this writing project, I felt small and puny compared to the forces advocating the other side of the argument. It all seemed so hopeless. I recall distinctly one day, feeling this discouragement, wondering how what I had to say could possibly make a difference and how any of the children could escape from falling for the propaganda for sport sex. I cried out in my heart, "But how can the youth not get swept up in the sex craze? It's everywhere, and they are so young." The sweet impression came into my mind,

"Where is your faith? They are children of light. They can tell the difference between light and darkness." You are children of light! Rise up and fly!

You may have already taken the first step—to want to be one of the stars to restore the forgotten virtue. I want to congratulate you! I have heard it said, "You'll never have a better opportunity to be a bigger hero than in this generation, because there are so few willing to do anything." Few are willing to pay the price to love "pure and chaste from afar," but if you are one of the few—the precious few—I promise you the greatest adventure of your life, and probably the greatest challenge.

In the beginning you will feel very lonely; few take the road less traveled. You may feel like you are fighting against a tidal wave, and that is just exactly what you will be doing. You will feel it even more every time you listen to the radio, watch television or go to a movie; honorable sex is rarely profitable. You will likely be surrounded by people who don't understand. They will say, "What? You're waiting until what? Are you serious? Why would you ever do that?"

Remember when Aldonza, shocked to meet a man without hidden motives, asked the Man of La Mancha, "Why do you do these things?"

He answered simply, "I hope to add a measure of grace to the world." Women of the nineties are like Aldonza; they're not used to men who love with honor. They don't know whether to be complimented or insulted by a man who won't jump into bed with them. A good man <u>is</u> hard to find, and with so few good men around, it takes time to trust the few. On the other hand, men who have known only women who surrendered too easily, or seduced too quickly might think that you—a woman of integrity—are strange, maybe even a prude.

Few will understand, but those few who do will bond together in respect and maybe later in romance. It is only natural. Men who have restored moral virtue in their own lives will search for women with the same values; women who have virtue will do the same. Those who choose to take the road less traveled won't be alone for long; there are others—however few. Maybe it will take more than one generation to see the restoration of virtue in our society. Maybe you won't ever be really understood until one day your grandchildren will say, "My grandmother (or my grandfather) lived during that dark period in America that they called the sexual revolution, but he/she stood against it and gave us children the legacy of loving honorably. I am so grateful."

My heart is with you, and I want you to know that whatever the price, the wealth of loving with honor is worth it. Even if no one ever understands, you will.

One of my favorite movies is "Man of La Mancha." As I have mentioned, it is the story about a man in his fifties who reads and despairs over the cruelty of life. Then in his blackest hour he makes a decision that changes everything for him. He decides not to look upon life as it is, but as it should be. In one scene he and his chubby sidekick, Sancho, are riding horseback on a desolate and deserted road. Quixote asks,

"Well, Sancho—how dost thou like adventuring?"

Sancho answers, "Oh, marvelous, Your Grace. But it's peculiar—to me this great highway to glory looks exactly like the road to El Toboso where you can buy chickens cheap."

Quixote replies that like beauty, "tis all in the eyes of the beholder." As we travel through life we can either decide that it's a highway to glory, or merely a road "where you can buy chickens cheap." Take the HIGH way to the wealth of loving with honor, and you will always be on the road to glory!

About the Author

Mollie Hobaugh-Sorensen is married to Norman Sorensen. Together they are the parents of five daughters and six sons. She has authored two books, A New Spirit Within You and A More Perfect Union, and numerous articles on political and family issues. She graduated from Brigham Young University with a degree in American Studies, Family Science and English. She was chosen for the Extraordinary Women in the Napa Valley award (1988) by KVON radio station. She is founder of American Family Leadership Seminars.

You can e-mail Mollie at:

mollie@mollie.com

For more information please visit the web site at:

http://www.mollie.com

About the Author